D0714163

WORKING WITH CLAY

WORKING WITH CLAY

THIRD EDITION

Susan Peterson

Professor Emerita, Hunter College at the City University of New York

Jan Peterson

Prentice Hall Inc.

Library of Congress Cataloging-in-Publication Data is available on request.

Editor-in-Chief: Sarah Touborg
Senior Editor: Amber Mackey
Editorial Assistant: Theresa Graziano
Executive Marketing Manager: Wendy Gordon
Senior Marketing Manager: Kate Mitchell
Senior Managing Editor: Mary Rottino
Senior Operations Specialist: Brian Mackey

Credits and acknowledgments borrowed from other sources and reproduced, with permission, in this textbook appear at the end of the book.

Copyright © 2009 Laurence King Publishing Ltd.

Published by Pearson Education, Inc., Upper Saddle River, New Jersey, 07458. Pearson Prentice Hall. All rights reserved. Printed in China. This publication is protected by Copyright and permission should be obtained from the publisher prior to any prohibited reproduction, storage in a retrieval system, or transmission in any form or by any means, electronic, mechanical, photocopying, recording, or likewise. For information regarding permission(s), write to: Rights and Permissions Department.

Pearson Prentice Hall™ is a trademark of Pearson Education, Inc.
Pearson® is a registered trademark of Pearson plc.
Prentice Hall® is a registered trademark of Pearson Education, Inc.

Pearson Education Ltd.
Pearson Education Australia PTY, Ltd
Pearson Education Singapore, Pte. Ltd
Pearson Education North Asia Ltd
Pearson Education, Canada, Ltd
Pearson Educación de Mexico, S.A. de C.V.
Pearson Education–Japan
Pearson Education Malaysia, Pte. Ltd

 This book was designed and produced by Laurence King Publishing Ltd, London.
www.laurenceking.co.uk

Every effort has been made to contact the copyright holders, but should there be any errors or omissions, Laurence King Publishing Ltd would be pleased to insert the appropriate acknowledgment in any subsequent printing of this publication.

Editor: Elisabeth Ingles
Designers: Andrew Shoolbred and Gregory Taylor
Typeset by Marie Doherty
Printed in China

FRONTISPIECE: **Barbara Nanning**, Vessel form, press molded, pigment and sand; 17 × 5¹/₂ ins. (44 × 14 cm)
TITLE PAGE: **Ann Agee**, Teapot, thrown and hand-built earthenware, majolica decorated; 12 × 15 × 6 ins. (30 × 38 × 15 cm)
FRONT COVER: **David Beumée**, Porcelain bottle, 13¹/₂ × 8 ins. (34 × 20 cm)
BACK COVER: **John Glick**, glazed plate, 8¹/₂ × 8¹/₂ ins. (21 × 21 cm)

CONTENTS PAGES
Village potter, India, applying rice-paste decoration to bonfired local clay vessels; 24 ins. (61 cm) high
Susan Peterson, Floor vase
Lucy M. Lewis, fine-line design painted with a yucca brush and natural ground hematite pigment on Acoma pueblo kaolin-type clay, bonfired; 10 ins. (25 cm) diameter
Ernst Häusermann, pyramidal sculpture
Dora De Larios, part of a dinnerware place setting for the Carter White House, intricate cobalt overglaze painting, majolica style, c/10 porcelain
Robert Brady, coil sculpture, engobe decoration; 5 ft (152 cm)
Kirk Mangus, *Dead Soldier*

Prentice Hall
is an imprint of

www.pearsonhighered.com

10 9 8 7 6 5 4 3 2
ISBN 13: 978-0-13196-393-1

CONTENTS

SUSAN PETERSON, c. 1980

VILLAGE POTTER, INDIA, c. 1997

LUCY M. LEWIS, c. 1975

CONTENTS

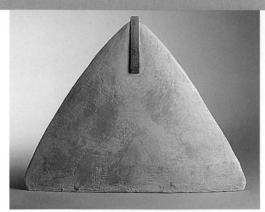

ERNST HÄUSERMANN

DORA DE LARIOS, 1975

CONTENTS

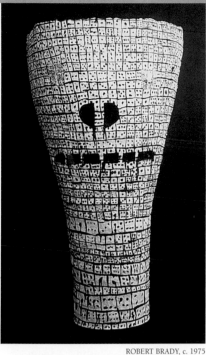

ROBERT BRADY, c. 1975

KIRK MANGUS, c. 1995

Temperatures in the book are generally given in figures on the Orton Cone Scale. Refer to Compendium, page 223, for Fahrenheit and Centigrade equivalent temperatures for Orton (USA) and Seger (world) cones

PREFACE TO THE THIRD EDITION, 2009

We have written *Working with Clay* to inspire and to teach beginners particularly, but also to give new ideas to advanced ceramists about clayworking through colorful photographs and descriptions of the various processes involved. The book is richly illustrated with step-by-step demonstration photographs of me or of Jan in our studio as well as incredible photographs of artists' work from around the world, pulled from the newest additions to our archive of 1,500 potters' portfolios.

This book also aims to give beginners, advanced students, and collectors a perspective on historical and contemporary ceramics. My long career as a professor of ceramic art and a practicing potter enables me to pass on my experience. To this end I am grateful to the artists all over the world who help me by sending photographs of their own examples and notices of their exhibitions, who tell me of new emerging artists, and send suggestions—please keep them coming!

In this third edition we have made a number of important changes. Highlights of this new edition include:

- a new chapter on ceramic sculpture
- an unprecedented portfolio of tests at low, medium, and high firing temperatures of fire-engine red, orange-orange, and lemon-yellow commercial brands of prepared glazes—new to the field due to the development of encapsulated cadmium oxides
- an expanded list in the Compendium of projects for clayworkers to do in each fabrication method and notes on how to think about the functional or sculptural requirements of each one
- over 80 new illustrations of work by contemporary clayworkers.

Much is changing in the ceramic world. We receive photographs of fewer functional pots and information from fewer production potters, but I know that hundreds of you are out there, operating in your own communities and not seeking wide publicity. More of you are using prepared clay and glazes instead of experimenting and mixing your own (sadly, in my view), but there is a return to basics in the trend toward building your own kilns and trying old-fashioned firings such as wood, raku, pit, or salt. Many of us are grasping for larger scale, necessitating experiments with new techniques, but enabling us to work in the public scene.

The situation in the ceramics departments of the universities, in the number of potters and ceramic sculptors, and in the market, has not always been as active as it is now. When I began teaching in 1950 there were three universities in the Los Angeles area, one or two community colleges, several art schools, one or two galleries showing ceramics—and the same was true worldwide; today there are many of each nearly everywhere. It has been an amazing journey for those of us who have seen all the changes since the 1950s.

Here are some names to remember, because these artists initiated the expansion from traditional functional ceramics to ceramics as an art form, which now makes clayworking a viable means of earning a living. The inventor of contemporary "studio pottery"—meaning that one craft person does everything involved in creating a pot by hand as opposed to industrial means—was Bernard Leach (1883–1979) of St. Ives, England, in the 1920s and his colleague Shoji Hamada (1893–1978) of Mashiko, Japan, national treasure of Folk Art, who with Leach traveled, lectured, demonstrated, and wrote books while exploring their new concepts of "mingei" and East meeting West, from the Twenties until their deaths. Following on from Leach and Hamada were Willem Koge in Sweden, Kaliki Salmenhara, potter/designer at Arabia Fabriker, and Kai Frank, glass and ceramic designer of Itola Fabriker in Finland, who continued Leach's ideas in Europe. Michael Cardew, another Englishman, worked with African potters using Leach's techniques. Beatrice Wood, Gertrude and Otto Natzler, European expatriates who came to America in the 1930s, brought the Leach attitude, but developed a more colorful track. The biggest change came with Peter Voulkos, whose name is synonymous with the new age of ceramics, who was the exciting pump primer in the 1950s, along with Carlton Ball, Michael Frimkess, Vivika and Otto Heino, Mac MacClain, John Mason, Harrison McIntosh, Ken Price, Jerry Rothman, Paul Soldner, Toshiko Takaezu, Henry Takemono, and myself. And more. Some are deceased, many of us are in our eighties, a few are younger, but this is the crew that negotiated the "explosion of the fifties."

From a few contemporary ceramics galleries across the world before World War II, the gallery scene has grown to encompass almost every hamlet on the planet, and we have seen prices rise from under $100 to many thousands since the 1950s. Museums that did not give us house-room some years ago are vying to build ceramic collections. Books and magazines abound. Exhibitions are almost continuous, and craft fairs are everywhere; websites delight. All of these changes present a brilliant future of possibilities in many facets of working with clay today for all of us who are passionate about this material.

Where do we go from here? Whenever it seems there is no place left to go, something innovative or just extraordinarily good hits the scene. Many clay artists today are unaware of Leach and Hamada, let alone others who paved the way, and therefore have no traditional baggage and can begin with themselves as the base. Coupled with readymade materials to use, computerized programs and the internet, workshops and demonstrations to attend, and our book, *Working with Clay*—this all helps to bring new ideas and more vitality to the surface, and it already has! Witness the annual juried international exhibitions of new work at NCECA, the national ceramic organization's meeting every spring. The ceramic arena is just incredible and the market is unbelievable. Period!

Acknowledgements

We are saddened that many of the wonderful images you submit must be left out because of space limits. My daughter Jan has helped me greatly with this book; her process photos have appeared in previous books and she has always been involved with my work. For help with this edition, we cannot thank enough: Margie Schnibbe for extraordinary research time and for organizing everything; studio assistant K.C. O'Connell, who for eight years now has run the many tests for the books until we get it right, mixes the clay bodies, does the glaze experimenting, fires the kilns; photographer Craig Smith of Phoenix, who takes the demonstration photographs; Marilyn Zeitlin, director, and Peter Held, curator, of the six-year-old Ceramic Research Center (CRC) that Ms Zeitlin and I founded with world-class collectors Sara and David Lieberman at the Arizona State University Nelson Art Museum; Laurence King, my publisher and friend, and his staff at Laurence King Ltd, London; Lee Ripley, Publishing Director of Laurence King, who oversees the project; Simon Walsh, production; Elisabeth Ingles, my superb editor, without whom I could not do; and designer Andrew Shoolbred, these last five all in the UK. My gratitude to all these friends.

I have written this in Cornwall, England, at St. Ives, where Bernard and Janet Leach's old pottery has just reopened (March 2008) as a museum and gallery, directed by Judith Twomlow and with master potter Jack Doherty producing new work on site making Leach's "standard ware." New kilns have been built, and residency studios for ceramic artists are being established. Somehow this resurrection, along with the Hamada museum in Japan at his working and living compound, seems to have brought closure to the exciting ceramic events of the twentieth century, and salutes a remarkable path to the future.

Susan Harnly Peterson, May 2008
PO Box 13780, Scottsdale, Arizona, USA, 85267
Email: shpeterson@aol.com

Early Minoan figure from Crete, c. 2500 BCE

Rose Slivka

Rose Slivka, who died recently, was one of just a few persons responsible for pushing the "ceramic revolution" of the 1950s, to which all of us who make and sell our work are indebted. Rose edited the magazine *Craft Horizons* for the American Craft Council from 1955 to 1979, where she wrote seminal articles like "The New Ceramic Presence" in 1961 and published many good writers on the subject. We are all beholden to Rose; we shan't forget her.

Rose Slivka, editor of *Craft Horizons*, the magazine of the American Craft Council, and Peter Voulkos, at the retrospective of Pete's work prior to the opening of the San Francisco Museum of Modern Art

THE SAFETY ASPECT

It is important to be aware that there are potential hazards involved in creating ceramics. Common sense is essential.

1. If you have allergies or respiratory problems, wear a mask when handling or working in the same room as powdered materials and clay dust, and while mixing glazes or spraying. Have a respiratory check every few years if you work in ceramics regularly.
2. Wear surgical gloves if you have skin troubles.
3. Keep all working areas well ventilated, preferably by opening windows.
4. Never light a closed kiln, only a partially open one.
5. Do not use electric tools or switch on electric kilns with wet hands, or if the tools are damp for any reason.
6. Standing on a rubber mat is the surest way to be safe when working around an electric kiln. Don't touch the elements when loading, and keep objects at least one inch away from all elements. Electric kilns can be ventilated, gas kilns should be.
7. Some glaze formulas are highly toxic. Take great care with glazes that have cadmium, chrome, barium, and lithium in the formula; do not use lead-based glazes—substitute non-lead formulas. Do not brush face or handle food until you have thoroughly removed all trace of glaze from your hands, and do not bring food or drink into the studio. Dispose of toxic mixtures sensibly; do not pour them down the drain where they will contaminate water supply (this is illegal anyway).
8. Remember that toxic fumes may be given off during firing of any kiln: gas, electric, wood, salt, and the like. Excessive reduction in a petroleum-fueled kiln will emit potentially deadly carbon monoxide gas, and consequently adequate ventilation all around is essential. It is preferable to install and fire gas, oil, and wood kilns out of doors. Use only organic material in sagger, raku, or pit fires—not plastic or styrofoam, which give off noxious fumes. Do not use styrofoam for armature.
9. When checking cones by looking into the fiery interior of a kiln, protect your eyes against heat by wearing goggles or dark glasses. Some eye specialists think that prolonged viewing into a chamber of red heat, 1300° F (700° C) and above, can cause retinal disease. You are safer if you peer into a firing kiln through a black-smoked glass or cobalt lens.
10. Take basic precautions around all machinery; watch for sharp edges; keep hair, long sleeves, and so on, tied back.
11. Raw lead oxide—such as in litharge, galena, red lead, or lead carbonate—is acknowledged by the industry as an unsafe compound in glaze compositions for functional ceramics for food or drink. Lead in so-called "frits," produced by international manufacturers such as Ferro Corporation and others, has been rendered insoluble and non-poisonous by high-temperature processes. Nevertheless, controversy still surrounds the use of lead frits; many schools currently advise against them.
12. Many glaze chemicals in the raw state are toxic, especially if somehow ingested. Please use them wisely and within proper conditions. Care and understanding with sensible precautions must be your rule.
13. For beginners, clay for throwing should be relatively soft to guard against strain on wrists; advanced potters should be aware, too, but they can use stiffer clay, so that the piece will stand up longer during throwing.

To call attention to particular hazards, the following icons have been included throughout the text where appropriate:

Corrosive liquids: liquid glazes contain minor amounts of alkali and acidic materials that may be harmful to some people's skin. Protect hands with pharmaceutical gloves; be careful to avoid splashing liquids, and keep arms and legs covered as much as possible. Certainly do not ingest these liquids, or any ceramic materials.

Heat: avoid opening a kiln until the temperature is below 300° F (150° C) on the pyrometer. Do not put hot pots or kiln furniture on to surfaces that will mark; do not put very hot articles on to very cold surfaces, for fear of bursting the ceramic. Handle hot wares or kiln bricks with thick protective gloves at all times.

Dust and fumes: plaster or glaze powders and other chemicals are liable to blow about and enter the lungs. Do not work with these materials in a draft. Try to work with chemicals or powders with proper ventilation, so you must arrange your work space so as to have ventilation without drafts. Wear a good mask, as indicated above, when working with these materials for long periods. Never sweep the studio without using a non-toxic sweeping compound, or while a gas kiln is firing. Keep the dust down by using water to mop the floors and sponge working surfaces.

Eyes: protect from corrosive liquids, dust, and fire by wearing goggles, as described above. Take real care around hot kilns.

Hands: take precautions as above when handling hot articles or corrosive liquids. Take great care when using sharp implements such as trimming knives, and keep hands away from sharp metal edges and out of moving machinery.

1

THE WORLD OF

CERAMICS

INTRODUCTION

CLAY AND POTTERY

The art of the potter dates from the beginning of humankind. From earliest times people knew that a certain kind of "mud" could be molded into any shape and would retain that shape on drying. Some time later in prehistory the potter understood that fire would harden the clay shape so that it was no longer fragile and would hold liquid. For 30,000 years or more, the working properties of clay and fire, and the necessary processes and tools, have been directed toward specific functional needs such as pots and water pipes in most traditional societies of the world.

Today these age-old concepts and methods are still valid. The artist-craftsperson or anyone who explores claywork uses the same materials and techniques as our long-ago ancestors. **To work in ceramics is to know the whole world and to learn about all times and cultures.**

FACING PAGE **Betty Woodman**, *Aeolian Pyramid* (detail), glazed earthenware, epoxy resin, lacquer, and paint, 120 × 168 × 91 ins. (305 × 427 × 231 cm). Installation view at Metropolitan Museum of Art, New York, 2006

In recent years scientists have discovered new elements to be added to the atomic table, and have reexamined old ones. The new knowledge has expanded our understanding of what constitutes ceramic products. In addition to the familiar brick and flowerpot of low-fire ceramics, called "earthenware," the utilitarian jugs and heavy clay products produced in "stoneware," and the fine, dense, sometimes translucent clay body termed "porcelain," many new products exist today of even higher-fired ceramics made of non-clay materials that are still silicates in the ceramic definition. Artists are concerned primarily with the "clay" part of a ceramic definition.

The space age is the ceramic age. Computer chips, airplane parts, machine components, submarines, and space

Geological types of natural clays and the temperatures to which they are fired in kilns are the two determining factors that produce the common coarse brick or the delicate piece of porcelain. A brick will never be a piece of porcelain because the type of clay is different, and usually the firing temperature is different too.

vehicles are routinely made of high temperature ceramics. **We live in the age of ceramics, no longer in the age of metals.** Ceramic materials have the highest melting point of any material known on the face of the earth.

The potter works in a temperature range of 1300° to 2500° F (700° to 1370° C), and space scientists, with their esoteric ceramic materials, probably (it's classified information) use several thousand degrees of temperature higher. Here we are concerned only with the potter's range.

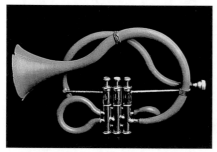

ABOVE Clay can do many things, including make musical instruments that really play: **Brian Ransom**'s ceramic flugelhorn, earthenware, mixed media

As any kind of pure clay dries, it shrinks and becomes hard. Clay has no real strength until fired in "red heat" (1300° F or 700° C) or above. In the firing process the clay mass fuses into a compact structure, with the glaze and decoration forever fired in, making a product of strength and durability that will never change. So a piece of ancient pottery appears today as fresh as when it first came from the fire.

Kripal Singh (India) is well known for his porcelain-like but clayless low-temperature soda-based body, rather like Egyptian paste (see Compendium p. 220); *overglaze enamel painted and fired* to about 1800° F

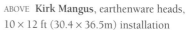

ABOVE **Kirk Mangus**, earthenware heads, 10 × 12 ft (30.4 × 36.5m) installation

LEFT **Nino Caruso**, "Dionysos Arch with Bacchante," stoneware installation, Italy

HISTORY'S INFLUENCE ON THE CERAMIC ART OF TODAY

At the beginning of this century ceramic products are much used in daily life, but objects of clay are now taking a more important place in our aesthetic lives.

Ceramic vessels, bricks, mosaics, and even huts have been part of the human environment for thousands of years. The Chinese developed a porcelain clay body and glazes about 3,000 years ago; the Egyptians probably made the first potter's wheels about 5,000 years ago, and developed glass too; most of the world, including China, had used the common low fire rust-colored clays for thousands of years until the Chinese discovered their own

1   2   3

Nature is a design influence

Design in nature: 1. Chillies from New Mexico; 2. Yucca, California; 3. The sea from the Big Island of Hawaii. Follow the lines, mass, and movement from nature in your claywork

natural deposits of porcelain clay body and figured out how to fire at high temperatures, somewhere around 2,000 years ago.

Marco Polo carried Oriental porcelains to Europe in the 13th century, which prompted Europeans to look for white clays and to try for the density and translucency they saw in the porcelain wares with cobalt blue brush decorations.

The Persians discovered that they had deposits of the rare cobalt, and began to paint blue decorations on low fire white clays under clear and matt glazes; the Dutch and later the English took over this technique and transformed it into Delft ware. The Persians also developed luster glazes, and the Italians found that metallic oxides could be painted on top of white glazes to give fused patterns when fired, a technique now called *majolica*.

Bernard Palissy in the 1560s in France experimented, and J. F. Böttger in Meissen, Germany, succeeded in making porcelain about 1710. In 1760 Josiah Wedgwood discovered how to make a porcelain clay body from English china clay and bone ash, and to fire it to high density—hence the term "bone china."

After the furious pace of mass-production resulting from the industrial revolution that was completed by the 1850s, history witnessed a period of revolt against everything looking alike. William Morris, in England, was one of the first to call for a return of the individual craftsperson and craft techniques. In the 1860s he reestablished the "workshops" and "guilds" we had seen in Renaissance times, and craftspeople began to collaborate. In 1925 a large German workshop, the Bauhaus, inspired a revolutionary new trend in design that

1

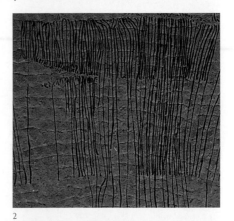

2

Clay surfaces reflecting the design ideas of nature

1. Detail of weave from a clay basket by **Rina Peleg**
2. Detail of stain drawing with hypodermic needle over a coiled, glazed surface by **Bruno Lavadiere**
3. Unglazed colored almost paper-thin porcelain layers, detail of a sculpture by **Marylyn Dintenfass**

3

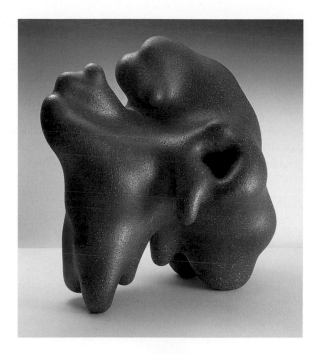

LEFT **Ken Price's** recent ceramic sculpture bears the illusion of glaze, about which this artist knows a great deal, but the surface is in fact a meticulous rendering of various *acrylic paints on fired clay*

RIGHT **John Mason's** vertical sculpture, "Figure Ember," 62 × 23 × 23 ins. (157 × 58 × 58 cm), is a brilliant example of *slab-building* technique astonishingly engineered to stand upright at c/10 reduction firing, 2000

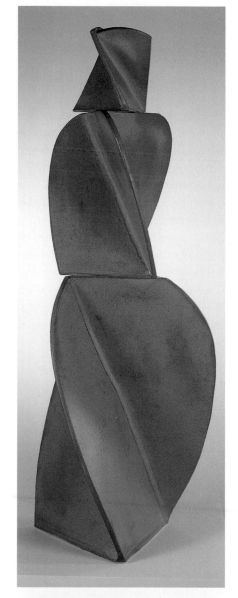

LEFT **Bernard Leach** (1887–1979), the so-called "father of studio pottery," worked in stoneware and porcelain at his well-known pottery in St Ives, Cornwall, UK, from 1920 to his death; this stoneware pot with *engobe and sgraffito design* dates from 1950. He wrote an early handbook for potters, which remains hugely influential

RIGHT **Shoji Hamada** (1894–1978), the famous potter and ceramic National Treasure of Japan, sitting in the lotus position at his Chinese chestnut hand-powered wheel, throwing a tea ceremony bowl in his studio at Mashiko, c. 1970

FACING PAGE **Peter Voulkos'** (1923–2002) *thrown and altered wood-fired stoneware* "stack," 45 ins. (114 cm) high; a magnificent piece that reconfirms how influential this artist has been in the ceramic world

is still influential today; the schools at Weimar and Dessau laid emphasis on ceramic art among other art media.

Before and after World War II, various countries began to investigate new ideas and to become known for their own design criteria. Scandinavian design, especially that of Sweden, promoted bright colors and simplicity of form; the ritual of the tea-ceremony emphasized the role of clay in Japanese culture; folk art, particularly ceramics, in such countries as Mexico and other parts of Central and South America, Morocco, Turkey, and the like, exerted great influence on their other arts. Europe in general responded to the Bauhaus influence,

REMEMBER

● Creative expression is an individual need; it is not a specialty reserved for the "fine artist."
● Clayworkers direct their materials, their processes, and their techniques into an expression of their personalities.
● There is no definite line between craft and art, they are both of a piece.
● A "pot" is not necessarily a container, nor any longer needs to be thought of only as functional.
● Today ceramic art is a characterization of our time, continuing to be an energizing and captivating challenge to clayworkers as one of our most important methods of self-expression.

while the trend in the United States was toward the freedom of Abstract Expressionism in painting and in craft. All these trends continue today.

Early American ceramics came with the European settlers after 1620. From that point up to the 1800s ceramics began to be made in small potteries on the eastern seaboard: slipware, salt glaze, Delft, peasant redwares, luster, some with an aristocratic aesthetic. Ceramic chemistry in the New World embraced the three types of wares already current across the Atlantic ocean—earthenware, stoneware, and porcelain.

The western coast of the United States was influenced by Spanish and Mexican earthenwares, and by the porcelains brought by early Chinese settlers. The USA became a melting pot of world clay styles and cultures, until in the early 1950s a change occurred, causing a revolution in ceramic art that still goes on.

In California, about 1954, a young Pied Piper named Peter Voulkos began to handle enormous chunks of clay in a radical manner on a potter's wheel and to alter the shapes created on the wheel by cutting them, slashing them, beating them, and combining them into large sculptural forms. Jack Peterson and I had designed the first variable-speed electric potter's wheels west of the Mississippi. Voulkos and Paul Soldner used this wheel design but added more horsepower, so more pounds of clay could be thrown at one time. With Mike Kalan, a ceramic engineer, I designed the first high temperature fast-firing open-fire up-draft gas kilns in the country. These developments made possible the huge thrown and hand-built forms that other ceramists began tackling in the Fifties and that are part and parcel of the ceramic objects being made today. **We should not forget that the**

contemporary ceramics movement is only about fifty years old, but ceramic art is as old as time. A group formed around Peter, each experimenting individually, that included myself, Paul Soldner, Jerry Rothman, Henry Takemoto, Mac Maclain, Michael Frimkess—Pete's students—and John Mason and Ken Price, my students, among others. (I had come to Southern California in 1950 and was already teaching at Chouinard Art Institute when Voulkos came to teach at the nearby Los Angeles County Art Institute.)

About the same time I brought British potter Bernard Leach, who had written the formative *A Potter's Book* in 1943, his old friends Shoji Hamada, the foremost potter of Japan, and Soetsu Yanagi, the scholar of Zen Buddhist aesthetics, to Chouinard for several weeks of lectures and demonstrations before an invited audience of clayworkers. The work, writings, and philosophies of these three mentors spread across the world and, even after their deaths, are a powerful inspiration today.

Of course there were other important clay artists in the world at the same time, but the force of the Voulkos personality, and the awesome work that was flowing out of the group in Southern California, provided the major factor in the rapid evolution of ceramics from a functional, utilitarian concept to an art form.

The world has become smaller, communication is easier, ceramic schools, workshops, suppliers, and museums proliferate across the globe. The transformation is spectacular. Ceramic art can vie for prices and clientele similar to those for painting or sculpture. Furthermore, working in clay is a fascinating experience for nearly everyone who comes in contact with it.

FUNCTIONAL VS SCULPTURAL

Recent generations have debated the old argument of functional versus sculptural, of art versus craft, and still not solved it. Historically the controversy has been considered from the monetary standpoint as well as from the point of view of aesthetic values. Ceramic sculpture today sells for higher prices than functional vessels. So-called "fine art" has usually sold to collectors for more than so-called "decorative art."

In past ages there were countless potters throughout the world making functional pots for daily use. Many of these were indigenous potters, fitting the folk art category, as the one million potters of India still do, or those in Morocco, Mexico, Africa, Japan, Indonesia, and elsewhere. Many others were individual potters who worked alone in their studios making objects for everyday use. Today functional potters are still a very active part of the scene, but many clayworkers seem to be entranced by a sculptural attitude.

Some of the functional potters exhibited and became famous as artists. Among the more traditional are the late Shoji Hamada, Bernard Leach, Michael Cardew, Marguerite Wildenhain, and in our day Warren MacKenzie, Sandy Simon, Jeff Oestreich, and their ilk in Europe—but they might not call themselves artists.

There is a fine line between, on the one hand, functional pots for daily use or functional shapes that might or might not be used, which could be called sculpture, and on the other, forms that are traditional but into which one would not think to put food or drink but which instead one would use for decoration or contemplation—as in sculpture.

A sculpture is more particularly defined as a non-functioning object that exists in space, is meant to be looked at, and generally carries intrinsic meaning to the observer. Ceramic sculpture can—but does not have to—expand into a mixture of media using clay and other materials, or into installations that assemble groups of ceramic objects, with the possibility of other added materials (see Chapter 4).

Claywork goes on the floor, on walls, on the table, in the garden, on façades of buildings, and into space technology. **The beginner in clay must learn the basics, then proceed toward determining the final goal, and ultimately execute his or her own ideas of ceramic art. Fine functional vessels produced by hand or wheel are still valued, though little publicized. The feel of a beautifully crafted cup, mug, or plate is unquestionably serene.**

TYPES OF CERAMIC WARES

The differences between a red clay brick and a white translucent porcelain teacup are different clays, different density, and usually a difference in the firing temperature. All clay products, from bricks to porcelain cups, are the result of these two variables, clay and temperature, both of which produce a fired density.

That said, we classify ceramic wares as *earthenware*, *stoneware*, and *porcelain*. Although we think of earthenware as made at low temperature and porcelain as requiring high firing temperature, in fact each type of ware can be made at any temperature if we understand what creates density (page 33). It is possible to make a dense porcelain-like clay body at low temperature, and we can make a porous earthenware-type clay body at high temperature by changing some ingredients. See pages 30–31 for a chart of various mined clays showing their absorption (density) percentages at different temperatures. The following pages will discuss clay body formulation to meet our definition of ceramic wares. The chart shows clays available in the United States, but all five geological types of clay are available almost everywhere in the world.

Earthenware

A fired claywork that is porous, relatively light in weight, easily chipped, and makes a hollow sound if tapped with your fingernail is called "earthenware." Most tribal societies such as American Indian, African, Aboriginal, and other outback peoples use **common surface clays** because they are at hand, and fire them in low temperature open fires to produce earthenware. So-called sophisticated

EARTHENWARE: *Wheel-thrown, burnished, raku fired* bowl with stain decoration by **Carol Rossman** (Canada)

EARTHENWARE:
Hand-built plaque
with commercial
glazes by **Annabeth
Rosen**, 16 ins.
(41 cm) wide

STONEWARE: A huge *coiled and thrown* sculpture by **Toshiko Takaezu** *shows the throwing marks* of centrifugal motion in contrast to the vertical splashes of glaze, 72 ins. (182 cm) high

societies make earthenware plant pots, tableware, and similar items, plus sculpture and installations, because they want to. Low density produces low shrinkage and lighter fired weight and low firing temperatures produce brighter glaze colors on ceramic wares.

The technical definition of earthenware is that it will have an absorption of 10 to 15% of its unglazed weight when a test piece is boiled one hour in water. China/ball clay bodies fired low will be very porous; most contemporary earthenwares used by artists are composed of common surface and fire clays.

was brought to North America by the early settlers who arrived from Europe.

For a clay body to become stoneware a higher firing temperature is usually needed than for earthenware, or more flux can be added to high temperature clays to make them dense at low heat. Stoneware bodies generally begin with fire clays, but for more fine-grained or lighter-burning bodies start with china and ball clays; again, consult the charts.

The technical definition of stoneware is that a test piece absorbs 2 to 5% of its unglazed weight when boiled in water for one hour.

Stoneware

A fired claywork that is quite hard, holds liquids, is not easily broken, and rings when tapped is called "stoneware." Stoneware developed in China over 2,000 years ago, and in Europe during the Middle Ages; the technique

STONEWARE: This unglazed plaque shows a heavy, utilitarian, coarse body; the piece is textured by *ripping and attaching layers*, and accented by the crispness of density achieved in a high-temperature fire. Sculpture by **Claudi Casanovas** (Spain), 36 ins. (91 cm) diameter

Porcelain

A fired claywork that is hard, dense, and vitreous, usually translucent if thin, and generally white or off-white, is called porcelain. As previously stated, we think that the Chinese were the first to make it, several thousand years ago; they were the first people to understand the effects of, and how to get, high temperatures in an enclosed chamber such as a cave or a kiln.

The technical definition of porcelain is 0 to 1% absorption of the weight of an unglazed piece after it is boiled in water for one hour. Because fired porcelain is so nearly glass-like, porcelain clay body ware must be evenly dried to prevent warping and will deform in the fire if the shape is not properly engineered.

Earthenware, stoneware, and porcelain products can result from clay body components **at any ceramic temperature** as long as they fit the above definitions.

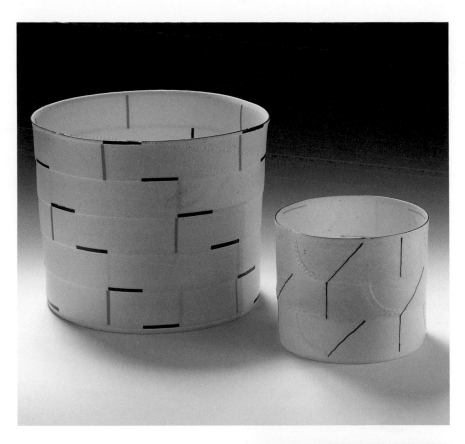

ABOVE PORCELAIN: **Bodil Manz** (Germany) makes extraordinarily thin, translucent cast porcelains with her own *handmade black and red decals, drawn with oxides and stains on decal paper,* transferred to the ware; lines show through to the inside. Multiple high firings, gas kiln c/12, with c/05 electric for red, produce even greater transparency

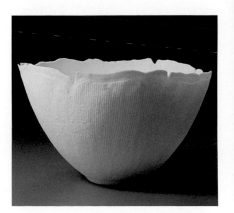

PORCELAIN: **Enid Legros-Wise** (Canada) has *carved and textured* her hand-built, vitreous, high-fired bowl so that it is translucent

PORCELAIN: **Nobuhito Nishigawara,** *hollow-built* sculpture, *burnished to a marble-like surface,* c/12, 17 × 16 × 10 ins. (43 × 40 × 25 cm)

FACING PAGE STONEWARE: *Hand-built:* the *sharply shaped and smoothed* sculpture with black matt and lustrous glaze requires a silky, fine-grained clay body. Sculpture by **Mutsuo Yanagihara** (Japan)

WHAT IS CLAY?

As long as we have a world, there will be clay. Clay is a mineral mined or dug from the earth, composed of alumina, silica, and chemically combined water. Its chemical formula is $Al_2O_3- 2SiO_2- 6H_2O$. Clay is continuously being formed from igneous rock—granite, which itself was formed through a process of fire. The great granite mountains of the world decompose, so to speak, through physical processes, such as rain, wind, earthquake, and glacial movement, and chemical processes, such as weathering from the acids and alkalis of the earth's atmosphere. How clay has been weathered and where nature moves it determines its ultimate color and workability; the more impurities it has, the more plastic it is, while the fewer impurities, the less plasticity (see Glossary).

Geologically speaking, all native clays fall into five general categories.
1. China clays. The first clay that forms at the base of the mountain is virgin, with few impurities. It is the whitest-burning, most heat-resistant, least plastic, and rarest on the face of the globe, and we call it *kaolin* or china clay. Clay that has not moved from the spot where it was formed is termed "primary" or "residual"; hence *primary kaolin*. When primary kaolin is carried away by whatever natural means, contamination occurs, the clay becomes more plastic from the movement, and the color on firing is somewhat off-white. Clays that have been moved are called "secondary" or "sedimentary." *Secondary kaolins* are not as rare, and are more workable than primary china clays. Both types

of kaolin become hard, dense, and vitreous (glassy) by themselves when fired at temperatures of 3100°–3300° F (1740°–1785° C). Most china clays are found in Asia, Britain, Germany, and several in south-eastern USA.
2. Ball clays, the next in purity and the most plastic of all clays, are always secondary clays and have always been moved by water. Because of their fine particle size, brought about by water movement and rock-grinding, these nearly white-burning clays have high shrinkage in drying and firing, and become dense at 2300°–2500° F (1260°–1370° C). Kaolins and ball clays are the usual components of porcelain.
3. Fire clays, readily found in mountain and desert areas of the world, are the work-horses of ceramics. These clays have particle sizes of varying coarseness and flat or round platelets depending on their formation. In addition to the clay molecule, fire clays include extra uncombined silica. Beige, tan, gold, red, brown, are the colors that these clays fire; most become dense and vitreous around 2200°–2400° F (1205°–1260° C). Potters like these clays for their resilience, their strength, and their ability to stand tall. Industry uses fire clays for firebricks, flue linings, blast furnaces, and other heavy clay products.
4. Stoneware clays. This category is debated by geologists: is it really a separate kind of natural clay? So-called stoneware clays are very rare—in the USA we have Jordon (not mined now), Perrine, and Monmouth. A few other stoneware clays have been found in Europe, China, Japan, and India. Because stoneware clays have the properties

of both ball and fire clays, they are remarkably workable, firing dense, in off-white to brown colors, around 2200°–2300° F (1205°–1260° C).

The commercial process of washing china clay (kaolin) removes all impurities

Yellow and beige fire-clay deposit being commercially mined

Slaking and screening natural clay in Kitagoya, Japan; after about three weeks in water the clay slurry is ladled into plaster tubs to dry to the plastic state

5. Surface clays. The most prevalent clays on the earth, under your feet everywhere, are rightfully termed *common surface* clays. Because they are rich with impurities, and have enjoyed millions of years of movement, they are very workable, and are generally the only clays that can constitute a "clay body" and be used entirely by themselves with no additions of flux or filler (see below). **All indigenous societies use common surface clays, with little or no addition, to make functional vessels, effigy figures, bricks, and water pipes.** The usual fired color is rusty red, but common surface clays can fire to any color—except white—depending on the metallic oxides that have combined with them in the earth.

Clay, as opposed to dirt, when mixed with water will form a plastic mass that can be molded into any shape and will hold that shape. When left to dry, most clays will shrink in size as much as 10%. Further shrinkage takes place in the firing. When fired in a bonfire, approximately 1300° F (700° C), all natural clays become somewhat hard and durable, but probably will not hold liquid for longer than it takes to have a drink from a vessel.

1

2

Many types of clay and combinations of clays with other materials are used for clay bodies in ceramic art:

1. **Ron Fondaw's earthenware** sculpture has *additions of turquoise "Egyptian paste,"* which was developed over 3,000 years ago by the Egyptians (see Chapter 8)

2. **Jun Kaneko's** museum installation of 8 ft by 2 ins. (244 × 5 cm) slabs was *constructed in a low-shrink clay body* at the Otsuka factory, Shigaraki, Japan

WHAT IS A CLAY BODY?

Inert or active materials can be added to natural clays to alter the basic properties of the original clay. This combination of clay and other ingredients is called a "clay body," and is built according to the visual and structural needs of industry or artists.

To the basic clay component (one or more natural clays) we add:

1. Filler, to subdue the sticky quality of plastic natural clays: sand, dirt, ground-up particles of already fired clay called "grog" or "temper," silica sand (fused silica), or pure silica. Some of these additions also add texture to the fired clay body.

2. Flux, to change the normal firing temperature of a given clay or group of clays. This can be feldspar, found all over the world, or bone ash—found mostly in England, hence "bone china"—or ground glass, or combinations of other low-melting minerals such as soda ash.

Thus a clay body consists of three components, clay, filler, and flux. The clay body should contain at least 50% clay, plus the added materials,

A famous natural clay body is found in YiXing village, China, well known for traditional and avant garde teapots in this special clay. **Zhou Ding-Fang's** (China) teapot with mouse, 7 × 5 ins. (18 × 12.5 cm), is an example. She is one of the few female potters to have made a name in China

to keep plasticity; a better ratio for excellent workability is 70% to 80% clay plus added material. The clay content can consist of several clays for different reasons, such as color, degree of fine or coarse particle size, temperature required for a particular density, and fabricating specifications. Experience will help you figure this out. Without a good clay body you cannot hope to make good claywork.

Most clay artists know exactly what they want in a clay body. The artist sets up standards for a clay body to suit a particular kind of claywork: how pliable does it need to be? Must it stand up and hold weight? Is color important? What density or porosity is required for the finished product? The artist then makes up his or her own mix.

Clays of most geological types are mined in various parts of the world and can be purchased in bulk, or dry, ground to 200-mesh, easy to mix. Feldspars, ground glass, and other fluxes exist everywhere; everyone likewise has access to various fillers. **Make up a clay composition, test it, and revise it until you like it**. Anywhere in the world you can probably buy these materials, or prospect your own from the earth.

Alternatively, a ready-mixed clay body can be purchased from a ceramic supplier, ready to use in the plastic state in 25 lb (11 kg) bags, or dry in larger quantity. You should specify your requirements for workability, fired color, and the temperature you will fire. You hope the ceramic material supplier can give you a ready-mixed clay body to fit your needs, although the company will keep the ingredients secret.

PAPERCLAY

Today some artists are using the ancient idea of mixing paper and clay to make a body that will do strange things that a regular clay will not, albeit fragile and purely ornamental. In past ages papyrus, paper, cloth, adobe earth, and other materials were added to clay to make it more easily fashioned into varieties of complex shapes, or very thin shapes, or to enable functional and decorative use without firing. Today we see an experimental revival of those practices.

Paperclay body. Begin by trying all kinds of paper and all types of clays or clay bodies, mixed about 50–50 by hand or with an electric blunger.

PAPERCLAY: **Bryan Hiveley**, *2000 Kiln Ritual*, glazed, 67 × 32 × 31 ins. (170 × 81 × 79 cm)

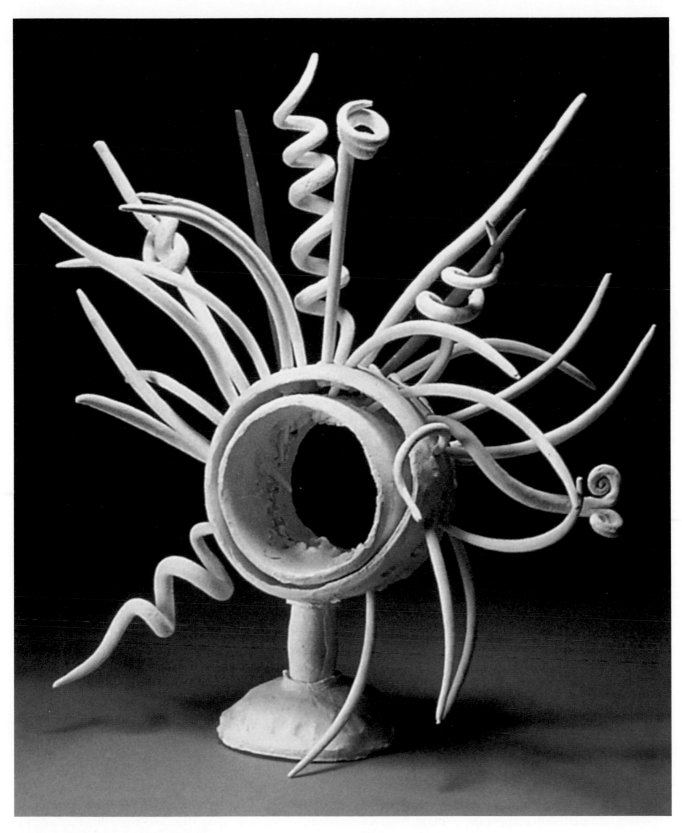

PAPERCLAY: **Graham Hay's** (Australia) sculpture illustrates the amazing versatility of a paperclay body. 43 × 47 × 24 ins. (110 × 120 × 60 cm)

Graham Hay
(Australia),
paperclay form,
earthenware,
22 × 11 × 8 ins.
(57 × 28 × 21 cm)

ALTERNATIVE CLAYS AND ADDITIONS

Adding any inert material to clay lessens its propensity for thermal-shock destruction, often adds texture or color, and may remove most shrinkage—it's like working with a material that is not clay.

Adobe, natural mud-earth that has some clay chemistry, is another age-old material that can work well for certain sculptures and installation art. It sets in air or can be fired; it has strength and can be built tall. So-called primitive societies used adobe for cookstoves and fireplaces; American Indians use it for outdoor bread-baking ovens today. Because adobe has low shrinkage, it is excellent for adding stones to give color and texture; if firing is not necessary for hardness and durability, additives such as shells, glass pieces, metals, and the like retain their personalities in the work.

Concrete, a member of the ceramic family, is another possible addition. Experiment by adding concrete in varying percentages to your own clay body for unusual air-set or fired forms; try finishing at different temperatures, which yield different textures. Concrete bodies have minimal shrinkage, can be glazed and fired and will withstand most weather conditions.

Nails and other hardware, wire, and the like, pressed into or wrapped around a clay piece before firing, over glaze or not, produce unique results.

Popcorn or firecrackers can be placed inside any of these compositions to create various effects during firing in the kiln, for fun, for experimenting with spontaneous form, but perhaps unwise in schools.

Graham Hay, of Australia, one of the most inventive artists working with this material, mixes it in various consistencies – slurry, like whipped cream, plastic, for hand-building and for use in plaster molds, and drier for rolling thin flat slabs. Parts can be made individually, dried, and attached together with paperclay slip before firing, or dried parts of other sculptures can be put together into new forms. Hay says he throws paperclay on the ground to create large slabs with earthy texture (see page 50).

  Dust and bacteria are important issues with paperclay. "I tell people to think about paperclay pottery like gardening: both have organic material for bacteria to grow in, especially if your environment is warm and damp. My advice is to wash with soapy water before coming into the house or eating food."

Make a paperclay slip to repair cracks, patch chips, reattach pieces, or build new parts, in the raw or bisque state of your work. Mix your own regular clay body with soft tissue paper by hand or in a blender when you are ready to use it because it won't keep; you won't notice the patches after glazing and firing.

The resurrection of the ancient concept of mixed paper and clay has been a boon to contemporary artists and to students. The easy manipulation allows for extraordinary squiggles, cantilevers, degrees of thinness, and easily fabricated large scale. Paperclay is best for decorative objects because it doesn't have as much strength as regular clay bodies. It makes excellent lightweight wall hangings that can be huge. Prints from stencils, rollers, free brush, and lithography techniques are appropriate.

Hollow forms can be quickly molded and attached wet or dry as shown in this **Graham Hay** (Australia) sculpture, **paperclay body, earthenware**, 15 × 15 × 11 ins. (37 × 37 × 27 cm)

CLAYS PLUS FELDSPARS AND SILICA EQUAL A CLAY BODY

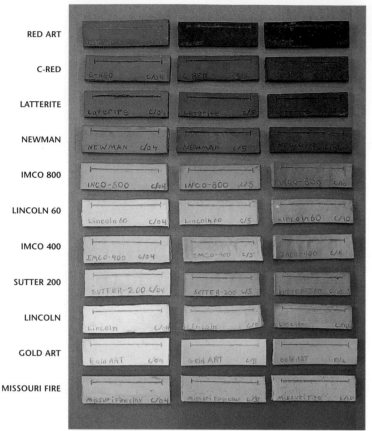

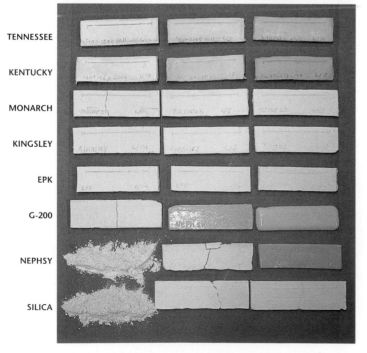

A good clay body is paramount in doing good claywork. A bad clay body will present problems from start to finish. If you can understand this, you will be miles ahead. However, some artists—especially traditional ones—have enjoyed the challenge of working with poor clay bodies. Shoji Hamada, one of the 20th century's best-known and finest potters, said of the coarse, unreliable clay that was dug for him on a hillside near his studio in Mashiko, Japan: "It is better to make good pots out of a bad clay than to make bad pots out of a good clay."

Concoct your own 100% clay body batch by choosing according to color, texture, and temperature, from available clays that you dig or buy, common surface clays, fire clays, ball clays, and/or china clays—plus a flux (feldspar) and a filler (silica).

Generic clays mined in the USA, illustrated here, were pressed in wooden bar molds to keep the clay bars exactly the same size, then marked with a 3.9 in. (10 cm) line that can then be measured for shrinkage, fired arbitrarily at c/04 oxidation low fire, c/5 oxidation median fire, and, to show the difference in color between oxidation and reduction atmosphere, c/10 high fire reduction. Absorption is recorded for each fired tile (right). G200 is a potassium feldspar, and nepheline syenite is a soda spar. Silica and nepheline syenite remain powder at c/04.

The first 11 bars are fire clays, representative of all fire clays. All but Red Art and Gold Art, from Ohio and Missouri, are from California, USA.

Tennessee and Kentucky are ball clays from USA. Monarch and Kingsley are primary china clays, EPK is a secondary china clay, from USA.

Note the differences among the clays and the fluxing agent spars; the spars we tested are only two of many. Use the figures on the chart opposite for these clays or similar clays, for similar feldspars, and for silica, to develop a blended clay body to suit your needs for throwing or hand-building, for low shrinkage, and for desired density. Remember, earthenware has 10–15% absorption, stoneware 2–5%, porcelain 0–1%. More density means higher shrinkage. Test your own local materials by making bars like these and firing them at these mean temperatures, or just the temperature at which you want to fire. Make two bars of each, and take the average.

		% SHRINKAGE									% ABSORPTION		
		c/04			c/5			c/10					
		WET TO DRY	DRY TO FIRE	TOTAL	WET TO DRY	DRY TO FIRE	TOTAL	WET TO DRY	DRY TO FIRE	TOTAL	c/04	c/5	c/10
FIRE CLAYS	**Red Art**	6%	2%	8%	6%	4%	10%	6%	9%	15%	14.5%	1.5%	1.0%
	C-Red	10%	0%	10%	10%	3%	13%	10%	5%	15%	19.9%	14.9%	10.5%
	Latterite	5%	3%	8%	5%	10%	15%	5%	12%	17%	25.5%	14.0%	10.9%
	Newman	9%	1%	10%	9%	5%	14%	9%	6%	15%	24.5%	18.7%	11.1%
	Imco 800	9%	2%	11%	9%	6%	15%	9%	12%	21%	21.8%	7.1%	1.6%
	Lincoln 60	8%	1%	9%	8%	10%	18%	8%	11%	19%	21.5%	6.8%	1.4%
	Imco 400	10%	1%	11%	10%	7%	17%	10%	8%	18%	20.4%	3.7%	1.6%
	Sutter 200	7%	4%	11%	7%	16%	23%	7%	18%	25%	27.2%	1.9%	1.3%
	Lincoln	6%	3%	9%	6%	12%	18%	6%	13%	19%	28.0%	9.5%	0.7%
	Gold Art	6%	2%	8%	6%	6%	12%	6%	9%	15%	12.7%	4.8%	1.7%
	Missouri Fire	5%	3%	8%	5%	7%	12%	5%	9%	14%	13.5%	5.0%	2.9%
BALL CLAYS	**Tennessee**	8%	3%	11%	8%	6%	14%	8%	7%	15%	22.5%	11.8%	4.5%
	Kentucky	10%	3%	13%	10%	5%	15%	10%	7%	17%	19.9%	7.5%	1.2%
CHINA CLAYS (Kaolins)	**Monarch** (primary)	5%	1%	6%	5%	4%	9%	5%	5%	10%	30.2%	26.4%	25.0%
	Kingsley (primary)	3%	4%	7%	3%	5%	8%	3%	8%	11%	29.0%	26.0%	19.0%
	EPK (secondary)	6%	7%	13%	6%	7%	13%	6%	12%	18%	19.3%	17.9%	17.4%
FELDSPAR	**G-200**	0%	0%	0%	0%	melt	melt	0%	melt	melt	20.0%	soft	melt
	NephSy	powder	powder	powder	2%	3%	5%	2%	melt	melt	dissolve	3%	soft
	Silica	powder	powder	powder	0%	0%	0%	0%	0%	0%	dissolve	21%	25%

Testing

Shrinkage: a) Measure the line on the bar wet (10 cm), then dry, then fired, one bar for each of the three temperatures. **Formula**: a) Shrinkage wet minus shrinkage dry divided by shrinkage dry × 100 = percent unfired shrinkage. b) Measure the 10 cm line of each bar fired at the three mean temperatures. **Formula**: Dry shrinkage minus fired shrinkage divided by fired shrinkage × 100 = fired shrinkage for each bar fired at each temperature. **Dry and fired shrinkage together give total shrinkage wet to fired.**

Absorption: 1) Weigh each bar after firing at the three mean temperatures; record. 2) Boil each fired bar covered one hour in water. 3) Remove, blot dry, weigh immediately, record for each temperature. **Formula**: Boiled fired weight minus original weight divided by original weight × 100 = percent absorption for each temperature.

Most potters enjoy testing individual clays, as shown on our chart, and testing any clay body they are using, commercial or homemade, so that they can understand how much their work will shrink at a given firing range, how dense it will be, and what if anything should be done to change or better it. **Ideally a clay body should shrink half in drying and half in firing, to avoid extra strains on the work during drying.**

WHY MIX YOUR OWN CLAY BODY?

The best reason for developing the proportions of various materials on a 100% clay body batch and then mixing your own clay is that you will know exactly what is in it. You will understand the properties of the individual components, which will help you to do exactly what your ideas demand. Almost any combination in a "clay body" will be termed earthenware at low fire, but at high fire it may be dense or *it may be a glaze*: **you must test!**

If you are determining your own clay body—and clay is the basic first thing in making any ceramic object—you will be thinking of the whole project, of the whole piece and of the final result. You will be starting at the beginning and can set your own boundaries. Furthermore, if you mix your own clay body you will do so in a rather large quantity, perhaps as much as 100 lb (45 kg). When we buy plastic-bagged clay made commercially it usually comes in relatively small amounts, rectangularly shaped. Mentally we are restricted by the size and shape of that bung of clay, which limits the mind and the work. If you have a big mound of wet clay on the table or floor in front of you, ready to work with, there are no limits to your conceptual thoughts.

METHODS OF MIXING CLAY BODIES

Besides combining your clay body from refined materials such as those on our chart (pages 30–31), you might dig from the ground a natural clay, which must be treated and tested as follows. It should be dried out and pounded into small bits, then screened to remove sand, leaves, and debris. Next, add water and test the clay for workability by making a small pinch-pot. If the clay is sticky, add filler. Fire the pot if you can, and if it is too porous or fragile at the temperature to which you fired it, add flux to the clay, make corrections, work it, and fire a new sample. Repeat until you have a good, usable clay body mixture.

Mix a plastic clay body without a machine:
1. Mix the batch dry—thoroughly—by stirring, sifting, or rolling in a closed container.
2. Next, hand-mix wet:
a) put clay and water in a bucket,

REMEMBER

A clay body consists of:
- **The plastic material**—any clay or clays
- **The flux**—feldspar, glass, or bone ash
- **The filler**—silica, sand, ground shards, or grog (also called chamotte)
- Check the charts on pages 30–31.

Whether you use materials from nature or buy 200-mesh refined materials, your clay body needs several ingredients. You must mix them thoroughly, with or without a machine.

stir to smooth slurry, remove excess moisture on porous surface to plastic stage;

or b) make a 4-in. (10 cm) high mound of the dry body mix, make a center depression, add water, mix, and knead to plastic stage—a large quantity of clay can be mixed this way on the floor with a hoe or your feet, or mix a small amount with your hands.

3. Miss Mary Muffet method: layer finely powdered dry clay (about an inch at a time); with a watering can sprinkle water over each layer until you reach the top of the container, cover and wait several days for workable clay.

Mix a plastic clay body with a machine:

1. Blunger. Put your dry batch in a barrel with water and mix liquid with an electric drill modified with a metal stirring blade on the end of a rod.

2. Clay mixer. For 100 lb (45 kg) of plastic clay, put about 4 ins. (10 cm) of water in the bottom of a commercial clay mixer, add the dry ingredients, and mix for about

> An example of a generic clay body that will fire at almost any temperature is:
>
> 70% clay (any kind or combination)
> 20% feldspar (any kind)
> 10% silica (red clays may melt at c/10—use with caution)
>
> At low fire this body will be porous, at high fire it will be dense, depending on the materials chosen.

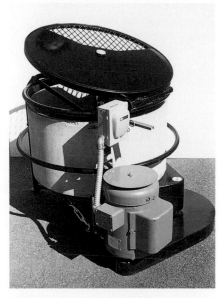

An example of a clay mixer. This one was designed by **Paul Soldner**, but there are innumerable types available all over the world. Most clay mixers blend the dry materials and water with a revolving paddle into your desired plasticity

20 minutes. Note: for mixing deflocculated clay body slip clay for casting in molds, see page 60.

STORING THE CLAY

Clay dries when exposed to air, but will keep moist if it is stored airtight. Metal garbage cans used for clay storage should be galvanized and lined with several sheets of plastic. Plastic containers are satisfactory if lined with sheets of plastic and kept moist with damp towels. Other possible storage containers are wooden tubs, bath tubs, old sinks, or the like. If the clay does dry out, pound it into bits, remoisten, and keep it airtight a few days until it becomes plastic again.

How important is fired shrinkage and absorption?

As shown in the illustrations of fire-clays, ball clays, china clays, feldspars, and silica (pages 30–31)—the components of a clay body—you will note the variety of shrinkage and absorption percentages at three mean temperatures: c/04 = 1922° F (1035° C), c/ 5 = 2150° F (1162° C) and c/10 = 2350° F (1273° C).

Clay shrinks as it dries in air, shrinks more as it fires, depending on how dense it becomes on firing. **Percentage of absorption—i.e. porosity—is the degree to which a fired clay will absorb water. Shrinkage and final density are particularly important when building and firing large claywork.**

Many ceramic sculptors use high-firing clays at low temperatures so that the shrink factor will be small, but porosity and fragility may be great. When clay becomes very dense, it will have maximum shrinkage; high shrinkage can cause deformations but dense work will be strong!

Thus a fired porcelain piece may turn out to be 20% smaller than it was when it was made; the density it attains could necessitate making several to get one correct form. Density in porcelain contributes to the visual effect. Functional pottery often has a higher percentage of absorption: cups, bowls, and the like should be dense enough to hold liquid or food without leaking. Low density—high porosity—makes for fragile, easily broken (but less costly to make) ware, hence earthenware dinnerware is in general cheaper to buy than stoneware or porcelain.

Density or conversely porosity is

controlled by the firing qualities of the clay itself and by the amount of *flux* that is added to lower maturing temperature and increase density. Silica, almost always added to a clay body to alleviate stickiness, will lessen shrinkage. Concocting your clay body focuses your attention on the kind of workability your ideas require, on the shrinkage your forms can stand, and on the density or porosity demanded by the function, or the "look."

How to reclaim scrap clay

Clay is only workable in the so-called plastic, malleable stage. The more you work it, the more it dries and loses its plasticity. To make it usable again:

1. If it is leather-hard (semi-dry, like cheese), poke finger-holes in the chunk, add water, wrap in a plastic sheet and store in a lidded container for a week or so until the clay softens.

2. If the scrap is bone-dry, collect it in a wooden box or some low, flat receptacle, pound it into powder, and—in a metal, wood, or stoneware container—add that dry powder in layers alternating with sprays of water. Cover with damp cloths and plastic, leave for several days and the clay will be workable again.

3. Or, add the ground dry powdered clay to an excess of water; in a few weeks it should be a slurry that can be dried to a workable stage on a plaster or wooden table.

4. If you add leather-hard, partially dry, and bone-dry scrap in various lumps to water, you will never get an un-lumpy mass of clay. Don't do this!

White earthenware clay body vase with *low-temperature matt and glossy glazes* by **Elisabeth van Krogh** (Norway)

WHAT IS GLAZE?

Glaze is a type of glass, which melts in a fire at a given temperature, but does not melt enough to run off the object it coats.

Unlike glass, which stands alone, **glaze needs to be bonded** to something like clay or metal.

Glaze is made of silica (the glass-forming oxide), plus other oxides that cause the refractory silica to melt at lower temperatures. In glass the fluxes are generally soda or lead. In glaze the fluxes vary according to the temperature required to mature the clay.

Glaze contains one more component than does glass. It needs the addition of an oxide that will hold the molten glass on a surface. That oxide is alumina, which acts as a binder and a viscosity controller. Remember, clay contains alumina. It turns out that clay is one of the important constituents of a glaze, in addition to silica, which is the same oxide that is a filler in a clay body. Both clay bodies and glazes, therefore, contain clay and silica in different proportions.

Glaze can be matt (dull) or glossy; transparent (see-through) or opaque in varying degrees; rough or smooth; colored with metallic earth oxides or left uncolored. Glazes can be mixed by you or commercially purchased ready-mixed, but of secret composition, or a company can mix your own formula.

Glaze provides:
• An easily cleaned, sanitary coating.

• A vehicle for decoration and color.
• Acid and chemical resistance.
• Durability.

Glazes can be "made up" from:
• An original molecular oxide formula.
• Experimental tests of various raw materials in different percentage combinations.
• Batch "recipes" found in ceramic books or magazines.
• Original batches, altered according to experience or caprice.

Glazes are colored with:
• Small percentages of oxides of a few metals that resist high temperatures, such as cobalt for blue, iron for brown, chrome for green, copper for turquoise, vanadium for yellow, and others.
• Salts of various metals such as carbonates, sulfates, nitrates (e.g. copper carbonate, copper sulfate)—sulfates and nitrates are less strong, carbonates are stronger but oxides are strongest, used with appropriate percentages.
• "Stains" that are commercially prepared from metallic oxides and other chemicals that are stable at certain temperatures and that provide a much wider palette of color than the basic oxides.
   More about glazes and glazing in Chapter 5.

FIRING CERAMICS

Humans made and used pottery for many thousands of years, knowing that sun-drying did not make the pieces durable, but not aware of what else to do. They added papyrus, dirt, and

Peter Hayes (UK) pulling a red-hot piece out of a raku kiln (see finished piece fired this way on p. 64). Usually artists use metal tongs or a shovel mechanism to extract large pieces hot from the kiln, but properly refractory gloves, as shown here, also suffice

other organic materials to the clay to increase the vessel's sun-dried strength. But in rain the clay reverted to mud, and disintegrated with use.
   No one knows how humans discovered that the heat of a real fire was necessary to produce the chemistry in clay body ingredients for a modicum of hardness and stability. 1300° F (700° C) is the measurable temperature of flame in an open fire. This "red heat" is the lowest temperature at which minerals in a clay vessel can achieve minimum durability, but it will still be fragile and liquids will seep out. When potters learned to enclose the heat, they realized greater density and permanence. Pots stacked for bonfiring could be covered with brush and a thick coating of clay all over to enclose the fire. American Indians used cow chips around their wood-fired pots. The first "kilns" were probably caves cut deep into hills, blocked up with stones after the pots and wood were placed inside. The cave idea progressed

to kilns built like a dragon, upward on sloping ground with fire at the bottom and a flue at the top.
   Potters found that different temperatures and lengths of time in the heat created different colors in the same clays. White-burning clays didn't change, but colored clays stayed lighter at low fire and darkened if temperature and time were extended. Ceramic chemistry has been called the earliest science. Museums are full of the evolution of pottery from earliest times, showing a variety of clay colors, shapes, and forms. We don't know why the Chinese were the first people in the world to determine, thousands of years ago, how to build kilns that would stand up under the high temperatures they were learning to attain—nor do we understand why they were the first and only culture to want to try.
   Clay does not like thermal shock—it breaks. Ancient potters put "temper," ground shards of broken fired pots, pulverized nutshells or bones, grains, sand, or volcanic ash into clay to make it more resistant to an instant flame. When clayworkers used enclosed chambers, which we call kilns, they also worked out how to control heat with flues and dampers in extraordinarily complicated ways.
   In a kiln, clay can be fired slowly, especially in the initial stages, to expel the moisture that made it workable and the water that is combined chemically with the alumina and silica in the clay molecule. Generally a six- to eight-hour firing curve, consistently rising to top temperature, is sufficient for normal claywork; cooling must be slow also. Exceptionally large works require much slower firings, which can take several days or even weeks.
   Look for more about firing in Chapter 6.

1

2

3

2

THE CRAFT OF WORKING WITH CLAY BY HAND

GETTING STARTED

Hand-building is the oldest method of clayworking, probably beginning at least 30,000 years ago.

Throwing developed in Egypt, China, and Mesopotamia about 5,000 or more years ago. Throwing on the potter's wheel (see Chapter 3) is the most direct way of shaping a clay piece. Thrown work made round on the wheel can be altered to make other shapes. Working on the potter's wheel is a skill that requires many years of practice, but it is only a skill and anyone can learn it.

FACING PAGE An extraordinary vertical *slab-built* sculpture by **John Mason**, $62\frac{1}{2} \times 13\frac{1}{2} \times 13\frac{1}{2}$ ins. ($159 \times 34 \times 34$ cm), built 1991, glazed 1997

INSETS The techniques shown here for making large pots are necessary because the wheels, or the potter's skill, are too imperfect to throw the shapes. Beginners can take advantage of these methods, too:

1. **A potter at Tulsi Farms, Delhi, India,** *turns and coils* a large container
2. **In Nepal, a potter** *paddles a shape inside and outside,* expanding a thick form into a thinner one; the potter must be very skilled
3. **A potter in Maheshwar, India,** *paddles the thicker shape* into the final one at the far right

There are many ways to shape clay forms with your fingers and hands, as you will see in the next pages. The earliest humans may have pressed clay against rocks or over a "found object," or shaped clay forms inside or around a woven basket, in addition to the pinching, coiling, and slab-building techniques that are ancient methods still applicable today.

Duplicating the same shapes in a fired-clay or plaster mold is ancient too. The Egyptians and Greeks mastered mold-making by 2000 BCE. Today commercial ceramics are made mechanically, by mold reproduction processes called slip-casting, jiggering, and ram pressing. Some processes done by machines turn out hundreds of wares automatically every day. Potters can use hand variations of these methods.

Space ceramics involve other ways of forming, which may one day be part of the potter's vocabulary.

The clayworker decides which method to use according to the special requirements of the piece that is to be fabricated. His or her emotional response to a particular method may also affect the decision.

If the skills are not known, then they should all be learned and practiced in order that an intelligent choice of method can be made. The clay body, as we have said, must be the best, or the best pieces will not be made.

TEXTURE

These modern tools imitate natural ones that might have been used by indigenous peoples

Rolling or pressing plant material into clay for pattern-making is an ancient technique

Today we often use "found objects" such as shells to obtain textures and forms in clay

Barbara Sorensen's contemporary shield sculpture, inspired by prehistoric images, is *encrusted with textural impressions and earth oxide colorings*; stoneware, stones, and mixed media, 27 × 15 × 4 ins. (68 × 38 × 10 cm)

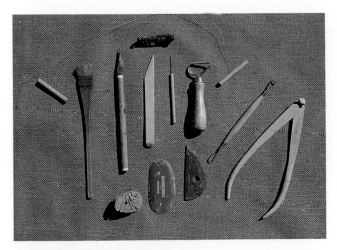

Potters can use hundreds of tools, or a few, or none, but a basic set is probably a good idea. Shown here are *a flat and a round brush* for decorating, a twisted *cutting wire*, a small *finishing sponge*, a *wood knife* for texturing and trimming, *a rubber and a wooden rib* for shaping, a *needle on the end of a stick* for cutting, a small *level*, a small and a large *wire-end trimming tool*, and a *calliper* for measuring lids or attachments

Exotic tool choices, left to right: YiXing wooden slab-pounder and paddles; buffalo horn scrapers; ribs; wooden, bamboo, plastic turning tools, carvers; brass trimmers, wood egg for rounding interiors; varying sizes of circle cutters and measuring sticks. More tools from China are available in the USA from Guangzhou "Po" Zhou (above), Li Jiansheng, and Luo Xiao Ping (see p. 234)

It behooves you to take time to develop or find a good clay body. If you are a student you may be limited to what is in your school. If you are working on your own, you can afford the time to experiment and test until the right mixture proves itself.

On the following pages we will show you beginning steps in the wonderful vocabulary of claywork. Some of the photographs of finished pieces may seem too complicated for beginners, but it's OK to try. It's also OK to feed your brain with lots of ideas and images, to keep your mind flying high.

TOOLS FOR WORKING

Potters can use many tools, or just a few, or none. Most clay artists make collections all their lives of various tools—or objects that will function as tools—from the hardware store, from their attics and garages, and from nature.

Water is essential in the handbuilding process, but should be used very sparingly. A plastic squirt bottle of some sort is required to spray water, as work must be kept uniformly damp throughout construction. Part vinegar can be substituted for water, to keep physical shrinkage lower.

Basic tools for claywork:

- Metal knife and wood knife
- Small sponge or chamois
- Cutting wire
- Half-moon-shaped wood or rubber rib
- Texture tools such as rocks, sticks, buttons, shells, etc.
- Metal scraping tool, wire-end tool, hacksaw blade, metal rib
- Silver or steel fork, knife, spoon
- Wooden paddles
- Two pairs of different callipers

WEDGING CLAY

Clay must be in the best possible plastic condition for working, without hard lumps, without air bubbles, and absolutely even in consistency throughout. *Wedging* is the hand process by which we get clay into working condition. Industry, as well as some schools and potters, use a pug mill to "wedge" clay, but even then, more hand wedging is essential. Wedging puts the clay into an even condition while the potter is "feeling" the clay. Clay will tell

HOW TO WEDGE

1. Start with a relatively soft ball of clay slapped into a rectangular shape, on end, pointing up to the right.

2. Left hand grasps the left side of the lump, fingers toward the back; right hand rests gently on top of the mound. Left hand presses down into the clay,

3. Right hand pivots the lump to the left, counterclockwise. After the pivot, left hand presses downward again, right hand pivots.

4. Repeat until the clay feels even. Wedging dries clay out—expect it to get stiffer as you work, add water. Although all forming methods with clay require the potter to be ambidextrous, to use both hands equally well, left-handers may want to reverse the above directions. Beginners should practice "petal wedging" every time before starting work.

5. This wedging routine results in "petal" shapes, and is called chrysanthemum or petal wedging.

Beginners can check their wedging capability by using two different colors of clay and wedging until they are completely amalgamated into a single color:

Turn the ball of clay on its end, push the left hand down into the clay, and…

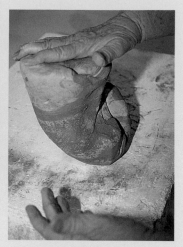

… pivot with the right hand. Repeat the process, left hand down, right hand pivot, until consistency is even. The air is forced out through the petal layers you can see developing above

---

you what it wants to do, what it CAN do. See also page 69 for more on the wedging process.

Of course you must start each project with an idea of how the finished object will look. Some balls of clay just do not feel as if they want to become wide bowls or tall bottles, in which case change your perception of what you wanted to make, or try another ball of clay. Ideas always should come first. Flawless wedging is the initial step.

"Cut and slap" is a method often employed by beginners for wedging from a commercial 25 lb rectangular chunk of clay: cut—with a twisted wire or string—a slab of clay 2 or 3 ins. thick, throw it noisily down onto the wedging table; cut again, slapping this slab down over the first slab, and so on and on, making certain no air remains between slabs. This is easy and fun, but runs the risk of trapping air in the clay. Remember, wedging puts clay in condition for working.

BUILDING BY HAND: INTRODUCTION

Because ancient peoples first made pots and clay figures by hand processes, and only later on the wheel, we sometimes think that the making of pottery by coil and slab techniques is easy.

Actually, learning to control shapes made from coils, slabs, and pinches by hand, or learning to support the line of the profile and the weight of the form, are techniques almost as difficult to master as wheel-throwing.

If a piece cannot be finished all at one sitting, it must be kept moist with rags and plastic wraps to keep the condition almost the same as any new clay that is to be added. It should remain so until the work is finished. Beware of spraying too much water on a piece or it might collapse. Remaining clay for working tomorrow must be kept moist in an airtight container to keep it uniform during the fabrication period.

"When the claywork is leather-hard," as Bernard Leach said, **"like cheese, take care not to squeeze or change its form; your last shaping must be finished before the clay becomes leather-hard."**

Solid clay shapes are used as models for making plaster molds, into which clay, plaster, or even molten metal may be cast. **Hollow clay shapes:** clay shapes to be fired, whether vessel forms or sculpture, should be built hollow; solid shapes thicker than 1 or 2 ins. produce firing problems.

Some clayworkers build forms solid but carve them out while the clay is still moist; this does not allow for an even cross-section, and disaster is likely in the firing. Thick, solid clay shapes can be finished in a very elongated kiln firing and cooling period. Bricks, one of the thickest clay shapes, may take weeks to fire. The larger and thicker the clay form the more slowly it must be fired.

Shrinkage. Furthermore, clay shrinks as it dries. Thin walls dry and fire most easily. Understanding the movement of clay from wet to dry to fired is the first and most necessary step in thinking of clay shapes. Clay is a living, moving thing until after it is out of the kiln. Clay moves because it shrinks physically from the wet to the bone-dry stage; more shrinkage takes place chemically in the course of the firing. The maximum shrinkage that a potter will experience, over the wet-dry-fired sequence, takes place in a vitreous porcelain piece.

Cantilevered shapes, that is, wide bowls on tiny feet, or pot-bellied bottles on small bases, are likely to slump or warp in any direction, or to crack. It simply is not feasible to create the same shapes in clay that can be achieved in wood or metal.

Allowing for the movement during shrinkage is crucial to the fabrication and the design in all claywork. Build especially large work on 1 to 2 ins. (2.5 to 5 cm) thick newspaper or thick cloth to facilitate the piece during shrinking and drying.

HAND-BUILDING TILES

Ron Kovatch devised this simple, quick method for students. Extrapolate for any size module:

- for instance, hollow out a 12 × 2 ins. (30 × 5 cm) thick slab of clay like a picture frame
- decorate a 7 ins. (18 cm) square stoneware tile with a punctured design, to fit the frame
- make a white porcelain thick slurry and fill the stoneware frame
- squeeze the tile into the slurry
- sagger fire with charcoal, dried food, pine needles, sawdust, salt, and the like. Tumble-stack tiles together

Temperatures from c/5 to c/11 work best, with a long firing

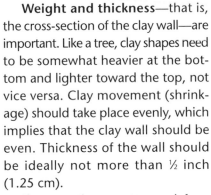

STONEWARE: fire clays 80%, china clay 10%, feldspar 10% plus coarse grog
PORCELAIN: china clay 50%, soda feldspar 25%, silica 25%

Weight and thickness—that is, the cross-section of the clay wall—are important. Like a tree, clay shapes need to be somewhat heavier at the bottom and lighter toward the top, not vice versa. Clay movement (shrinkage) should take place evenly, which implies that the clay wall should be even. Thickness of the wall should be ideally not more than ½ inch (1.25 cm).

If cross-sections vary too much from thick to thin over the entire piece, then drying and shrinking will also be uneven. **This is almost always the reason for cracked pots.** Cracks resulting from uneven drying may not be seen until after the first firing, the so-called "bisque" firing. Sometimes the clay waits to crack until there is further shrinkage, at the stage when

the glaze is fired to higher temperatures. But the strain will almost always have been the potter's mistake, set up during the fabrication and the drying.

The clayworker is in total control when using the basic hand methods such as pinch, coil, and slab. In throwing, the wheel determines a great deal of the weight and wall of a piece.

Combustible cores: it is possible to use materials that burn out in firing, as cores for supporting difficult shapes in the hand-building process. Again, you have to understand what you are doing. If clay is fastened against paper, cardboard, or fabric without room to move, then it cannot shrink properly and it will crack at the pre-fire drying stage. Combustible cores are supports that burn out in the fire, but they must be soft enough

Bruce Howdle builds a wall 23 ft (7 m) long against a wooden easel, carves directly into the moist clay, keeps it damp with plastic covers for the weeks of work, and will cut it into sections for firing, following along the lines of the sculptured forms rather than traditional squares— a very important concept

to allow movement of the wet to dry clay before firing, or must be covered with layers of soft paper or cloth that will give as the clay moves. Cores may also be removed before firing.

Wooden or metal armatures should not be used unless they can be removed before firing, unless the cracking that ensues can be part of the design, or unless the armature is stainless steel or nylon wire and is not removed (page 101). Sculptors who work in stone or bronze often make solid clay models on metal armatures as "sketches," or work clay on metal armatures from which a mold is made for further casting in metal. Potters are limited to hollow, relatively thin and even-walled work. **Ceramic sculpture is best made by building hollow, bottom to top, controlling wall thickness and weight all the while.**

Children enjoy making small clay figures or objects solid, and they can be successful, especially if they are shown how to poke needle or pin holes through the thick clay for even drying and firing. Something children particularly like is to put little groups of figures or objects together on a flat clay pancake, making a whole story on a stand of clay.

Some of the most beautiful objects ever made in clay have been made by hand techniques, without the use of a wheel or template. Today some of the best ceramic sculpture on an architectural scale is made this way. If you respect the technique and learn to use it properly, if you understand the principles of hand-building, there is no limit to size or design (see Chapter 4).

HAND-BUILDING TECHNIQUES
Pinching clay

Pinching a ball of solid clay into a hollow form, with the fingers and without tools, is one of the oldest methods of building with clay. Pinching can be combined with coiling or with paddling, so that larger shapes can be obtained. Much satisfaction— akin to meditating—can be gained from holding a ball of clay in the palm of one hand, making a hole in it with the thumb of the other hand, and then rotating the form and pinching the wall up and out with the thumb and fingers.

Pinching is the first technique to use with any new clay, or with clay you have just prospected in nature. It is the ideal method for developing that absolutely vital sense of the clay wall thickness. The best way to measure clay thickness is by feel, although you can push a needle through the clay wall to measure it. Feeling the wall is also the proper method of teaching yourself to sense whether the clay is in good condition, that is, without lumps or air bubbles that will cause trouble in firing. Gaining these perceptions takes practice; pinching a clay form is a good way to practice (see page 44).

Coil method, smooth or textured

As old as time, this is one of the most difficult ways of making clay forms. We give kindergarten children the assignment of making a coil pot, and then expect them to do it!

Ropes of clay are rolled out, one at a time, and attached to each other by a process called **luting**. Each coil is scored with a knife, the tines of a fork, a comb, or a similar tool. The scored edges are moistened with water or with a clay slurry (a thickish mixture of clay and water) and attached sturdily. **Scoring must be deep so that each coil mates solidly with the other.** Scoring and using water or slurry to

Coils placed one on top of the other will cause the vessel to grow tall and straight; a coil edge placed outside the previous one will expand the vessel outwardly; a coil edge placed inside the previous one will move the shape inward. Thus a shape is easily controlled, whether straight up or out and in.

attach may not be necessary if the clay body is very moist so that clay welds to clay naturally under a slight pressure (see page 45).

Coils must be added while the clay is moist, or "leather-hard," not dry.

Stoneware clay body **coils** from a hand-pushed extruder mound together in a large sculpture by a Hunter college student, New York City

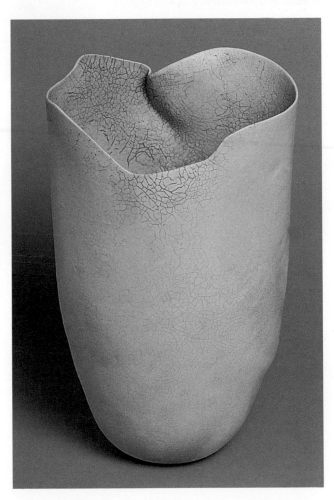

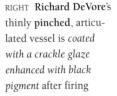

RIGHT **Richard DeVore's** thinly **pinched**, articulated vessel is *coated with a crackle glaze enhanced with black pigment* after firing

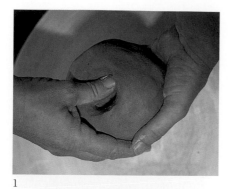

1

2

PINCHING A CLAY POT

1. Begin a small pinch-pot from a ball of clay you can hold in your hands. Press a hole downward with your thumb, turning the ball in your hand

2. Thumb inside, fingers outside, or vice versa as here, squeeze and pinch upward while rotating the ball; repeat to perfect the form

3. Turn pot upside down, fingers squeeze up a foot pedestal, thumb indents

4. Finished form can be pinched thinner, wider, taller, right side up; a paddle can refine the form or add texture
Large pinched forms are possible in similar fashion to almost any scale

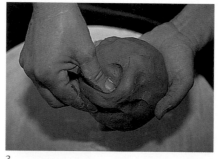

3

4

ABOVE **Maria Martinez** (d. 1980), San Ildefonso Pueblo, New Mexico, **pinching out** a form which she has started from a solid ball. The 50–50 clay–volcanic ash composition causes the body to become moist and sluggish quickly, making it difficult to control. Maria used to build jars as tall as 3 ft (90 cm) and bowls equally wide, but by her 90s, above, her arthritis prevented large-scale pieces and she preferred only shapes she could hold in her hand

BELOW A large pillow form by **Marea Gazzard** (Australia) illustrates the **pinching** technique and is a good example of the concept of enclosed space. *It is quite difficult to give the feeling of volume in clay sculpture*

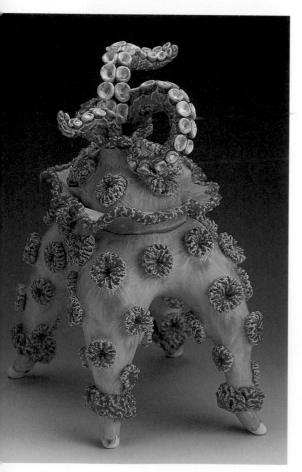

LEFT **Carla Potter's** *Late Bloomer Box*, a combination of **coil and pinch** construction, *surface smoothed during building*, is coated with *high fire underglazes*, c/10 oxidation, 11 × 8 × 6 ins. (28 × 20 × 15 cm). Coil and pinch methods are often used together, complementing each other

Because clay shrinks and must dry uniformly, the piece must be constructed all at once in the same state of wetness, even if this means keeping it damp for weeks until the fabrication is finished.

Weight, thickness of the wall, and the profile line of the form are the determining factors in whether or not a coiled piece will stand up without cracking or warping in the fire. The texture and pattern of the coils can be kept as part of the design of the work, or the coils can be smoothed inside and out with a tool. Evenly rolled coils make evenly controlled lines, but unevenly rolled coils can be interesting too. Coils rolled into rosette shapes, or snakes, or U's and W's, laid sideways or vertically, will achieve pattern and structure at the same time.

If a smooth surface is desired on very large works, build with fat coils that can be flattened before they are attached. Usually one coil is wound round to form one circle and the two ends are luted together. More complicated forms are possible if the coils are kept narrow in diameter, but the building process is slower. It is also possible to wind the pieces round and round in a continuous coil, which will create a different kind of texture and form (page 43).

Lucy Lewis (d. 1992), Acoma Pueblo, New Mexico, **coils** and textures a storage vessel. In order to achieve the traditionally rounded bottom, she is working in an old clay shard

COIL-BUILDING

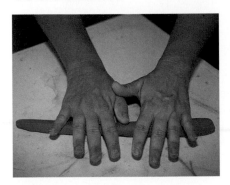

Two hands may be easier than one hand for rolling a coil of even thickness and roundness; roll from center out, on canvas, plaster, wood, or towel. Coils can be extruded too

Attach coil to a patted-out base: score base and coil deeply with a sharp tool, moisten, press together strongly. Score (lute) both ends, moisten and join

Exposed coils can form arbitrary patterns during building of the shape, or coils can be obliterated with a tool for a smooth surface

Rolled coil forms for building or decoration …

… can add decorative elements to finish the work; be sure to score and wet both sides for the attachments

The base of the form can be indented with your fist or palm, for ease of drying and firing

ABOVE **Jennifer Lee** (UK) is a master at **pinch and coil** technique *using stains and metallic oxides* added to a variety of clay bodies for a range of colors and textures. She works one pot at a time over several weeks; pinch and coil marks are *smoothed with bamboo and wood tools; some surfaces are scraped, some are burnished.* Pots are once-fired, oxidation, to c/9; no glaze is used. 6 × 9½ ins. (15 × 24 cm); 3¾ × 3½ ins. (9.5 × 9 cm)

Joanne Emelock's large **coiled** floor pot, 42 ins. (106 cm) high, meticulously *carved and textured*, has been coated with low-fire earthenware glazes

Slab-building

Coil-building is for round shapes, slab-building is for squares or angles and sharp edges. Slabs can also construct round forms where there is not much profile change, and coiled shapes can be pounded into off-round objects.

Depending on the size of the work to be constructed, one slab can become one whole vertical wall, or a number of slabs may be laid vertically one on top of another in a manner similar to building with the coil process. A natural line-change takes place where slabs join, making an artful conjunction if you want to use it. Fabricate slabs against a canvas board, or other porous surface from which the clay will be easily released.

Different ways to make a slab:

1. Roll a lump of clay flat between two horizontal sticks; the width of the sticks will determine the thickness of the slab, usually ½ to 1 inch.

2. Shape a lump of clay into a rectangle; hold two sticks upright either side of it, with a string or wire stretched between them; pull the string or wire through at different levels to obtain a number of slabs.

Clay that comes to you in 25 lb (11 kg) bungs in a plastic sack has been mixed in an auger and extruded in a rectangular shape. Clay is like an elephant, and never forgets. The strains of the commercial mixing should be overcome by vigorous wedging. Tip: For rolling out a slab from a plastic bag of clay, cut off a chunk across the grain instead of vertically to counteract the spiral caused by machine mixing, then wedge.

3. Pound a lump of clay into a flat slab with your fist; turn it over and pound the opposite side; repeat

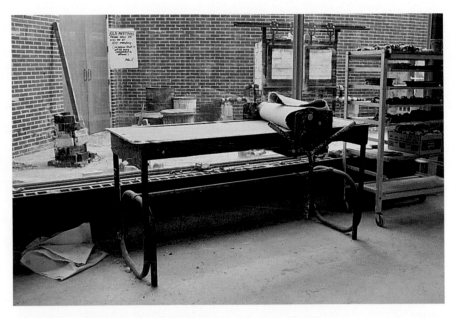

Slab roller, a mechanical means of producing slabs of varying thicknesses

SLABS ARE BEST FOR ANGULAR FORMS

Cut shapes from preformed slabs (see **Different ways to make a slab**)

With a sharp tool, deeply score mating edges, and moisten with water; repeat several times

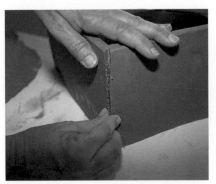

Squeeze scored, moistened surfaces together tightly; paddle both edges to strengthen the bond

A thin coil can be pinched into the interior seam for strength; reinforce the seam with a tool

several times for structural strength (page 51).

4. Several slabs can be luted together to make one large clay blanket.

5. "Throw" out a slab: hold a flattened lump of clay from its top with both your hands and fling the clay down toward the table, repeating several times until it has expanded to the desired size. This method works for small or huge slabs, once you get the hang of it, and yields a relatively even cross-section (page 50).

6. Use a rolling pin and roll a lump of clay as if it were pastry dough (page 52).

7. A "slab rolling" machine helps, especially in making extra-large slabs (page 47).

8. Cast a liquid clay slab against plaster (page 53).

9. Cast a thicker slab into a sand mold (page 58).

10. Press a slab from plastic clay in a mold.

Slab construction is ideal for large scale; it is a faster method of building than pinch or coil. Slabs for large work can be laid over combustible cores made of cardboard wrapped in fabric, or scrunched-up paper, or sand-stuffed pillows—the sand must be let out as the piece reaches leather-hardness. Clay can be rolled against nylon screens, which burn out, or against stainless steel screens, which will stay in the structure up to 2150° F (1175° C).

Potters through the centuries have added inert materials to the clay body to enable the handling of large, weighty constructions in the moist plastic state. Today short nylon fibers can be wedged or mixed in clay bodies to serve this purpose. Clayworkers need to become magicians with inventive ideas.

Màrta Nagy's (Hungary) charming **slab-built** sculpture is constructed of stoneware and porcelain, *decorated with engobes and gold leaf*, multi-fired from c/12 down, with added accessories and silk

| Some of these slab methods will give a more even, some a relatively uneven result. Select the method most suited to your design concept. |

1. The late **Marilyn Levine's** slab-built suitcase with **slab** buttresses is encased in plastic and taped to keep it damp and ready for the top to be added. She was one of the first to use nylon fibers added to clay for hand-building to give strength and flexibility

2. **The artist applies an oxide patina** after the whole piece is finished, before firing. After firing, wax is added for leather-look

A SLAB-BUILT FIREPLACE

OPPOSITE BELOW **Paula Winokur** is well known for slab-building large sculptures of porcelain clay body. For this commissioned and installed fireplace she began with a clay maquette presentation to the client. To do the work she:

• Cut large-scale cardboard templates for the sections for the entire piece, allowing for 14% fired clay shrinkage

• Rolled the clay slabs according to design; allowed them to stiffen; scored edges, and moistened several times before attaching sections of surface slabs with torn edges.

• Fired porcelain shapes were grouted together, installed on site, with Paula's hearth of flat tiles

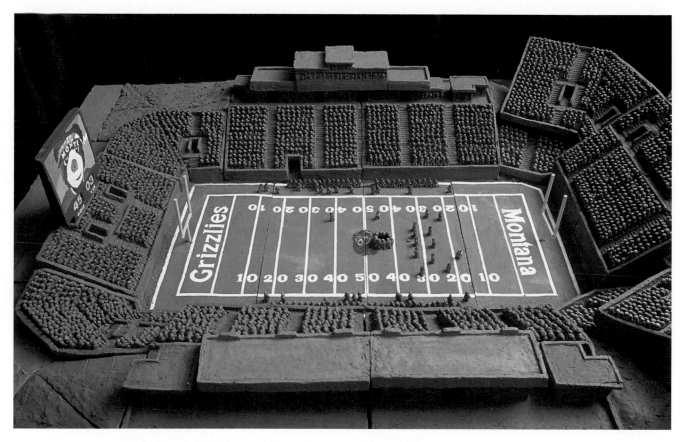

Doug Baldwin's stadium detail of a sculpture with 3,300 ducks: earthenware, hand-built of local clay with *engobes and underglazes*, 48 × 36 ins. (122 × 91 cm)

SLAB-BUILDING: THROWING OUT

1

2

3

David Middlebrook "throws" out a slab:
He picks up the flattened slab and . . .

. . . **flings it down on to the table, pulling the clay as he goes.** *It's a throwing out and dragging, pulling motion* so that the clay will thin out and expand. If you throw the slab in the same direction each time it will become longer; if you throw it in opposite directions it will become round or square. *Several slabs can be luted together* to make one huge slab

John Mason's large pentagonal form, 26 × 26 × 14 ins.
(66 × 66 × 35.5 cm), is a virtuoso piece of **slab-building**,
as well as of *graphic surface decoration*

SLAB-BUILDING: POUNDING

Shao Junya (China) uses the famous YiXing natural clay, prospected near her home, to fabricate teapots of traditional and avant-garde forms

She pounds clay slabs hard many times, with a heavy wood hammer, to achieve a very thin, even thickness of 3/16 in. (5 mm)

Very thin and rounded slab is attached to base, scored, and moistened (slabs *can* make round forms)

Cylindrical form is paddled round (a "turntable" can be used)

Carefully turned upside down, the teapot foot is shaped

Right side up, she turns and gently paddles the final shape, which rests on a pad of clay to turn pot without scratching foot

Hand-formed spout attaches at tea-straining holes; slab has been attached at opening, will be cut to leave an edge for lid

Hollow formed handle is placed directly opposite spout

Lid with flange and knob is similarly fabricated; this whole process may take several days

1

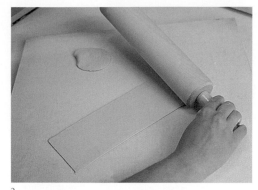

2

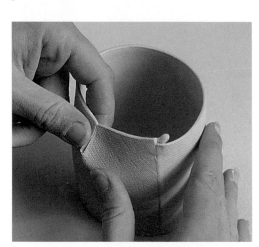

3

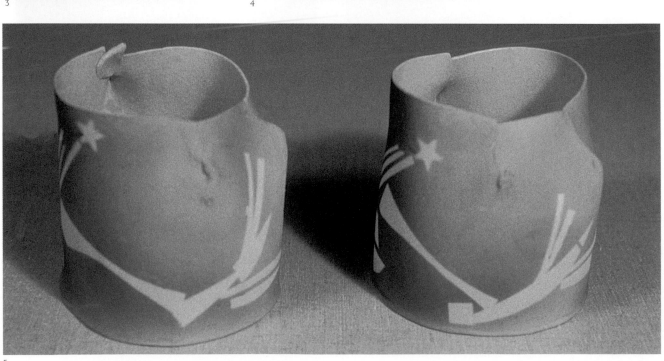

4

SLAB-BUILDING: ROLLING

1. Using a very clean canvas board, **Jan Peterson** pats out a porcelain clay pancake

2. She rolls very thin slabs from the pancake and cuts them to size for a tumbler

3. **The cylindrical shape**, thin enough to be translucent, is placed on an equally thin slab base, and the two are scored and luted together with a slurry made of the clay body and water

4. She cuts and folds the edge to alter the shape

5. **Finished tumblers**, glazed inside, unglazed outside, with *airbrush and tape resist stain decoration*, c/10 oxidation

5

SLAB-BUILDING: POURING

Jan Peterson hand-builds a porcelain plate from slip-cast slabs laid over a plaster hump mold

Leather-hard slabs, cut into patterns from the poured liquid clay ones, are "set up" enough to handle; they are laid over a plaster hump form; moist slabs are rolled together for strength and design

Pouring liquid clay on to plaster to create flat, thin slabs

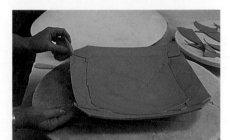

Plate turned right side up shows pressed pattern created by the slabs; edges are smoothed with a damp sponge

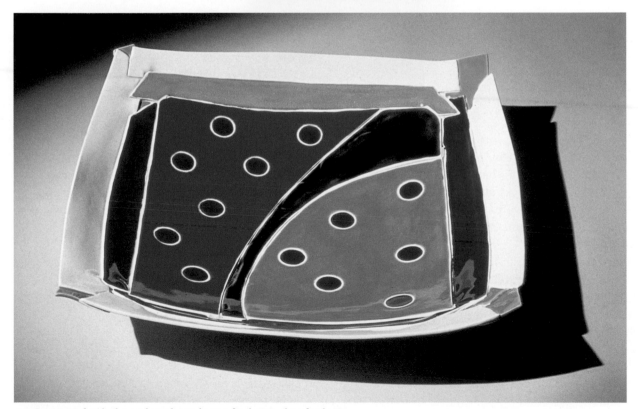

Jan Peterson's finished porcelain platter, bisque fired c/10, glaze fired c/04

LEARNING FROM TECHNIQUES USED BY INDIGENOUS PEOPLES

These techniques are still widely applicable, and are well worth practicing whether you are a beginner or not.

Methods of forming

1. Using a natural form as the interior shape:
• Coil over a convexly curved rock.
• Lay clay over or into a reed basket.
• Shape clay over a ball of wax, melt wax out.
• Form clay over a ball of bark, twigs, or string, pull the fiber out of finished piece.
• Lay slabs or coils of clay over fruits or vegetables such as melon or squash.

2. Pushing natural forms into solid lumps of soft clay to create a pot:
• Use sticks, starting with thinner ones, working up to sticks of successively larger diameter.
• Ram solid clay with smooth, elongated rocks.
• Dig down into a soft lump of clay with clam shells or pot shards, turning the clay and widening it with the shape of the shell.
• Shape a hollow piece by paddling the outside with a stone against a paddle inside.
• Use a wheel made of bamboo or an old tire.

One-hundred-year-old oversized coil-built Ayyanar horses in a hidden shrine in Tamil Nadu, South India; wood-fired, some are as tall as 13 ft (4 m)

An Indian pot at Tulsi Farm Pottery, Delhi, *is supported on a grain bag while it is burnished with a smooth stone*

ALTERING WHILE BUILDING

Texture a fresh clay surface with:
• Paddles: carved of wood in various shapes, or wrapped with string, weeds, or fabric, or made of bark from different trees or brush.
• Roulettes: natural forms that can be rolled against soft clay, such as bones, pine cones, seed pods, animal teeth, wads of leaves, rocks, carved wood rollers.
• Combing: pull a toothed or serrated edge across a clay surface.
• Stamping: use carved clay stamps, dried or fired, or vegetables, shells, bone ends, twigs, or broken pots.

Changing clay surface

• Burnishing: polish the leather-hard clay with a smooth water-washed stone or a gourd to produce a sheen.
• Resin: drip tree resin or pitch against a hot pot as it is pulled from the fire.

Rocks containing mineral oxides are ground for paint pigment on a stone *metate* at Acoma Pueblo by **Emma Lewis Mitchell**, one of Lucy's daughters, who, with Dolores, helped their mother in her later years

BELOW The late **Lucy Lewis** uses the ground pigment for painting, with her yucca-frond brush, her famous fine-line design (see Contents pages). Painting this size of jar would take her three to four weeks of daily work, sun-up to sun-down, on the electricity-free Acoma mesa

Coloring with mineral/vegetable matter

• Add to water the powder from grinding metallic oxide rocks such as hematite or copper, for painting on the clay surface.
• Use plant juices—almost any plant will do, but yucca is a favorite—painted against a burnished surface to produce a dull matt design; some plant juices cause color on the clay in the fire.
• Change all the clay colors by smothering the fire or making smoke.

It is stimulating to increase your awareness of all the ceramic processes that have been in use for centuries by primitive and studio potters. If you have a chance to travel in rural areas or in countries where clay is still the prime material for functional objects, take note of the various techniques and adapt them for yourself. Books and photographs of these areas are also a wonderful help.

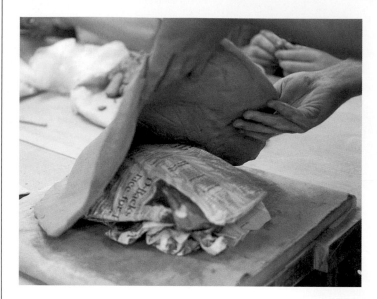

MASK MAKING

Students at Highland High School, Gilbert, Arizona,
enjoy making monster masks as a ceramic project. Piles
of newspaper, of almost any size and height, form the
basic shape; stoneware clay slabs are laid over to form
the mask. With the paper core support, facial features,
pinched, coiled, or slabbed, can be added. When leather-
hard the mask will be lifted off the paper, decorated with
colored clay engobes and fired to c/10. Finished mask
above right is 10 × 6 × 3 ins. (25 × 15 × 7.5 cm)

John McCuistion, *Miró mask*, c/10 reduction, bisque with
acrylic paint, 13 × 10 × 6 ins. (33 × 25 × 13 cm)

WORKING WITH PLASTER

Potters use plaster as a means of reproducing ceramic forms, or as a form against which to work. Plaster can also be used as a mold for casting metal, but then so can bisqued clay. As potters we usually use plaster for making molds, into which liquid clay slip is cast, or into or over which plastic clay is pressed. Sometimes mold techniques are used to make component parts for adding on to thrown or handbuilt work.

Plaster is a gypsum (calcium) product, available from lumber yards, hobby shops, hardware stores, and the like. Good pottery plaster is *not* the same as dental plaster. Most pottery plasters are labeled as such in all parts of the world, yet there can be many types. For instance, in the United States, U.S. Gypsum and Blue Diamond, the most noted companies, have different trade-names for types with various setting times, and different plasters for degrees of hardness. Potters usually prefer a setting time of 20 minutes from when the plaster enters the water to when it is the proper consistency for pouring; stirring the plaster shortens the time, as does hot instead of cold water.

It's a good idea to maintain a separate area for making plaster models and molds as well as for casting and pressing into molds. Plaster bits will cause holes or blow-outs in the kiln if they mix with your ready-to-work clay, in good condition for handbuilding and throwing. Taking care to keep clay and plaster separate is really important.

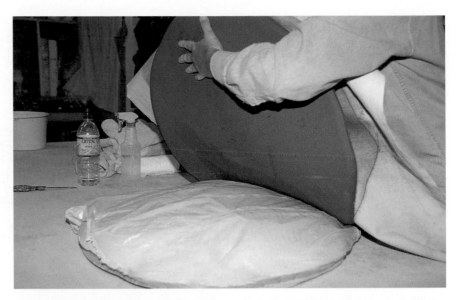

Linda Speranza creates outrageously large platters from previously made plaster one-of-a-kind hump molds. She layers paddled chunks of clay on the canvas bed of a slab roller, sometimes using fiberglass strands between layers, to give strength for the large proportions of her slabs

The carved plaster face of the mold imprints the clay slab laid over it; a coiled foot attached to the back several inches high supports the piece or, when pierced with holes, forms a rack for hanging

Linda Speranza's finished platter, glazed and reduction fired c/10, 28 ins. (71 cm) diameter

How to make a mold

To make a mold requires making or acquiring a model first. The plastic clay you use for hand-building is the usual substance for a **model** you create yourself, but Styrofoam, cardboard, sand, wood, newspaper, or fabric can be used, as well as "found objects" such as rocks, fruit and vegetables, tools, and so on, which can provide images for conceptual pieces.

"**Undercuts**" determine the number of pieces a mold will have. An undercut is a line that goes under from another line or curve. Your face would need at least a two-piece mold, divided either around the head or down the middle from the center of the top of the head, over the forehead, down the nose, over the lips, over the chin, and down the neck. If you make a solid model of a head you will make all the planes and curves recede from that center line. *Think about how you will detach the mold from the model.* You must be able to lift it off, so if there are undercuts, necessary to form such fea-

BELOW AND RIGHT **Virginia Scotchie** constructed two-piece molds from street lamps, kick balls, beach balls, baseballs, for a large multi-balled site sculpture. Clay was pressed 1 in. (2.54 cm) thick into both halves of the plaster molds, which were joined at the edges; balls were removed leather-hard

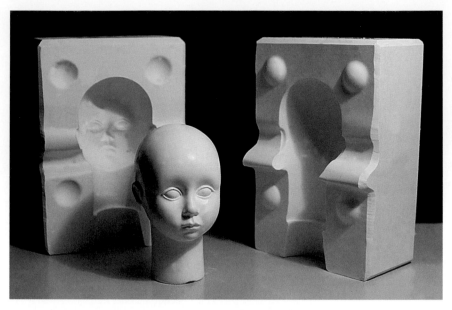

A Lennox china doll head model with its two-piece mold for hollow-casting

One-piece mold (left). A two-piece mold is necessary if there are "undercuts" (right)

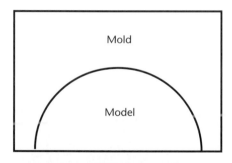

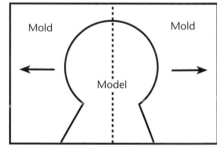

CASTING SLIP INTO MOLDS

> **Hollow-cast molds** (also called drain-cast)—either one-piece or multi-piece—are *open voids that form only the outside shape*; clay slip is poured into the top of the shape and poured out as soon as a cross-section of ³⁄₁₆ in. (5 mm) or so sets against the plaster.

> **Solid-cast molds** *shape the inside and the outside* form of the piece; the hollow between the two or more pieces of the mold fills with slip and *nothing is poured out*. Plaster is porous and absorbs moisture from the clay slip, so that the skin of the piece hardens in minutes. Molds cannot be used more than a few times a day or they become too wet.

tures as nostrils or ears, they will necessitate further pieces of the mold.

If the model is made of clay, metal shims can be inserted to be used as a separation line, against which to cast the first piece of the mold. If the model is any other material, the separation line could be a slab of clay, or a thin slab of plaster. After you have cast the first piece, use Vaseline or potter's soap between each section of the plaster mold to separate the pieces as you cast the plaster over your original model. You now have a mold. When the clay that is cast into the mold is set, the various parts of the mold come apart and are removed; the piece then stands alone. It is **not** advisable to re-use casting slip that is poured out of molds; you can try it once or twice.

Try to keep a clean table for fabricating claywork with molds, allowing plenty of room for initiating and removing the pieces from the molds; working a number of molds at one time is prudent. Pour casting slip into each mold from an appropriate-sized vessel—depending on the volume of the mold—all at once without stopping, or an unpleasant line will remain on the piece.

A hollow-cast mold, also called a drain-cast mold (see page 58), is an open void with the outside shell being the profile of the model; *characteristically the cross-section of the cast piece will be an even thickness all over*. After filling the mold with casting slip, allow approximately 30 minutes for a hardened clay shell ³⁄₁₆ in. (5 mm) thick to form against the plaster; then drain the remaining slip out of the mold quickly, leaving it supported upside down until the piece drops gently to the tabletop. A two-piece drain-cast mold can be held together with rubber bands; its image will be poured and released by taking one side of the mold off first.

A solid-cast mold is always in at least two parts, that is, two sections of plaster formed against the front and back sides of a model; the cast piece will look exactly like the model, with a *characteristically varying cross-section*. Casting slip is poured into a small hole on one side of the two-section mold, filling the void that is the shape of the model; no slip is drained out. The mold must be pulled apart as soon as the sections will release from each other, or else the enclosed piece will dry and crack.

TOP **Gilda Oliver** has removed the top half of a two-piece hollow-cast mold, revealing the face of the sculpture (which was slip-cast—it could also be pressed in with plastic clay). The mold was made (see p. 58) over a solid clay model. The mold has been removed as soon as possible so that the head is still soft enough to refine and add details

ABOVE Glazed earthenware sculpture

Jan Peterson's hollow-cast porcelain cups make a sculpture if grouped, or can be used individually; bisque fired c/10, glaze fired c/04; 6 × 5 × 4 ins. (15 × 12.5 × 10 cm) each

RIGHT **Karin Bjorquist**, detail of tiles with articulated sections, slip-cast to fabricate a screen in Stockholm, Sweden

BELOW Tiles for wall installations can be slip-cast in previously carved or textured plaster molds; these are by **Karin Bjorquist** (Gustavsberg, Sweden)

MAKE YOUR OWN CASTING SLIP OR BUY IT READY-MADE

Clay casting slip that is poured into hollow or solid-cast molds is a specially **deflocculated** clay body. If we make clay liquid enough to pour into a mold just by adding water—three to four times the weight of the clay would be needed—the proportion of clay becomes so tiny that when the water evaporates there is not enough clay left to hold the form together.

Deflocculating a clay slip means adding a catalyst, called an electrolyte. A percentage of 0.2 to 0.5% of deflocculant will make a batch of 100 parts of clay body plus a maximum of 40% water into a liquid that weighs 1.7 **specific gravity**, just a little heavier than water. If it weighs more, add water or add a measured small quantity of deflocculant to your 100 parts, which usually thins the slip; if it weighs less, add dry clay body to bring the sample to proper weight. You can duplicate additions by multiplying according to the measured large volume of casting slip you want to use. **Of course, it is also possible to press plastic clay into or over plaster molds.** The most satisfactory deflocculant is usually sodium silicate (also called waterglass) or soda ash, or a combination of both, although tea, dishwashing soap, or manufactured chemicals such as "Darvan" also work.

Any clay body will deflocculate, *but tests should be made with small quantities before mixing a large batch.* Store the casting slip as airtight as possible. If it seems less liquid when you come to use it, add a small quantity

ASSEMBLING MULTIPLE MOLDED FORMS

Karen Massaro's porcelain slip-cast conical elements, to be freely arranged in varying "installations," are *finished in underglaze stains and glaze*, fired c/10; *china-painted overglaze decoration* c/013

Mold forms of various units can be cast individually and assembled in different ways, as shown in this porcelain sculpture, one of a series of outdoor installations by **Patriciu Mateiescu**, 6 ft × 6 ft × 6 ft (182 × 182 × 182 cm)

Victor Spinski's *trompe l'oeil* installation, assembled from ceramic objects which have been pressed or slipcast from plaster molds taken from real life

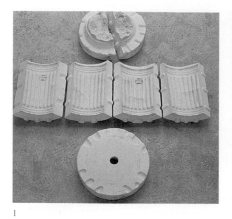

1

2

CASTING MULTIPLE-PIECE MOLDS

Richard Notkin assembles a six-piece mold of a garbage can (1), ties it together, pours slip into a cone placed on top of the assembled mold (2); the cone holds excess slip, and when a cross-section of clay hardens against the mold, he removes a plug to drain the excess (3)

4. Mold pieces being removed from the cast garbage can

5. Finished object in porcelain, celadon glaze, electric hardware and wood. Many more molds of the fantasy images were employed and slip cast to form the final composite

3

4

Casting a 6 ft (2 m) tall piece from multiple molds is challenging but fun:

• Clay must be removed from the molds as soon as possible.
• All shapes must be kept moist until final attachment.
• Or, shapes can be glued together after firing.
• Deflocculated slip must be kept at 1.7 specific gravity (s.g.) in an airtight container as long as the individual units are being cast.

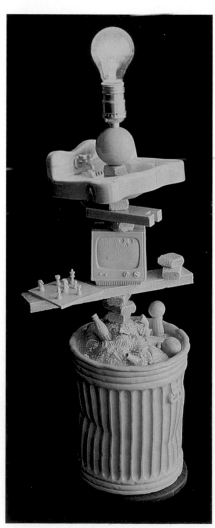

5

of water to the slip, or adjust it by weighing for specific gravity.

A hydrometer can be used to check the consistency of casting slip. This simple tool is easy to use by inserting the tube into the slip and taking a reading. You will always bring the slip to that reading if it dries out.

Readymade deflocculated casting slip can be bought in jugs ready to use. Alternatively, you can buy the dry casting body; make it liquid with 40% water by weight (as described above) and add the deflocculant. Clay bodies for earthenware, stoneware, and porcelain are available commercially all over the world. Potters in England and France are particularly lucky in being able to buy casting bodies from famous factories. Mixing your own casting slip gives you the advantage of knowing exactly what the ingredients are and how they will function.

HOW TO MIX PLASTER AND POUR A FORM

Some clay artists mix plaster and water willy-nilly, as bronze sculptors do, but sculptors use plaster as a throw-away material. Potters want their plaster models and molds to last a long time and to be used over and over. Therefore it is important to use the proper plaster/water ratio your particular brand of plaster requires and to mix in a regulated manner that will produce the most durable mixture.

This is a regular mix for bats, models, and molds, for use with Blue Diamond or Gypsum Pottery Number One plaster in the United States. Plasters in other countries are similar. **Do not use so-called Plaster of Paris.**

MAKING A PRESS-MOLD FOR PLASTIC CLAY

1

2

3

4

P. R. Daroz, a sculptor in Delhi, India, illustrates his technique of making molds for pressing images to construct a wall:

1. Clay model encased in wooden frame

2. Plaster is poured over the model within the frame; the image will be indented in the plaster

3. Pressing the clay slab into the plaster image

4. Detail is added to variations of the molded clay tile assembled into a wall piece

1. Calculate how much plaster is needed in cubic inches for the area to be poured. That is, measure the three dimensions of height times width times depth. If the area is round rather than cubic, multiply the cubic inch total by 0.8. Then divide the cubic inch total by 81, as 81 cubic inches of space require one quart of water plus 2¾ lb plaster (generic ratio for most plasters). (Metric equivalents: 1325 c. cm, 1.18 litres, 1.25 kg.)

2. Measure the correct amount of cold or lukewarm water into a plastic, rubber, or metal container; weigh the correct amount of plaster.

 3. Shake plaster into water slowly—not too slowly—so it mounds up in the bucket; allow plaster to slake a few minutes in the water until it all seems moist.

 4. When stirring plaster, use gloves or a wooden stirrer to avoid an irritation from the lime. Stir with your hand around the bucket in a wide motion, then a figure-of-eight motion on the bottom, palm up, moving upward to the top of the mix and around again. As bubbles come to the surface, scoop off with a paper towel.

5. As soon as you can make a mark that holds its line slightly on top of the mix, the plaster is ready to pour. **Pour down the side** of the wood or linoleum coddle surrounding the model, or down the side of the mold area, so that the plaster fills up the space and air comes to the top; shake the bench or table under your mold, to break the bubbles. **Remove the cast mold** when the plaster becomes hot to the touch, at which point it pulls away most easily; otherwise you may need an air hose to part the plaster from its core.

Peter Hayes' (UK) raku fired sculpture (6 ft, 180 cm, tall) was fabricated in *plaster press molds*

Charles Nalle makes his living designing tiles to be fabricated in plaster press-molds for clay and slumped glass shapes which are fired together at low temperature. Detail, 22 × 22 × 3 ins. (56 × 56 × 7.5 cm)

6. If there is excess plaster, pour it on to newspaper to set, and discard it. **Do not pour plaster down a household or schoolroom drain**. Rinse the container in lots of cold water.

Making molds is a complicated process. Frequently, artists use casting or pressing mold techniques to create multiple images or exact replicas of objects for use in sculptures. Molds are also used as a means of reproducing forms when many similar items are needed, such as for dinnerware or accessory sets. Some artists use plaster as a sketch mechanism to see form quickly.

Carved plaster makes innovative stamps for decorative pressing into clay. To explore the capabilities and experiment with plaster requires explicit instruction. Don Frith has written the definitive book on making and using plaster molds (see Bibliography).

Pat Kenny Lopez's earthenware bottle, slip-cast in a mold with hand-built additions, is *clear and matt glazed* c/04; 10 × 6 ins. (25 × 15 cm)

3

THROWING ON THE POTTER'S WHEEL

ANYONE CAN LEARN TO THROW . . .

The potter's wheel has not changed much in 5,000 years. We think that in ancient times a large wooden or stone disk was placed on a rock or stick fixed in the ground, and it bounced as it rotated unevenly. More sophisticated means of achieving balance and stability were gradually incorporated, until thousands of years later, in the 20th century, an electric motor was added. The purpose of the potter's wheel—to revolve evenly and smoothly under the pressure of the potter's hands—has always been the same.

FACING PAGE **Elsa Rady's** *thrown wall piece is an altered porcelain form* on a painted aluminum shelf, 13½ × 14½ ins. (34 × 37 cm)

INSETS **A village potter in South India** *using coil and turn technique: a long, fat coil is rolled from very plastic clay and attached to the* previously turned vessel. The clay is very soft and fingers pinch an even wall which the potter turns into symmetrical shape. Eventually the huge vessel will be enlarged and refined by hand with a paddle

It is a good idea to hand-build before starting to work on the wheel. It is important to learn to feel the clay, and to gauge its reaction to your hand pressure. These sensitivities are important through all claywork, but really important in throwing. You should have made at least a pinch pot with the clay you will be throwing to test plasticity, before trying to use the wheel.

Throwing on the wheel is the fastest way to get a hollow clay shape, ready to be finished or to be combined or cut up and added to something else ("thrown and altered"). But it is the fastest method only when the potter is skillful and has total command of the wheel. This accomplishment can take ten years to acquire, although some people have a natural skill that allows them to develop control faster.

Throwing is a process of working clay by hand on a revolving wheel that is kicked, rotated by hand, or motor-driven at speeds up to 120 rotations per minute. It is the only process by which a form can be so spontaneously created, so quickly made, involving the most direct communication between the creator and the material. Potters work a mass of clay under their hands, in tune with the speed of the wheel and the rhythms of their bodies, into a shape determined by their own sensitivity and skill.

A potter at Tulsi Farm, Delhi, India, wedging clay on the floor

A village potter in Maheshwar, India, working on a large, slow-moving disk wheel of wood or bamboo turned by hand with a stick. This type of wheel rotates a long time, allowing several shapings from one twirling effort; the large diameter keeps it going. At the beginning the potter can stand or squat. Pot at right is similar to the one he will throw

During the process of learning, everyone will feel the sense of being one with the clay, of feeling the clay take shape—any shape—under the pressure of the hands. Not everyone will acquire enough skill to make thrown clay into an art, or be able to say the things an artist can communicate with this method, yet all who work on a potter's wheel will feel an expression of self. This degree of personal satisfaction can make throwing on the wheel an end in itself. M. C. Richards, a potter-poet, wrote a book called *Centering*, about the process of centering a ball of clay which she likened to centering oneself.

Consistency is very important. The clay must be soft enough to respond easily to any pressure. No hard lumps or foreign particles should be present in the clay body, except small impurities used for texture or color. Clay for throwing can be softer than clay used for hand-building.

TO THE BEGINNER

If you will read the following pages on throwing many, many times over, you will fix the words and steps in your subconscious memory. Your fingers will respond quickly because they are really being told what to do by my words in your mind.

It matters not if you are left or right-handed: both hands are equally important. Left hand is inside, right hand is outside if the wheel goes counter-clockwise (mostly in the West) and right hand inside, left hand outside when the wheel is traditionally rotated clockwise (Britain, Japan, and the East).

Throwing takes years of practice before you will be in complete control of the clay and the wheel. But even in the beginning you can respond to the clay, react to the motion of the wheel, and make something, or

make something that you can make into something else, by hand. The pleasure of throwing will be enhanced as control and skill improve.

Practice the whole process of throwing. "The whole is greater than the sum of the parts." Practice centering and opening the ball first. Then wedge five small balls of clay (approximately 5 lb/2 kg each).

After some days of practice at centering and opening the ball, then practicing the shapes (page 72), now begin to analyze where you are having problems and practice the trouble spots. When you have managed all the shapes pretty well, do the same thing again with balls of clay twice as large.

Remember the motion of the wheel. No change in the movement of your hands should be made until you feel that the clay has revolved under your hands one or more times, so that it has reacted to your pressure all the way round.

Remember that the smallest pressure point gives the most control. The smaller the area of clay that your hand or fingers touch, the less drag on the clay, and the better leverage you will have. Beginners tend to want to put their whole hand, or both hands, against the clay. This never works. Just a small point at the base of your thumb, or the tips of the fingers, should touch the clay.

Remember to pull from the bottom to the top every time you draw. This keeps the motion and rhythm of the lift. Finish the shape at the bottom first, then the top. Put your fingers on each side of the wall, feel the form from the bottom, as you move up, being careful not to exert pressure, except where you wish to further the shape.

Once you know intuitively where the pressure really is, and can feel the clay respond immediately, then you can make your own way.

STEPS IN THROWING ON THE POTTER'S WHEEL

Wedging

This potter in Morocco throws hundreds of functional tajines and jars from local clay every day. He will fire them stacked up in a tall updraft wood-burning kiln, unglazed, for his domestic market. Note the mound of clay behind the potter

We have mentioned wedging in the hand-building chapter but must speak of it again here. The process of making a ball of clay into just the right consistency for working is more important for throwing than for hand-building. If the clay consistency is uneven, a really centered form is impossible. Any method of kneading clay works, but wedging petal-fashion is best: one hand rotates a lump of clay and the other hand presses the sides in, giving a chrysanthemum-petal look (see page 40).

Clay should be wedged free of air so that subsequent moisture pockets will not cause the piece to "blow up" during the bisque firing. If the clay is too wet, wedging against a porous surface will stiffen it; if it is too dry, water can gradually be wedged in to moisten it.

Practice makes perfect for petal wedging. Since many potters buy clay ready-mixed and already pugged by machine, little wedging is necessary. Bought clay also tolerates the **"slice and slap" method of wedging:** wire-cut a slice of the clay bung, slap it down on the wedging table, cut again, slap, many times, building a tower of slapped slices, being careful not to trap air between the slices.

Many times in learning to throw, the clay will fall apart or be so off-center that it cannot be rescued. The potter should re-wedge the lump and begin again with the same clay, until it is too worn out to be made into a satisfactory form. At that point, re-wedge the rebellious clay, wrap it in plastic, and put it into your storage bucket; get a new lump of clay and begin again, repeating until you too are worn out.

Wedging is so important that we are giving the instructions again here:

1. The basic ball
Take a lump of clay the size that your two hands will go round without quite touching.

2. Wedge clay
a. Left palm pushes into clay, right palm pivots the ball; continue and keep a steady rhythm.
b. Spiral shape develops which shows that the clay is moving and the whole chunk is being properly wedged.
c. Proper wedging removes air bubbles, puts clay in good condition for working; if dry, add water and wedge.

3. Put clay on wheel to throw
Pat into a cone shape, and put the wide part down against the wheel head or bat. Turn the wheel on or begin to kick it; moisten the clay with water.

Position at the wheel

The position of the potter at the wheel is crucial. Some wheels are made for sitting, some for standing, some for squatting; kicking a wheel usually requires sitting and kicking a rotating flywheel. European wheels are often treadle-style: you must stand on one foot and move a treadle back and forth with the other foot.

Preferably, the potter should sit at the level of the wheel head, or above it, close enough and high enough to bend the back and shoulders over the clay. Tilt the seat of a sit-down wheel slightly toward the wheel head, or use a wedge or a pillow on a chair, pushing your body forward to relieve pressure on your back.

Arms should be relaxed but held against the body, and the whole body including the arms should move in toward the clay as hand pressure is applied; if the arms move alone, they become unsteady; clay goes off-center. Hands, wrists, and arms must be steady and fairly rigid, although poised and relaxed enough to feel what the clay is doing. The body leans into the clay from the back and the shoulders, through the arms to the hands. **A steady, centered "self" is essential in learning to feel every tiny response of the clay. It is important to stretch and relax your body now and then.**

If the potter stands to a low wheel, it is usually to handle a huge amount of clay. The stance will be solid, with legs apart, arms braced from the shoulders. You work bent over the clay until the wall rises as high as you are and eventually you are standing tall, parallel with the clay. To make really large vessels or sculptures you may need to throw several shapes and attach them together, or to cut, patch, or paddle forms into other forms.

**The left hand centers the clay.
The right hand lifts the wall.
The left hand shapes a bowl.
The right hand lifts a bottle.
Two hands squeeze in to collar a neck.**

It is important to have only one pressure point on the clay at a time. If there are more pressures—more fingers or too much hand surface against the clay—the pot will absorb all those pressures and will be taken off-center.

In America the potter's wheel rotates counter-clockwise. In Britain, Japan, and some other countries it is rotated clockwise. It does not matter about the direction. The potter adapts to the motion and pulls up on the right side of the clay if the wheel goes counter-clockwise, or on the left side if it goes clockwise. The best spot for catching the clay with your pressure as it comes round is about 4 o'clock on the right side, or 8 o'clock on the left side.

It does not matter what shape the wheel head is, or the bat on which the throwing is done. What matters most is that the potter learns to feel the centrifugal motion of the wheel and the clay as it responds to that motion and the potter's pressure. **Learning to feel is one of the big issues in clayworking.**

Centering

All directions are for a potter's wheel revolving counter-clockwise.

1. Begin centering
Squeeze the cone up with the base of the palms of both hands, squeezing into the clay and lifting up (see picture opposite top left).

2a, 2b. Lean in and center
Center by leaning in with the edge of the palm of the left hand, at the 8 o'clock position on the left side of the clay (if the wheel goes counter-clockwise), or 4 o'clock (if it goes clockwise). "On center"

1. Begin centering:

Squeeze the ball of clay up with the bases of the hands opposite each other

2a. **Press the cone down to center** by leaning into the clay with outer edge of the left wrist flexed; push down also with base of the right palm held vertically, at right angles to left hand; left hand leans in, right pushes down. Squeeze up again and push down until clay is centered

2b. **Same centering position as 2a. but opposite view:** left photo from potter's side, right photo from side looking at potter. Heel of left palm leans steadily in at 8 o'clock, right pushes down simultaneously. Left hand makes a "V," inside of palm does not touch clay. Base of right hand lies next to left thumb

means running true with the centrifugal motion of the wheel— you must learn to feel that, but you can test it by holding a point against the clay; if it is centered the point will make a mark evenly all the way around.

3. **Right fingers push down.**

Opening the ball: steps

Opening position 1 (far right) All directions are for counter-clockwise rotation. (Reverse for a clockwise wheel.) Left middle finger centered on top of the clay, with middle finger of right hand over it; hold left finger rigid and push straight down, right finger guides.

3. **Tip of first finger right hand, buttressed by second finger, pushes at 4 o'clock position** straight down from the top to the bat; true-up base by pushing inward; clay is centered when it revolves true with no bumps

Open the ball by pushing straight down, (a) with the middle finger left hand supported by the middle finger right hand, as above, or (b) by the tip of the left thumb supported by the right hand, and pull toward you to widen the hole (see 1 and 2, page 78)

CYLINDER   HALF-SPHERE   WHOLE SPHERE   SPHERE AND CYLINDER   LOW OPEN FORM

The five basic shapes a beginner should practice over and over have to do with **form, not function**; *cylinder, half-sphere, full sphere, full sphere and cylinder combined, low open form*

Or **opening position 2**
Left thumb finds center on top of clay, middle finger of right hand on top of thumb; thumb pushes straight down, guided by right finger.
Push to bottom
Push down to within about ¾ inch (2 cm) from the bottom.
Open
Position 1: pull the middle fingers, one on top of the other, toward you, *or* Position 2: push left thumb, with middle finger right hand supporting, from the bottom center out to the left.

Pressure of either position will move to the wall of clay from the hollow now being opened; move far enough to make several inches of curved opening. Feel the thickness of the wall and try not to go all the way through.

Note: We are showing you traditional methods of throwing traditional shapes. Potters can invent their own techniques, and can be very creative in altering or scrunching up traditional forms. Creativity sometimes comes from lack of skill!

PRACTICE THESE FIVE SHAPES

Practice these five shapes, one after the other, in this order:
• Cylinder
• Half-sphere
• Whole sphere
• Sphere and cylinder combined
• Low open form

Repeat every day or as often as possible until you feel mastery over these five shapes.

We could give functional names to the above shapes, such as bowl, round vase, bottle, plate, but we prefer not to do this.

We prefer you to think of the geometric form, not function, when you practice shaping on the potter's wheel.

a) Pull up and shape a cylinder

1. Hand position
Left middle finger-tip, buttressed by the left first finger, goes *inside* to the bottom and sweeps over to the right wall. *Outside*, the right first finger crooks toward you, the first finger-tip pushes into the clay on the outside for almost an inch (2.5 cm) and begins to lift upward. Fingernails must be short!
2. In repeated draws the outside first finger, buttressed by the second finger, does the lifting. Press in hard to really cause the clay to grow; the inside finger does not push, only follows straight up.
3. Squeeze with both hands to narrow the cylinder and thicken the wall for a further lift.
4. Outside finger continues pushing inward, lifting up to desired height. Both fingers or a sponge keep the lip smooth.
5. If the lip is uneven, cut it with a needle or a wire held on the right side of the clay even if you are left-

1. "Knuckle pull," push in with tip of knuckle, and pull up to shape cylinder. Keeping hands connected helps control

2. "Finger pull," push in with tip of finger, and draw up for height

3. **With base of both hands squeeze and lift up** to narrow cylinder several times during cylinder-making

4. Continue pushing upward and lifting with finger or knuckle, squeezing with both hands and lifting upward between pulls each time

5. On right side of clay, **cut uneven lip with needle** from outside to inside finger, then lift

6. Wheel turning, straighten cylinder profile with wood knife against clay, then tool cuts under base to trim excess clay

7. Cut to release; both hands hold wire at back of cylinder, pull to right to sever, wheel turns slowly

handed. Push the point into the clay, wheel moving slowly for one revolution; quickly lift up the cut ring; smooth the lip.

6. With a wood knife cut excess clay from cylinder base several times while lifting the clay; at end, hold wood knife parallel to bat and cut into the clay base, then hold wooden point parallel to the cylinder and cut down to the bat; stop the wheel, remove excess trimming, and clean the bat.

7. Holding the cutting wire with each hand, pull toward you from behind the cylinder as the wheel turns slowly. Lift the cylinder off the bat with both hands.

Cross-section of thrown piece; beginners should try to pull an even wall, slightly thicker at base, thinner at top, then cut with a wire to see what you have pulled. This photo shows right hand first finger below left hand finger inside, to lift the cylinder taller

b) Half-spherical shape

(sometimes called bowl, see p. 71 for steps 1, 2, 3)

1. Center a low wide mound
Push downward with the wrist-end of the left hand on the top center of the mound, the heel of the right hand against the left thumb; lower the mound. **Push down to make the base of the mound as wide as you want the base of the shape to be.**

2. Open the mound
Same method as for the cylinder shape, but the inside opening will be wider because this mound is lower and wider than that for a cylinder.

3. Pull up the wall
Lift a low thick wall, with three or four draws upward.

4. Shape the half-sphere
Inside, the left-hand middle finger, buttressed by the curled first finger, drops from the wrist; it moves from the center out toward the right side. When the fingers reach the wall, the right-hand first finger, on the outside, curled and with the fingertip pointed into the clay, squeezes inward to meet the "feel" of the inside finger. On the inside, the left middle finger, buttressed by the first finger, pulls over to the right and up to the top. Pressure from the inside fingers controls the round shape. Both left- and right-hand fingers together, with the clay in between, draw out and up in the desired profile line.

5. Finish the shape
Continue bottom to top, pulling outward with the inside left finger toward the outside right finger, and upward until the half-sphere

Half-sphere: after opening a low, wide cylinder, expand the clay into a half-spherical shape (4) with the fingertips of the left hand exactly opposite the fingertips of the right hand. (5) Pull up and out three or four times, slowly, so that the clay will not fall; draw the profile line of the bowl shape you want, moving fingers from the base up to lip. It may help to have a drawing of the profile you want, near the wheel, while you throw

Some potters use a sponge or rib for support while throwing large open forms, as **Jane Dillon** is doing at this wheel. Note her assembled thrown forms on the shelves in her studio

is shaped and the wall is thin enough. True up the lip, cut if necessary, smooth it, and undercut the base with the wood knife, as in the cylinder. For beginners, the diameter of the initial mound of clay at the base should be 4 ins. (10 cm) less than you want the diameter of the half sphere. Carefully draw the curve on paper first as a guide.

1

2

3

SHINSAKU HAMADA THROWS A BOWL IN JAPAN

1. **He punches a hole** into a lump of clay, because his Korean kick-wheel moves too slowly for him to center a solid ball of clay

2. **He adds coils** to the first thrown base

3. **He throws the coils true**

4. **After straightening the cylinder** he sets a wide lip which will remain to reinforce the vessel

5, 6 **He expands the bowl**, being careful not to affect the lip

7. **He smooths the interior** with a thick wooden rib. Shinsaku's finished bowls can be 18 ins., 24 ins. as this one, or sometimes 36 ins. in diameter (46, 61 or 91 cm)

4

5

6

7

Susan Peterson's large thrown and altered bowl is stoneware, *glazed with reduction fired copper red and blue glazes*, c/10, 20 × 7 ins. (50 × 18 cm)

Stoneware bowl by **Viveka** and **Otto Heino**, *reduction matt glaze*, 12 ins. (30 cm) diameter

c) Full spherical shape (see forms p. 72)

1. Begin a half-sphere
Make a basic half-sphere, leaving a thick roll on the top lip. Shape the half-sphere curve from inside out, using the thick roll to lift up, out, and in toward the center in a diamond shape.

2. Expand the diamond
Push outward with the inside hand for the half-sphere, then the outside hand takes over to pull the diamond shape taller, rounder, and thinner. **Keep the curve moving up at all times**; don't push in horizontally, or the wall will fall in. Keep the top opening narrow; if you widen it to get your hand inside, narrow it again at the finish of each draw.

3. Make the full sphere
With one last draw, push out with the inside hand up to the middle, rounding the half-sphere, then "draw" the profile shape of a full circle with your two fingers opposite each other, one inside, one outside. The opening should be as narrow as you can make it.

4. Keep practicing
This is a difficult shape. Do it over and over.

See Toshiko Takaezu throwing a whole sphere or closed form on page 85.

Bowls come in all sizes and shapes, age-old containers for everything imaginable, or wonderful bases for glaze and decoration.

Bottles provide contrasts in form from wide to narrow, short to tall, round to angular, indeed any shape.

George Bowes's stoneware bottle, *brushed with engobes and glazes*

Andy Nasisse's thrown and hand-built jug, $15 \times 9 \times 7$ ins. ($38 \times 23 \times 18$ cm), is made of a white earthenware body glazed at c/02, then *overglaze decorated*, refired c/09

Fred Olsen's thrown stoneware bottle, *wood fire, ash glaze*

Michael Frimkess's stoneware bottle is *decorated with an Aztec design* in brushed glaze

d) Sphere and cylinder combined

(sometimes called bottle, see forms p. 72)

1. Center, open, lift
Pull a cylinder about as tall as you want this form to be. Don't pull all the way to the top – leave a thick roll at the top.

2. Shape the sphere
Go to the bottom with left fingers inside, opposite the first finger of the right hand outside, and expand the spherical shape, out and in, like a grapefruit.

3. Lift the cylinder
When the circle form is made, take the thick roll you left at the top and lift it into a cylinder. It will look like a ball with a stove-pipe on top. It will not look like a normal bottle, but as we said we want you to learn geometric form, not function, now.

4. Cut lip, trim base
Cut the lip even, sponge smooth. With wood knife, after cutting parallel to the bat, carve a nice indented line at the base by pointing the tool downward and cutting against the profile of the clay shape down and into base.

e) Low open form

(sometimes called platter, see forms p. 72)

1. Center a mound of clay
Press down and out to expand and lower the mound of clay to the diameter you want the base to be. Right hand presses down, left palm leans in to center the mound.

2. Begin opening the low form
Middle finger left hand supported

Bottle forms are made by keeping an extra roll at the top of the full spherical form from which to create the neck. Collar with the fingers of both hands squeezing in and lifting up. Use a tool such as a stick inside the bottleneck when your finger no longer fits in. Continue squeezing and lifting until the neck is the shape you want, ribbing from the lip down to smooth the neck

1. **Low open form**: center a mound of clay; open: *left thumb*, right fingers supporting, find center, push down to open. *Mound is the diameter you want the base* of the platter to be

2. Alternative way to begin opening the mound: middle finger left hand against the clay supported by middle fingers right hand on top, find center, push down to open

3. Use wood or metal rib to flatten interior of low open form

4. Shape edge between fingers; smooth with sponge or chamois

by right fingers pushes downward in center and pulls toward you to widen. You can continue lowering the entire mound while you open the center.

3. Use a rib

Move a rubber, wood, or metal rib from the center outward, pushing down to compress the clay and flatten the interior form.

4. Shape the edge

Left fingers inside, right fingers outside, pull the curve out and lift up to form a lip; press down to round and smooth the edge. Use wood knife to trim clay away from the base and clean the bat.

5. Cut under

With the sharp-pointed wood tool, cut into the base down toward the bat to shape the outside profile.

The five shapes you have just practiced are the basic shapes from which all pottery wheel forms come.

OTHER SHAPES ARE VARIATIONS
Pitcher

A pitcher is usually a bellied cylinder with a flared top for the pointed **pouring lip**. Make this by holding the thumb and third finger of the left hand outside against the pitcher neck, and with the right-hand first finger down inside the neck, pull up and out into a lip-shape. This can also be done reversing the two hands if you prefer. Sharpen and thin the lip to a sharp edge for pouring without dripping.

Most pitchers have a functional shape that is wider at the bottom and collars in to a flared neck which controls the liquid to be poured ABOVE **Lift a narrowed neck** from the full sphere shape

Collar in with fingertips of both hands and then flare the lip

Form the pouring lip by pushing in with the outside thumb and first finger against the inside finger, lifting and pulling over to form a sharp point to cut the drip, parallel to the bat

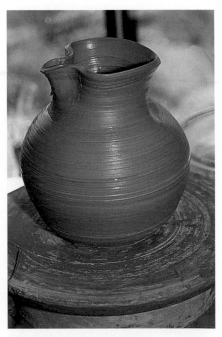

Wire-cut to sever the bottom from the bat (p. 81) and carefully lift the wet pitcher off, or leave it on the bat to get leather-hard. A pulled or hand-formed handle can be added to the wet pitcher, deforming it, or left to stiffen

Handles

Handles for thrown pots can be hand-built by pinch, coil, or slab methods, or cut from thrown cylinders, or carved from bamboo or wood. More usually a clay handle for a thrown shape is pulled from a solid lump of clay, just as the pot was thrown from a solid lump equalizing the strains.

Hold the well-wedged rectangular lump in one hand, moisten the clay and begin to pull downward, with thumb and finger of the other hand forming a circle around the clay; turn the pulling hand as you work to keep the handle shape even. When you have pulled a long enough, thick enough piece, pinch it off with your fingers, arch it, and put it on a board to stiffen until you can attach it.

Cups with handles: think of how the hand will hold the cup, with one or more fingers or the whole fist. Think function: a handle sticking too far up or out will break off easily; too thick a handle weights the cup unevenly; too thin a handle is not strong enough. Feel the handle as you make it, then it should feel right after firing.

Pull a handle from a wedged chunk of clay by holding the clay between thumb and fingers, turning the other hand from left to right, pulling from the top downward until the desired shape is achieved

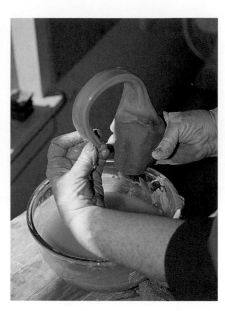

Curve the handle and set it aside to stiffen

Pitchers with handles: for functional success, attach a pitcher handle where the bulk of the liquid will be. Keep handles away from the lip of a pot, or else they break. Usually a handle is thicker at the top and narrower at the base, but this can be reversed.

Attach handles wet or leather-hard;

score both edges, moisten, and push firmly together.

The pitcher foot can be rolled easily without trimming, as can bottle feet. Or a pitcher foot can be wheel-trimmed (page 84) or hand-carved (page 85), or created by adding other clay shapes.

When the pitcher is dry enough to handle, **roll the bottom** against a flat surface to achieve a rounded foot. Cut the handle from its base, and fit it to the pitcher

Score and moisten the ends that will be attached

After scoring and moistening the attachment points on the pitcher, **fix the moistened handle on** and smooth it into the body

Casserole flange: make the flange on a lid by **pushing straight down on a thickened cylindrical wall** with the first finger of the right hand against the first finger of the left hand, which is underneath to support the flange

Cut the flange true with a needle at the 4 o'clock position

Measure with a wooden calliper the exact spot where the lid should sit, and throw the lid to fit. A flat lid for a casserole is made as shown on p. 82, but larger, and not thrown off-the-hump

Casserole

A casserole is a large half-sphere, **with a horizontal flange** where a lid will sit, or without a flange so that the **lid must have a vertical flange** (page 82, 2) that fits down inside the lip of the pot. Measure the opening the lid will fit into, or the casserole flange on which the lid will sit, very carefully because it is only a proper measurement that will make a lid fit. If it does not fit it is the potter's fault.

Lids and flanges

Lids for all pots are made in several ways, depending on whether they span very wide or very narrow diameters (page 82).

Create a flange for a lid from the lip of any pot by pushing down a ledge between left and right fingers. To wire-cut any pot off the hump, pull twisted wire at base from back to front through clay toward you, as wheel turns slowly.

Lids made right side up, with no flange, can be thrown directly against

THROW SMALL POTS FOR LIDS OFF-THE-HUMP

Center a lump of clay, then mark off a chunk for the pot size you want

Pot shape with a straight lip will accommodate a lid with a flange to fit inside the lip (page 82)

Left fingers hold the lip while right fingers flatten a flange for a flat lid (page 82)

Wire cut flanged pot off hump, ready for a flat lid; pull wire from back, through clay, toward you with wheel moving slowly (page 82)

a bat or off-the-hump, as shown here and on page 81. **Be sure to calliper the diameter of the lid and the diameter of the flange on the pot where it will sit**.

Right-side-up lid (1): center a mound for width of lid on a hump or against a bat; open the mound **away from center**, make knob, calliper diameter, leaving clay in the middle from which to throw up a knob.

A lid made right side up can also have a flange: press into the clay at the base to achieve proper diameter and height to fit in the pot. This flange can stay solid or be trimmed out later.

Wire cut the lid off the bat or the hump; when leather-hard check the fit of lid to pot.

Flanged lids made upside-down (2): lids made upside-down with a flange that fits into a pot can be dome-shaped or flat. Usually a separate thrown or hand-built knob is added later to the leather-hard lid.

Center a wide enough mound of clay—for the outside diameter that the lid should be—directly on a bat or off a hump, as shown here.

Open the mound, pull up a thick wall, then press in with outside finger against the inside finger opposite, to create the flange diameter.

Lift the flange as tall as it needs to be. Measure again exactly; finish lip smooth.

For domed lids made upside-down, belly-out a round shape under the flange with the inside fingers. Keep measuring the flange diameter after each draw.

Wire cut the lid or let it stiffen on the plaster bat; add a separate knob, or attach a coil and throw on a knob.

Always check the fit of lid and pot in leather-hard state, and make changes if needed. Don't handle the pot or the lid more than necessary or you will cause warping or crack-

LIDS WITHOUT AND WITH FLANGE

1. **Right-side-up lid:** center mound for width of lid

Check fit of lid on flanged pot after cutting it off hump; this can best be done wet on a small pot

2. **Upside-down lid:** lift flange for lid; larger flat lids must be thrown directly against a bat; don't touch until stiff

Check fit of flanged lid at leather-hard stage

Three bisque teapot variations: left, a pulled clay handle, middle, a Japanese bamboo handle, to be fitted on after the glaze fire, and right, a thrown lug handle; the right-side-up thrown lid shows the correct depth of the flange

ing later on. Almost all problems occurring in the firing are the result of too much touching with hands during wet to leather-hard stages.

Lids should dry on their pots. Lid and pot should bisque-fire together, but askew so that air and moisture can escape from the pot. For the glaze firing, scrupulously wipe the glaze from edge of lid and rim of pot so the two can be fired together. If you want the edge of the pot glazed, fire the lid and pot separately. If lid and pot fire together, put in a steam hole.

TEAPOT SPOUT

Throwing teapot spouts uses the same method as making a tall thin bottle neck, except that you can begin from a hump of clay and cut the spouts off, or throw each spout directly on its own bat. A thin sharp lip cuts the drip when liquid is poured.

Throw the teapot spout by expanding it at the base and collaring in at the top, in much the same way as a narrow-necked bottle is formed

Wire-cut the spout base at the desired length, and lift it off when it is stiff

Arbitrarily cut away a triangular section to help fit the spout to the body

Thin the cross-section of the spout with a metal knife and score it in preparation for attaching

Hold the spout against the teapot body and trace around the base where it is to go. Use a drill bit or other rounded tool to punch holes to strain the tea-leaves. Score both the spout and the area to which it is to be attached, moisten, and meld the two

Teapot, coffee pot

A teapot or coffee pot shape is one of the most difficult composite shapes because of the complicated parts, the assemblage, and the reference of the parts to each other, but beverage pots are among the most exciting forms for the functional potter.

The body of the pot is made first; then throw the spout separately. Make the lid with a deep flange so it won't fall off the pot when it is tilted. **The spout must be thrown so that, when it is attached at an angle, it is long enough for its narrow end to be as high up as the lid of the pot—otherwise the liquid will leak out.**

Pull the handle when the body is trimmed, then trim the lid if necessary. Next, attach the spout, making a full hole in the body, or punch small holes at the point where the spout fits, to strain the liquid from the leaves when pouring. The pulled handle can be attached opposite the spout or it can fit in an arc over the top of the pot. If you prefer the Oriental-style bamboo or reed handle, make two small hand-built clay lugs on either side of the top opening, for the ready-made handle. Coffee pots are taller than teapots.

Sets

Making sets, all items alike or proportionally related, is difficult for beginners. Weighing balls of clay helps, as does taking proper measurements or making a template for the profile changes. Keep wall thickness, edges, and feet alike too.

Sets do not need to be look-alikes; they can be related in function or with similar forms, or with patterns or colors. It is fun to think of all the ways that objects can interact, tell stories, or project similarities. Of course, these ideas are not limited to thrown projects (see page 94).

Closed form

Throwing a closed form is similar to throwing a spherical shape, except that you will pull the clay wall all the way over and close the vessel completely; use a rib to press down at the closure to insure the seal (make a pinhole to allow expanding air to escape). Prior to closing you may want to blow into the shape to fill out the form. See Toshiko throwing one opposite.

Do-nut

Throwing a do-nut shape is difficult. Begin with a low wide mound of clay the diameter you wish the outside to have. Make a hole, not in the center of the mound, but off-center; raise and shape the outside wall. Next, open the mound in the center and go directly down to the bat, clean up that hole with a tool, and undercut it for shaping. Raise that wall also and pull the two walls up and over to each other, closing their edges together in the do-nut form; you now have a hollow do-nut shaped ring with a void in the center.

Do-nut forms can create such vessels as wine-pitchers and flower-holders (see page 88).

Throwing off-the-hump

Off-the-hump throwing is a fast way to throw many pots. Start with a large wedged lump of clay and center the whole thing, or just the top for the first pot. Take a bite of clay the size you think you need by making a line at the base of the top centered chunk, open that ball, pull up and shape the pot from that line, cut with a twisted wire, and lift off with your fingers or two spatulas. Do another; continue until the clay is used up (see page 81).

This method is particularly useful for throwing functional vessels on a production basis; page 69 shows a Moroccan potter making many shapes, including the bowl being thrown on the "hump" of clay on his wheel.

TRIMMING FEET

Trimming thrown pots can be achieved in the classic fashion by turning the form upside down, re-centering it on the wheel, and trimming an indented, pedestal foot with a sharp tool; tool the profile on the right side of the pot if the wheel goes counter-clockwise and on the left side of the pot if the wheel goes clockwise.

Alternatively, paddle the foot shape, carve it, add legs or other standing supports, roll the bottom against a flat surface—or think of other ways. Ceramists are forever turning hand-made and commercial pots over to examine the feet, looking at the form, the texture, perhaps the design of the signature, and the rhythm of relation-

1. **Trimming**: a bottle form with a narrow neck must be trimmed in a chuck of some sort, whereas a bowl or plate can be turned upside down directly on a bat. **Level the pot in the chuck**, using a bubble level, and center chuck or pot. Beginners should paste the chuck to the bat with coils of clay

2. **Hold middle finger** in the center of the foot, push down gently to keep the pot in place. Hold a sharp tool steady on right side of clay, trim downward to "draw the line" you want, repeat until correct. Indent the foot by carving into the clay from the center out

Collectors and friendly observers who are reading this book, but are perhaps not involved in clay construction, will find that the information and perceptions outlined here are helpful in gaining a complete understanding of the ceramic medium.

LARGE FORMS FROM THE WHEEL

Another way to trim feet: Sequoia Miller's lidded jar is thrown and altered by adding a thrown foot and cutting it leather-hard, reduction glazed c/10; 10 × 5 × 4 ins. (25 × 12.5 × 10 cm)

ships. The foot often finishes the profile line of a thrown pot that begins with the lip, and progresses from the shoulder through the belly to the aesthetic conclusion.

Remember that it seems to take forever to learn to throw. No matter, a form of some sort will result each time you work at the potter's wheel. Use these uncertain shapes for glaze and decorative experimentation. Often beginner's luck creates really interesting works. Nothing is wasted; look carefully at everything you do, for inspiration, for self-tutoring.

Steps for easy progression in learning to throw will be found at the back of this book, as well as suggestions for individual projects that can be fabricated in any of the methods we have discussed, once you have gained some experience.

Making larger and larger shapes on the wheel comes after you learn the basic steps on so-called functional sizes. To increase your technique for larger forms, try adding 5 lb (2.5 kg) increments—start with a 5 lb ball, then a 10 lb (5 kg) ball, and so forth. If that is too much, reduce it to a 2½ lb (1.25 kg) increase at a time. Everyone can learn to throw, but some persons take longer than others—don't be discouraged, it *will* happen! Throwing larger shapes takes more time to learn. You can throw as tall as your arm is long, or you can throw what is comfortable, then add coils and throw each one up, or you can throw separate shapes and join them leather-hard (pages 86, 87).

Large thrown pots can be made several ways:

1. Throw and coil: throw as tall as you can, then begin to add large fat coils one at a time, each luted well into the last, and throw each coil up true until you have your desired height.

2. Make a number of thrown sections, measuring with a calliper where they will fit together, and attach them in the leather-hard stage. Do not use a ruler: it is not accurate enough.

Toshiko Takaezu makes a 7 ft (213 cm) tall sculpture by *adding flattened coils and throwing them true*. In the process of gaining height she *stiffens the clay with a bonfire* inside the vessel; eventually she encloses the form totally (see a finished piece by Toshiko on page 21)

COMBINING THROWN FORMS

1

2

3

4

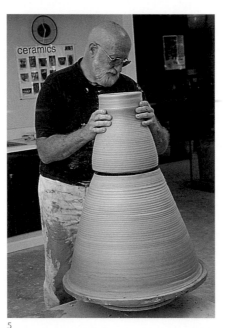

5

6

Bob Kinzie throws and attaches several forms, throwing them together:

1. **Throwing a huge piece on a low wheel**; note the position of the potter in relation to the wheel
2. **Raising and expanding the form**
3. **Stiffening the shape** with fire from a torch
4. **Turning the leather-hard shape upside down** on another bat on which the flat clay pancake base was thrown
5. **Adding another shape**, carefully measured to fit
6. **Throwing the two shapes together**

Neil Tetkowski throws a huge bowl on a larger wooden bat for one of his mixed-media wall pieces

Taäg Peterson assembles previously thrown sections by luting and rethrowing. In order to be able to stand above the pot he has placed a rock on the wheel pedal to keep the motor moving

ALTERING THROWN FORMS

1

2

1. Another **Bob Kinzie** piece: the thrown form is paddled into a triangle
2. Separate neck is thrown, attached off-center to paddled form; throwing marks are smoothed, surface textured; decorative carving begins
3. Finished thrown and altered stoneware, 40 ins. (102 cm) high; glaze should enhance texture and carving

3. Combine sections creatively. Make a number of thrown sections without measuring anything and put them together in a frenzy of creative passion, cutting, slashing, pushing the parts into a whole sculpture.

4. Combine after firing. If you don't have a large enough kiln to fire the monolithic piece, fire the sections and attach them with a good glue or plumber's cement, or put them together by other means such as nuts and bolts, wire, wood or metal appendages, or other decorative additions.

3

5. Some of the illustrated large forms are obviously a bit much for beginners, but you can scale the techniques down in size. Progress gradually; "discouraged" is not a word in our vocabulary!

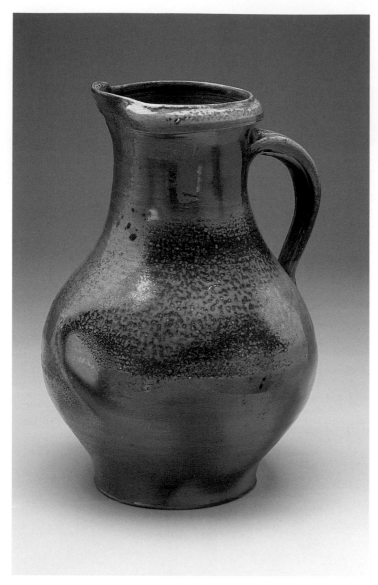

Linda Arbuckle, *majolica glaze* on terracotta-colored earthenware pitcher, 7½ × 6 × 5 ins. (19 × 15 × 13 cm)

Jack Troy, stoneware pitcher, *natural ash glaze*, four-day anagama firing, 16 × 9 × 9 ins. (40 × 23 × 23 cm)

PITCHER

Pitcher shapes are almost as old as time, but still provide creative fun for clayworkers.

Classic matt glazed stoneware jug by **Greg Miller** (Denmark), 8 ins. (20 cm) high

Rick Malmgren's thrown and altered pitcher is reduction fired c/6 stoneware with *an iron persimmon glaze*;
10 × 7 × 5½ ins. (25 × 18 × 12.5 cm)

Juris Bergins' (Latvia) cup metaphor is a composite of *porcelain forms, decals, china paints, transparent glaze, multi-firings,* oxidation c/10 to c/013; 14 ins. (35.5 cm) diameter

Nick Joerling's thrown and altered stoneware cup and saucer is *stain-decorated*

CUPS, SAUCERS, MUGS

Cups are functional forms that can be used every day or exist as sculptural objects.

Don Reitz stoneware mug with *engobe decoration,* 3½ × 4 ins., salt glazed

The openwork sections of these **thrown and pierced** porcelain cups by **Sandra Black** (Australia) are *covered by translucent colored glaze*

Deborah Smith's (India) lidded chapatti server **has an easily grasped knob** and is *decorated with brushed oxides over the glaze*

Harrison McIntosh's stoneware lidded jar has *engobe pattern under a translucent matt glaze*

LIDDED POTS

Lidded pots are a challenge, especially large ones, first for fit, second for good proportion between lid and pot. Lid and pot should glaze-fire together, with no glaze between them. Bad fit is potter's bad measurement.

Linda Sikora's porcelain tureen is *resist-patterned with glazes* and fired in a wood- and oil-fueled salt kiln, 6 × 12 ins. (15 × 30 cm); plate is assembled from thrown sections

Ray Meeker's (India) tiered and lidded set of serving dishes is *wax-resist and glaze decorated*, 14 ins. (35.5 cm) high

Randy J. Johnston's thrown teapot has been *touched with color in the woodfire*

Sandy Simon's porcelain clear-glazed teapot is *brushed with black and yellow glaze stains*

Farraday Newsome's teapot is earthenware, wheel-thrown, with press-molded protruding forms added at the leather-hard stage, glazed with *commercial pigments*, fired c/04 oxidation; 8 × 13 × 9½ ins. (20 × 33 × 24 cm)

TEAPOTS

Teapots or beverage pots are exciting to make but difficult to design and assemble. Think of the whole before you start.

FACING PAGE **Hwang Jeng-Daw**'s (Taiwan) thrown stoneware teapot of *multicolored clay* with hollow appendages, 15 × 15½ × 8 ins. (38 × 40 × 20 cm), is c/8 oxidation fired; many supports hold the pot during firing

SETS

Sets are great fun for the potter, because relating the various components to one another demands ingenuity as well as creativity.

Don Davis's slanted bowl group, thrown and altered porcelain, is *decorated with engobes, stains, resist patterns, glaze*; tallest bowl is 13 ins. (33 cm) high

Nina Malterud (Norway), sets of cups, thrown, stoneware, *underglaze stain decoration*, 4 ins. (10 cm) high

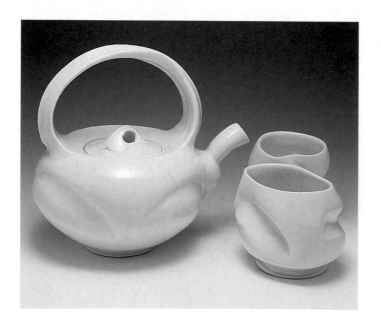

ABOVE Thrown earthenware tray set, *partly glazed with brush-strokes of commercial low fire glazes*, by **Woody Hughes**

LEFT **Chris Staley's** thrown porcelain teapot and cups were *altered in the wet stage*

ALTERED THROWN FORMS

Thrown shapes can be changed into many other kinds of forms in the wet to leather-hard stage. Hand-built appendages are often added to thrown forms and vice versa. Once you learn, throwing is the fastest method of making shapes and turning them into other forms.

Josh DeWeese's *thrown and altered* oil and vinegar set is soda-fired stoneware

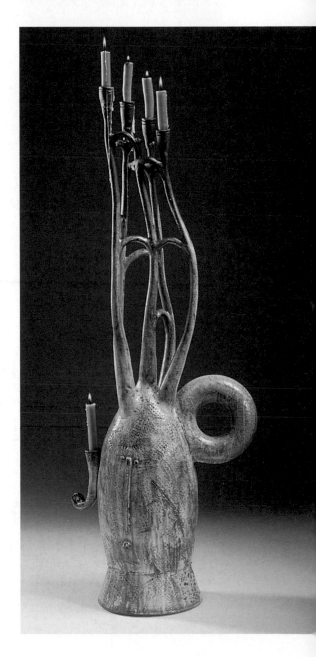

ABOVE **Matthew Wilt**'s server is *decorated with engobes* on a dark clay background; reduction fired c/10 stoneware, 16 × 15 × 8 ins. (40 × 38 × 20 cm)

LEFT **Tim De Rose**'s (Canada) thrown stoneware plate with *edge cut at leather-hard stage* has been *decorated with engobe and salt-glazed*

RIGHT **Curtis Hoard**'s thrown stoneware candelabra, nearly 5 ft (152 cm) tall, is a tour-de-force of *throwing and hand-building* technique

4

CERAMIC SCULPTURE

Michelangelo is said to have written that a good piece of sculpture is one that could be rolled down a mountain without anything breaking off. This definition is no longer applicable today, what with new ceramic materials like paperclay, advances in firing technology, and larger kilns—all of which allow ceramists to work in almost any size with multiple forms and varying surfaces.

Indigenous peoples have been making sculptural clay objects since the beginning of time, mainly, we think, for children's toys and for religious ceremonies, two uses that today keep clay images in use in tribal cultures. Much ancient sculpture has doubtless been destroyed, but we can still see: **a.** Emperor Ch'in Shih Huang-ti's hundreds of 2,000-year-old life-size horses and carriages excavated in 1979 at Xian, China; **b.** artifacts from other ceramic excavations in China; **c.** huge unfired clay figures in Japanese temples; **d.** the terracotta temples in India that really are ceramic sculpture; **e.** the effigy figures found in all civilizations; **f.** the ancient life-size storage jars preserved at Knossos, Crete; **g.** the huge water vessels of Otani kiln, Shikoku Island, Japan; **h.** the astonishing jars from potteries in Spain that are still producing them.

In China, archaeologists have found "kilns" that are hundreds of years old burrowed into the sides of hills with piles of ancient shards on the ground—caves are probably the earliest enclosures for firing ceramic objects. The life-size figures at Xian must have been fired by building individual chambers around each one, and the bricks would have been taken down after the fire. Firing ceramic sculpture presents more problems than firing the usual functional forms.

WHAT IS CERAMIC SCULPTURE?

By ceramic sculpture we mean a non-functional claywork that is hollow with a wall thickness of one inch (2.5 cm) to several inches, or a solid clay piece no more than two to three inches (5–7.5 cm) thick in any direction, that can be hand-built, thrown, or cast and will require a special firing schedule to avoid cracking or

Stephen De Staebler, *Two Legs with Black Knee*, built up solid and slashed downward, engobe, glaze, natural clay, stoneware fired, 35¼ × 15½ × 14 ins. (89.5 × 39 × 35.5 cm)

INSET Ancient sculptures: from top, Amlash animal (Persia); Haniwa figure (Japan); Minoan chariot (Crete)

DongHee Suh's (Korea) earthenware bird sculpture, solid clay, *sliced and carved*, 7 × 5 ins. (18 × 13 cm)

exploding in the kiln. We know that firing, from bonfire temperature of 1300° F (721° C) to porcelain temperature of 2300° F (1260° C), is necessary for permanence, but if kilns inhibit scale, artists may break up the raw sculpture and reassemble it later. If accidents happen from fabrication or firing, it's usually the fault of the maker, almost never of the clay or the kiln. Dealing with the many wild and diverse problems presented by our material means that sculpture in ceramics is arguably more difficult than in any other medium.

Any method of clay construction may be used for the purpose of sculpture, but hand-building techniques are probably the most versatile. A misconception is that sculpture must be large. If the piece is small and

BELOW In one of the largest ceramic projects ever undertaken, **Jun Kaneko** created monolithic shapes of extraordinary technical difficulty with conspicuous success:

1. **His slab and pinch-built "dango" shapes,** 11 ft 6 ins. (3.5 m) high, were constructed within a sewer-pipe kiln in Fremont, California

2. **Jun Kaneko** glazing an 11 ft (3.4 m) tall dango, following his doodles and codes for color notes. Jun has worked out his idea in drawing on the dango. It may be changed again when he paints

3. **The beehive sewer-pipe kiln** in which the dangos were built and fired was 30 ft (9 m) in diameter

4. **Dangos packed and ready to be trucked** for storage in Kaneko's Omaha, Nebraska studio

1

2

3

4

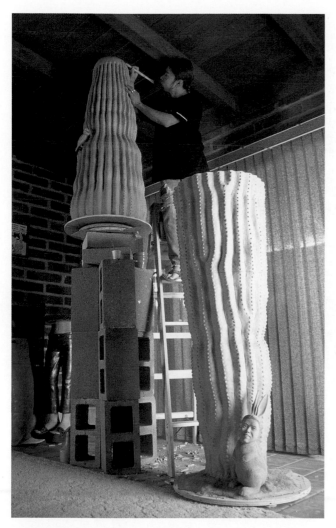

Hirotsune Tashima (Japan) is known for **building larger than lifesize figures and installations**, usually in sections to be assembled later

ABOVE Hiro is constructing a colossal stoneware cactus. *Engobe decoration* and glazing are done next; firing in a gas kiln takes place at c/5 to c/10 depending on the clay and colors

Here the clay figure, modeled after himself, using a mirror, is about to receive a head similar to his own. The base of the figure is kept damp by being wrapped in plastic; the cement blocks allow him to climb up to continue the piece

narrow, or if long-time firing is possible, the work could be solid. However, as we have said, it is best to think of ceramic sculpture as hollow, and to build it bottom to top as a pot is built.

Making a small solid clay model prior to constructing the large sculpture will help in the complicated thought process of building hollow from the bottom up. Parts of a sculpture can be made separately and attached when the clay is leather-hard.

Any size of work is possible, the only limitation being the kiln size. In fact, this can be overcome by making your piece in units that will fit the kiln and can be fired separately. These can be combined after firing by non-clay methods, such as glue, plumber's cement, nuts and bolts, wire, or similar methods. **The only real limitation is the clayworker's imagination, and even that can be strengthened and enriched with knowledge and time**.

Sculpture in other materials such as metal is often made by factories following a model from the artist, whereas ceramic sculpture is accomplished entirely by the maker, with possible assistants. **An interesting question: when does a vessel become sculpture? One answer is: when you place it on a pedestal.**

P.R. Daroz (India) is one of the very few artists creating large-scale ceramics in India. His monumental gateway, a private commission for a swimming pool in Gujerat, India, consists of four arches and six pillars, *slip-cast (liquid clay) or extruded (plastic clay)* in 2 ft (60 cm) stoneware blocks built to a height of 9 ft (2.7 m) and width of 5 ft (1.52 m). The relief design will be press-molded and attached leather-hard to the clay blocks; *iron oxide accents on a dolomite matt glaze*, fired in a tunnel kiln fueled with oil, are the finishing touch to the three months' work prior to the installation

Using an armature

Stainless steel will withstand 2150° F (1175° C), c/5, and such an armature will remain in the piece to give strength to large work, but must be wrapped with enough paper to allow for the clay to shrink against it. A clay body should be developed for minimum shrinkage.

Nylon mesh or nylon wire armatures may disintegrate depending on the firing temperature, but will add structure during fabrication. Supports of wood, glass bottles, or pipes must be wrapped and extracted before the plastic clay begins to dry.

If the clay piece is a model for a plaster mold or for metal casting, the armature buttress will remain in until the clay is removed from the mold.

Jerry Rothman's low-shrink clay body will be laid over this stainless steel armature, which will remain in the piece while the sculpture below is fired at a median stoneware temperature

Clay on the steel armature is supported by wood while it dries; sculpture from the 1970s

Drape in a hammock

Drape a cloth to form a sling of desired depth and width by pinning or nailing the fabric to the inside of a cardboard or wooden box, or suspend material from the legs of an upturned stool, or in any way you can, as a receptacle for a slab of clay. Platter and plate shapes are easily made in this manner. Alternatively, the slung clay can become the base for a sculpture, with pinch, coil, or slab additions. The hammock supports the clay until it is dry enough to be moved.

Several slings can be utilized at once, so that the clay forms may be joined together into hollow vessels or sculptures.

Over-the-hump slab building

(see also p. 53)

Choose a contour—a rock, a pot, a balloon, or the like—that will create the interior shape of the vessel when a slab of clay is placed over it. The form must be such that the clay will be released from the hump without getting stuck. It must therefore have no "undercuts" (see page 58), or the clay cannot be removed. You can create your own form from clay or plaster instead of a found object; fire the clay to keep it, or use it moist for one time only.

Place a sheet of plastic or paper or fabric over the hump before laying the

ABOVE **Jeff Irwin**'s glazed earthenware sculpture is *hand-built over a paper armature* using coil, slab, and pinch techniques

Susan Peterson lays a textured clay slab into a burlap hammock draped in a cardboard box

BUILDING ON A CORE

The late **Christine Federighi**'s unglazed figure is built over a cardboard core which burns out in the firing

clay slab on top, so that it will be released easily when it is lifted off. The hump method, the opposite of the sling method, provides the opportunity of working on the back of the shape, for instance if you want to add a foot or any other appendage to the vessel.

John Mason with the paper maquettes he makes before starting to build his sculptures. He says, "I now have over 60 file boxes of paper maquettes. I started making them in 1990 as a way to visualize the new slab constructions I was making. They are small constructions that are accurate visualizations of shape and the angles of intersection. They contain all the concept information. The scale of fabrication is open and flexible." See p. 114 for a finished sculpture

CATEGORIES OF SCULPTURE

Abstract This has no particular connotation other than that the piece does not relate to anything real, being a thing in itself, rather like a three-dimensional "design." Today it is possible to conjure up an abstract idea by first beginning on the computer. **Most potters start a sculpture using a drawing or a maquette**, but a com-

RIGHT AND BELOW ABSTRACT: **Ruth Borgenicht** casts rings in gang molds, removes them wet, cuts them to construct like chain mail; she bisques partial constructions to support weight of more additions, firing frequently for stability; wet rings can be interlocked with dry and bisque; final firing is stoneware, 20 × 19 × 15 ins. (51 × 48 × 38 cm). A similar technique extrapolates to large scale (see Mateiescu, page 61)

puterized virtual image can constitute the sculpture itself, or the computer can offer numerous ideas, viewing a piece from all directions, and, with the proper software, changing it over and over.

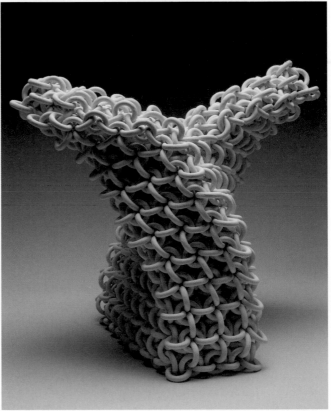

TROMPE L'OEIL: **Susan Margin**'s basket sculptures are fabricated with thin coils meticulously hand-woven, creating a calligraphic shape, inviting a touch to see if it's real; *stains and oxides are rubbed in before firing and inks are added after.* 14 × 12 × 10½ ins. (35.5 × 30 × 27 cm)

BELOW CONCEPTUAL: **Ruth Chambers** (Canada), one of 80 high fired, *very thin porcelains*, representing human organs (such as the heart and lungs), with *interior electric lighting*, suspended in a large gallery space. "This piece is a part of a series that looks at how I have attempted to locate vitality or the 'source of life' within various internal organs. The work is informed by metaphorical, medical and visceral processes"

CONCEPTUAL: Ideas of decay, transformation and entropy are central to the work of **Nidhi Jalan** (India): "In my installation, the reflection of wire-wrapped decomposing fruits hung over ceramic bowls filled with the essence of the fruits, explores the nostalgia of something diminishing"

Trompe l'oeil Here the artist uses an idea almost directly opposite in meaning to "abstract," super-realistically depicting objects or landscapes, creating in clay with hand methods, or from projected slides or photographs, or making molds of real objects into which clay is slip-cast or pressed.

Conceptual An idea that is a metaphor of something else, surrealistic or illusionary, relating to a real or made-up fantasy, sometimes referred to as "dada," a word first coined in Europe and brought to New York by the artist Marcel Duchamp in 1917. This, or any of the categories, can be unfired or

self-destructing. Often, text accompanies the work.

Installation A composite group of objects that are usually arranged together but not necessarily joined, that may or may not have a relationship to each other, that do not have to but may take up a great deal of space.

INSTALLATION: **Betty Woodman's** extraordinary retrospective of her life's work covered several major galleries at New York's Metropolitan Museum of Art in 2006. This installation, *House of the South*, earthenware, epoxy resin, lacquer and paint, 14 ft 5 ins. × 22 ft 9 ins. × 9½ ins. (4.39 × 6.93 m. × 24 cm) of unbelievable scale was the first expansive exhibit for any ceramic artist at this prestigious institution. Betty is shown here with one of the walls

LEFT NARRATIVE: **Sun-Koo Yuh's** (Korea) storytelling porcelain, glazed sculpture, 51 × 28 × 22 ins. (130 × 71 × 56 cm), represents his feelings about his South Asian culture

RIGHT FIGURATIVE: **Li Jiansheng** (**"Jackson Lee"**) (China), *Memory of a Box Song*. Hollow-built stoneware, 3 × 9 ins. (33 × 23 cm)

ABOVE MIXED MEDIA: **Gerit Grimm's** (Germany) installation, glazed ceramic, cardboard, paint, is inspired by personal memory: "There was a bakery in the Baltic Sea, posed previously on the edge of a cliff that eroded over the years, bringing the bakery closer to the edge and possibly the end. This bakery had the most amazing window display; sometimes we walked to it along the sea, taking nearly three hours." Detail of 9 × 8 × 8 ft (2.74 × 2.44 × 2.44 m.) installation

Figurative, Narrative Since time began, tribesmen have told their stories in clay with small vignettes of workers, families, games, and such, fired or not, and today figures seem to be important to clayworkers. Isolated ceramic figures, or groups of them on a scale from small to large, impart a real challenge in fabrication and firing.

Mixed media Clay in combination with one or more non-clay materials, usually metal holding the structure together, or found objects attached or not, perhaps supporting the piece, or wood or small units embellishing surfaces of the work—or almost anything. If glue is necessary, try using plumber's cement (after firing).

Most sculptures fit these categories. A good potter usually begins with one of these ideas, or makes an "installation" combining several different ideas. Having a picture in mind from the beginning is one of the hardest aspects of ceramics to learn, but working from a goal is always helpful when making art.

Beginners often find these concepts exciting, and can achieve success even before they have mastered fabrication and glazing methods. As you progress to more advanced stages of technique, your sculptures will probably become larger and more complex; the possibilities are overwhelming. Functional or so-called production potters may not have as much fun considering the turn of a lip or the placement of a handle, and may soon adopt a more sculptural attitude. *However, the functional potter may consider his beautifully crafted bowl a work of pure sculpture.* Many clayworkers continue to produce traditional forms as well as experimenting with sculptural ideas.

Granted, it is not easy to extrapolate from a small model to a life-size figure or whatever, and this is the main problem in working off-round and in large scale. **Beginners should not tackle large work all at once.** Start with a regular-sized ball of clay, say 5 lb, and work up until you are handling 25 lb pieces which may in turn be luted together or have more clay forms added, to make heroic sizes.

MIXED MEDIA: **Jim Leedy's** sculpture at Jingdezhen San Bao Ceramic Art Institute in China; handmade brick and other Leedy-built additions to the structure, engobe and glazes, with historic fragment; 18 ft high × 50 ft long (5.48 × 15.24 m.)

SCULPTURE TOOLS

The larger the claywork the larger the tools to be used in fabrication. For instance, where a paring knife would do, here a butcher's knife may be in order, or you may graduate from a rice paddle to a ping-pong paddle, and so forth. You will need a heavy clay scraper of some kind to refine line; a wood paddle to pound forms; a putty knife or a sawtooth tool or saw-blade to pull off chunks of clay; a yardstick or a calliper to measure when attaching coils or appendages; a large sponge; absorbent terry-cloth rags for keeping clay moist; a heavy duty banding wheel for building on and turning the sculpture. You will think of other objects that suffice for ceramic sculpture-making tools as you go along.

Judy Onofrio's "Make a Big Wish" is *ceramic and mixed media*, 93 × 36 × 36 ins. (236 × 91 × 91 cm)

MATERIALS

The composition of the sculpture clay body depends on the **temperature at which you wish to fire, the density you want in the finished object, the color you desire, and the degree of plasticity necessary for building—** these are requirements similar to those for more traditional forms (see Chapter 1). If the piece will be installed out of doors, the climate makes a difference: in cold winters too porous a clay would absorb moisture, then expand and crack, or too dense a body might suffer thermal shock and crack in freezing weather. Experiment by putting sample works into your refrigerator or freezer, and move them from hot to cold and vice versa.

Workability is always an issue. A clay body for throwing needs more fine-grained minerals in the body formula for plasticity, while a clay for hand-building needs to stand upright on its own and not slump (see Mason sculpture, page 36). If the piece is very large and the walls are of maximum thickness, you may want to lighten the weight and "open" the clay for ease of drying and firing by adding 10 to 20% grog to the mix. Adding paper to a clay body (page 26) allows more exotic forms to be made at the expense of strength. Any sculpture body can be colored by adding percentages of metallic oxides or stains to the dry batch, as we do in glazes and engobes (see Chapter 5), or a light-burning basic clay can be darkened with iron-bearing clays or iron oxide wedged into the plastic mass.

Adding 25% lignite cement to the clay body will make it possible to use the finished sculpture in or out of doors without firing, but concrete lessens plasticity and limits form, which probably makes this addition, with its possibilities and problems, a technique more suited to advanced clayworkers.

All-purpose ceramic sculpture body composition (see chart, pages 30–31; outside the USA find similar clays)

Fire clay (finer grained such as Hawthorne) 10–30%

Fire clay (coarser grained such as Missouri Fire) 10–30%

Ball clay (very plastic, such as Kentucky OM4) 10–30%

Potash feldspar (such as G200) 0–30%

Silica (200 mesh) 10–20%

From the above limits, make a basic composition adding up to 100%. Add various types and sizes of grog, from 5% to 30%, as **additions to the 100% batch.**

Grog is bits of fired clay; purchase it from ceramic suppliers or manufacturers, or make your own from grinding shards or by pressing plastic clay into 60 to 100 mesh screens and firing from 1800° F (982° C) to higher for a more dense finished look; make impressive colored grogs by adding oxides or stains to the plastic clay and firing. For other "openers" use just plain dirt; "pearlite" or other commercial fertilizers; burn-out materials such as ground coffee beans, sawdust, or wood chips; American Indian style ground pottery shards; beach sand or mineral sands such as crystal silica (granules fuse at c/10), and probably many others. Grogs will add texture to clay depending on how much is used, of what kind, especially if the raw clay surface is scraped during fabrication. Choose the feldspar amount according to the temperature you fire

at: none to some at lower fire for earthenware, while 0–1% absorption (porcelain) requires more.

Fired, the above batch (page 108) is a buff-colored body at low temperature and will get progressively darker brown as temperature goes up toward c/10. If you want a more iron-red color, substitute 10–30% of an iron-red clay in place of some of the buff fire clay. You might purchase a good clay body from your local brick manufacturer to use as is, or add to your regular clay; iron-bearing red clays can become glaze at high temperatures; be careful of the amount. **For ease of fabrication and for less difficulty, fire at mid range, c/3 to c/6; for bright color use oxidation atmosphere, for subdued color use reduction (see page 30).**

SCALE

Ceramic sculpture is often large—why do we think of sculpture as large? It's not necessarily true but it seems to be a universal thought. **When size is important, don't lose it in shrinkage.** Look at the chart (page 31) for clays with the lowest shrinkage for the temperature you fire at, make your own composition or make shrinkage bars from bodies that are available from your supplier or from those clays that you can prospect in the bush. It doesn't matter what the "brand name" of the clay is; as previously learned, only five geological types of clays exist anywhere in the world and you will find some everywhere to buy, or dig, that are similar to the ones on the chart.

Frank Matranga's wall sculpture for a client's koi pond incorporates a fixed fig tree and waterpipe; built on a huge easel in the studio, natural clays and glazes, fired in sections, stoneware, 13 × 4 ft (3.96 × 1.2 m.)

Low temperatures, ceramically speaking around 1800° F (982° C), do not usually cause much shrinkage of natural clays and basic body compositions, because these bodies remain porous. When a flux is needed to create density at low fire, such as ground glass or body frit, substitute it for feldspar (see clay body, page 108). At high temperature, around 2300° F (1260° C), most natural clays and body compositions have high shrinkage because many clays become dense at that heat; add openers to reduce shrinkage caused by density.

Moving a large sculpture from place to place during the building processes, getting a piece into a kiln, and finding proper firing techniques, are not problems at low temperatures or with highly porous clay body mixtures at any temperature. As soon as you want a fired sculpture to be dense, and to have the "look" of high rather than low fire, size becomes a problem. It is helpful to **a.** refine the composition of the clay body; **b.** change methods of building and what to build on for the best movement of the object; **c.** rectify systems of drying the work slowly and evenly; **d.** devise ways of movement without any strain; **e.** qualify schemes related to firing schedules.

Taking the weight out of the fired piece, particularly for wall hangings, is difficult to judge. The weight of an object can be lowered 20% to 30% with the addition of any of the nonplastic materials we have listed. Air around each of these inert additives will cause the total weight to be less, but if too much weight is lost, strength will also be lost. In an effort to lose the weight of a colossal sculpture, artists like Jerry Rothman (page 101), Jun Kaneko (pages 25, 98), and John Mason (pages 17, 36, 154) experienced monumental losses initially as they progressed to larger scale, and exper-

Zhang Wanxin's monumental sculpture is reminiscent of China's third-century warriors; coil-built with plaster-pressed additions; cut into sections for firing c/04, *glued; stains and glazes,* 84 × 25 × 18 ins. (213 × 63.5 × 46 cm)

imented to find usable body compositions and additives. Some of the mined clays that we in the USA had access to years ago, such as a flint-fire clay from Mexico, Missouri, were of naturally coarse and jagged particle sizes that helped clay to stand tall without slumping during the building; these clays are no longer mined. The challenge in finding alternative materials now requires using all your creative instincts, even for less advanced clayworkers.

FABRICATION TECHNIQUES

Begin a really large sculpture directly on a kiln shelf, covered with powdered silica to help shrinkage movement, or on a ½ in. (1 cm) thick plywood board (extending several inches out all around the sculpture) that can be moved into the kiln and burned away in the firing; the board should be covered with cloths and an inch or more of newspaper to allow the work to move and shrink evenly as it dries.

Coil, slab, and throw (see Chapters 2, 3): choose the method of building according to what you do or like to do best, or choose according to the required look of the finished object. Some ceramic sculpture appears the way it does because of how it's made. Some sculptures can't be classified visually according to technique—for instance, Peter Voulkos's stack sculptures could be thrown, slab-built, or coiled, but throwing was what Pete liked to do and did best. Some sculptures need the crisp feeling that comes from slab-building, such as John Mason's tall, crisp totems (page 36). Some sculptures require rounded shapes for which coil-building or

Paula Rice begins her sculpture with coiling and pinching process from bottom to top

Paula Rice's finished sculpture, *unglazed and glazed*, oxidation fired and *smoked*, 32 × 15 × 18 ins. (81 × 38 × 46 cm)

Conrad Snider adds 8 to 10 ins. (20–25 cm) each day to his enormous thrown pots; the wet clay *coil and throw* process takes about seven to eight days

Working alone, he devises a means of moving the pots using dollies, hand trucks, and forklifts. Drying takes six months and bisque and glaze firings are about five days each

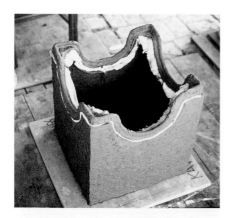

LEFT **Elaine Katzer** builds a 6-ft (1.83 m.) stoneware fountain in five sections with an internal flange and cloth between the units to ensure an exact fit; cloth burns out but allows sections to move as they drag. Finished work below

BELOW **Elaine Katzer**'s engobe-decorated, unglazed 7-ft (2.13 m.) totem, actually a model for a larger piece, is built in sections and installed outdoors with an iron rod and pea gravel for support

ABOVE **Val Lyle** constructs gestural figurative sculptures over hollow clay tube armatures, *manipulating soft clay slabs to drape the torso*

pinching will be more appropriate, such as Richard Devore's vessel forms (page 43).

Cast, pressed, in molds (see pages 58–65): large molds get very heavy when you pour or press into them, but you can divide the work into sections to be put together when the pieces are removed from the molds. Plaster molds last a long time and can be used for many different sculptures; pay attention to attaching molded pieces together to make larger forms, or attaching molded parts to clay segments made by other methods; score the attachment area well, use water or slurry at the joint, cover the whole sculpture for several days to help the attached seams dry slowly with the whole piece.

Remember that with density at any temperature comes shrinkage, perhaps as much as 20–30%. Make a clay bar (page 30) from your clay body, and measure the shrinkage at the temperature at which you intend to fire. If you have a small test kiln, fire samples at several cones to see the range of shrinkage percentages; alter the body as we have discussed. **We can't**

stress enough that you must be aware that the choice of clay and the clay body composition are the most important factors in making ceramic sculpture in terms of workability, shrinkage, and strength before and during firing. Casting slip should be tested for shrinkage, in the same way as plastic clay.

Nancy Jurs made this monumental sculpture, installed with forklifts and cranes at the new Rochester, NY, airport, by first building the entire piece in solid clay, then casting plaster molds in 18 sections and pressing a wall 2 to 4 ins. (5–10 cm) thick into the molds. Final carving was accomplished with a shovel and a two-man saw. The work was trucked to the room-sized kilns at Lapp Insulator Company for firing; c/5 stoneware, sigillata surface, 16 ft (4.8 m.) tall, 15 ft (4.5 m.) diameter base

BELOW LEFT AND RIGHT **Luo Xiao Ping** (China), figurative sculpture:

(a) hand-rolled, slab-built, hollow torso of thinly rolled slabs, *scored and pasted with clay body slurry*; the look of the figure explains the process

(b) finished figure, raw clay to be fired to stoneware

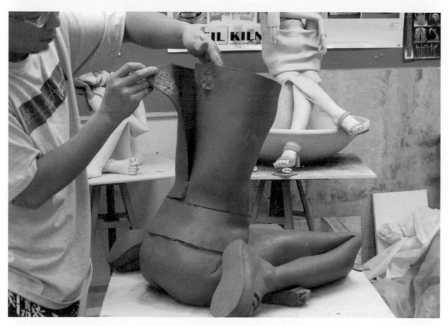

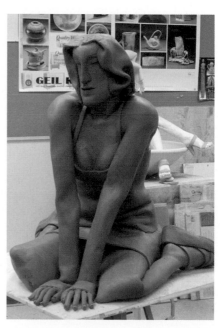

DRYING

Clay must be kept with the same degree of moisture content right through fabrication from beginning to end, even over many days if you are continuing to work on the piece. Damp cloths to cover the work from day to day are often used, but the weight of the cloths on the sculpture must be considered as well. Clay shrinks as it dries—how often have we said that! **Uneven drying** causes cracks later. Spritzing with a water bottle wets only the sculpture's surface unless you spray more or less all the time; if the form gets too wet it will collapse. If possible, elevate the hollow work several inches so the piece can dry from the bottom and inside up.

When a really large sculpture is finished, cover it with plastic all over so that it is completely air-tight; the next day (or so) punch one hole in the plastic, the next day another hole, and so forth for a period of about two weeks;

now remove the plastic, and let the piece air until it is bone-dry and does not feel cold to the touch. If you have built the sculpture on a kiln shelf or on a board, it can be lifted easily into the kiln. The board will become ash in the fire, letting the work down slowly as it matures.

COLORING

The possibilities for coloring clay sculpture include leaving the clay its natural fired color; adding colored clay engobes (page 120) to the moist clay; using metallic oxides or commercial stains on the bisque surface; applying glaze to the raw clay if it will be once-fired, or to a bisqued piece; adding "room temperature glazes" such as crayons or paint; or combinations of other alternatives.

Most ceramic sculpture does not benefit from a shiny glaze; exceptions are historic examples such as the Chi-

ABOVE **Lisa Wolkow**'s structurally complex sculpture combines *extruded and coil-built parts* and uses bricks to prop it up while drying and firing; earthenware, 34 × 20 × 10 ins. (86 × 51 × 25 cm)

John Mason, *Trans-orb*, gloss black with tracers, 2006, 11 × 14 × 14 ins. (28 × 35.5 × 35.5 cm). See p. 103 for Mason's maquettes

Keisuke Mizuno's miniature sculpture, not as mini as he often makes; multi-fired, c/5 glaze and *low fired china paints, layered colors on porcelain;* 9 × 12 × 12 ins. (23 × 30 × 30 cm). Firing many times, particularly feasible in an electric kiln, can eventually cause breakage from thermal shock

nese Tang dynasty horses (page 208) and Meissen porcelain figurines (page 211), among other models through the ages. Think of color for ceramic sculpture: **a.** depending on size—smaller seems to work best with bright glazes; **b.** placement of the sculpture; **c.** the color and texture of the environment outside or inside; **d.** in a natural setting see if muted engobes or the natural clay color will blend best with nature; **e.** if the structure is complicated, using commercial stains or oxide colors will enhance the details; **f.** or, zen-like, meditate and intuitively decide what will work best for the form. It behooves the potter to have more than one sculpture to experiment on, especially until you have accumulated experience, and as always, keep notes of exactly what you did and the results from firing. Ceramic sculpture is a never-ending challenge, with limitless possibilities.

FIRING

A low-temperature firing, about 1800° F (982° C), c/06, is really too porous for a substantial sculpture; a median stoneware temperature, c/3 to c/6 or so, is better for durability, but c/10 may be preferred for the more dense look of the clay body. A very large sculpture will probably be alone in the kiln, but a smaller work may have other shelves and clay pieces surrounding it; take care in packing the chamber. **Distribute the "mass" evenly so that heat absorption will be even during the firing**. Sometimes, colored engobes or glazes, or other surfaces, are applied to the raw piece, allowing for one firing from the beginning to the end temperature. Sometimes the bisque firing is necessary to prepare the sculpture for a particular glazing technique.

Firing for a large sculpture

From the beginning of the firing, increase temperature 50° per hour until the pyrometer registers 500° F (260° C) (about ten hours or overnight); increase the firing curve to 100° per hour until 1000° F (540° C) is reached (five hours), at which point the "water smoking" and oxidation stages are complete, allowing the fire to progress more rapidly from now. From 1000° F you can continue for two to three hours to the end, slowing down near your desired top temperature; **allow the last 100° on the pyrometer to take one hour**, to mature the body color and the glaze if you have applied one.

Before opening the kiln, allow it to cool for at least as many hours as it took for this firing. As always, keep a record of the firing schedule and results. Even if the piece seems to be whole when it comes out of the kiln, if the cooling time has been too short a mistake such as a crack can wait for weeks or months to reveal itself. Remember, like the elephant, clay never forgets.

Ceramic sculpture garners more money on the collectors' market than most functional vessels. Often it is evident that a sculpture took much longer to make and has survived more problems than a similar-sized traditional pot. However, some of this is due to our inbuilt feeling that functional work is not art, and sculpture is. Until we can change the universal public mind, you will decide which way to go, whether to make sculpture or be a functional potter, according to which area gives you most satisfaction in your life's work; we hope you won't decide solely according to the income it will bring in.

5

FINISHING TOUCHES

ENHANCING THE CLAY FORM

Since the beginning of time, human beings have felt a desire to embellish their claywork. Early in history, coiled pots were made with the coils showing, and perhaps stick-marks or indentations were made on them during fabrication. Often clays of other colors were added to the surface of a vessel and drawings were scratched through the added colors to the clay body. Sometimes clay cut-outs or decorative appendages serving no function were added to the surface. Many times, brush-strokes of a different-colored clay decorated the pot.

Thousands of years passed before glass and glaze were discovered, probably around 5000 BCE. With this achievement a variety of colors was possible and a shiny, easily cleaned surface was developed. More importantly, a transparent glaze could cover and protect the col-

ored clay paintings and textured surfaces with which primitive potters had been ornamenting their vessels.

The method of constructing the form does not matter: decoration of all kinds is possible on any clay shape. Industrial decorative processes do differ from hand processes, but some of those methods, such as the use of decals, can also be applied to handwork.

Engobes, also called *slips*, which are colored clays used to decorate surfaces (pages 120–122), and **glazes**, which become glassy coatings in the firing (pages 125–126), are both pigmented with certain metallic oxides or with manufactured glaze stains made from the oxides plus other minerals to widen the decorative palette. Engobes yield a raw-clay-like matt surface which seems natural, and glazes—from matt to high sheen gloss—give the work a voice and should be chosen to enhance the idea the artist wants to express. As in music or creative writing, the "tone" of a work can be highlighted through embellishment.

Jun Kaneko, detail of a 9-ft (2.74 m.) tall dango (a Japanese word meaning "round form") shows complex 3-D depths and intricacies of glaze over virtuoso engobe painting

DECORATING WITH CLAY

Texture

The simplest method of decorating clay, from earliest times, is to pattern it in the wet or leather-hard stage with any tool or object pressed into the clay to various depths. This includes use of the fingers in a number of ways; pressing imprints of objects from nature—seed pods, rocks, shells—or "found objects"—nails, screws, wires, and so on—into the clay; using stamps you make yourself from clay, textured, carved, and bisque-fired so they can be pushed into wet clay for decoration; pressing wooden paddles or rolling castors that you have carved yourself against your pots or sculptures. Anything can be used to make impressions on clay in random or organized patterns.

TEXTURING CLAY

Ah Leon constructed his 60-ft (18 m.) long bridge in his Taiwan studio over a period of several years; each segment was slab-built hollow, with interior buttressing, and different colored clays were used

Ah Leon meticulously *textured the clay to resemble wood* and fired in high-temperature reduction

Section of **Ah Leon**'s bridge; the entire piece was first shown at the Sackler Gallery, Smithsonian Institution, Washington D.C.

TEXTURING CLAY

Clay is so susceptible to marking that the simplest method of decorating it is to push something into it. Any number of objects or tools will leave an interesting decorative pattern (see above).

Marc Leuthold painstakingly *carves from a flat slab* a disk which will form the top surface of his sculpture

Marc Leuthold's finished hemispherical sculpture is fired at c/010 with a *cadmium glaze*

Gudrun Klix's (Australia) textured earthenware server has been *patinated with low fire engobes and matt glaze* to resemble bronze

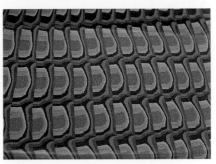

Detail of a **Katie Kazan** tray made with her *millefiore technique*. Sections of different colored clays are laid and pressed together into a solid rectangle to form patterns, then wire-cut across the grain to form slabs to build with

Texturing clay in the wet state gives a soft effect, as opposed to carving on the surface when it is leather-hard. After the piece is bisqued, colored metallic oxides can be rubbed into the indentations and wiped off, to highlight the patterns. This surface can be left unglazed to give a weathered or stony look; oxides without a glaze coating need firing at c/5 or above. Glaze can also be applied over the stained texture (not Ah Leon's style). Especially, transparent glazes will puddle in these indentations, which gives another quality to the texture.

Adding clay to clay

Clay forms of the same or different-colored clays can be appliquéd to the basic shape either wet or leather-hard; rolled, beaten, or torn slabs can be squeezed or pounded against moist clay forms; coils can be rolled into various shapes and added on, pressed flat or left to protrude; small balls of clay can be added in spots for emphasis; edges can be cut and folded to change the line. Experiment with many different additions to your forms—paddle, slash, and change the shape freely. Differing types of clays can be added to each other with varying results; shrinkage cracks are OK in "art."

Susan Peterson brushes black engobe into lines and around background of previously applied *wax-resist pattern* on leather-hard clay

ENGOBES

Engobes are liquid colored clays, also called slips, applied in coats, in patterns, or all over a clay form, in its wet or leather-hard state. Engobes bond only on unfired, usually leather-hard clay unless they are specially formulated for application on bisqued clay.

ENGOBE

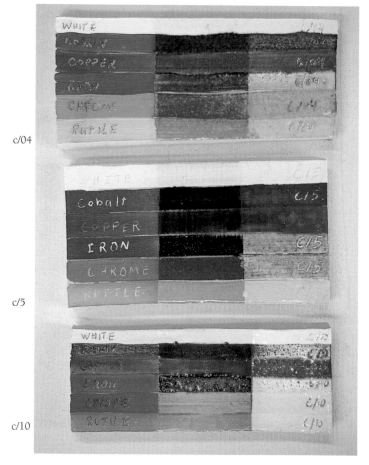

| | NO GLAZE | CLEAR GLAZE | OPAQUE GLAZE |

c/04

c/5

c/10

Basic engobe batch with 20% zircopax added for white, 20% cobalt oxide for blue, 20% copper oxide for blue-green, 20% iron oxide for brown, 20% chrome oxide for green, 20% rutile for tan, were each brushed across each of three tiles.

Each tile was left unglazed on the left, glazed in the center with the c/04, c/5, and c/10 transparent glazes, and on the right side with the c/04, c/5, and c/10 opaque glazes (see page 127), and fired in oxidation at the three temperatures.

Note the visual differences between the color unglazed, under the clear glaze, and under an opaque white glaze. If the tiles had been fired in reduction, the copper bar would have turned pink or red under the glazes

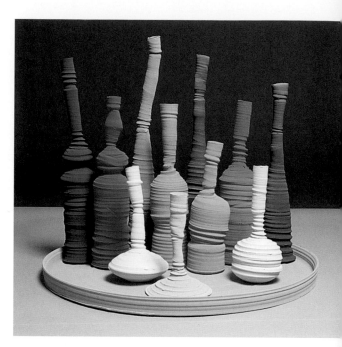

Engobes and glazes are colored with natural metallic oxides such as iron, cobalt, copper etc; but commercial blends of these oxides with other chemicals, called "glaze stains," or stains, for short, will give the potter a wider palette and can be purchased from ceramic suppliers everywhere in the world. Engobes may be covered with a glaze, or left unglazed

ABOVE A porcelain sculpture by **James Makins** was sprayed with stain-colored engobes and fired at high temperature oxidation, without glaze, which gives a very matt texture

BELOW **Makins** has added Mason stain 6005 to a basic semi-matt glaze to make a solid-colored glaze, c/10 oxidation. Unglazed solid-colored engobes, as above, and solid-colored glazes, as below, yield two different kinds of surface with the same pigments

Engobes (slips)

Engobes are made of clay, other materials, and colorants, that fire to the same temperature as the clay body and fit the body without cracking off. Sometimes the base clay of the engobe is the same as the clay body, or at least a similar composition. Engobes with a major proportion of clay content will be applied to moist clay; engobes made with 50% clay plus other inert materials can be applied to dry or bisque clay; engobe compositions can be made that will become dense and almost glaze-like, and are called **vitreous engobes**. White engobes can be colored with various metallic oxides or stains (see page 126). Engobes are only clay, and will not stick to the clay kiln shelf or any other pot during firing.

Add metallic coloring oxides or commercial stain colors to any batch in amounts of 20 to 50%; test the engobes on pots fired to your normal temperature with and without glaze until you reach the effect you want. The basic engobe batch is for use on wet to leather-hard clay. Adding sodium silicate, gum, or liquid wax may help engobes to brush better.

An all-temperature engobe batch for painting on bisque clay
> ball clay 50%
> talc 20%
> whiting 10%
> feldspar 10%
> silica 10%

A vitreous engobe batch for high fire; for low fire use ground glass or frit in place of spar
> ball clay 40%
> whiting 10%
> feldspar 30%
> silica 20%

ALL-TEMPERATURE BASIC ENGOBE BATCH

An all-purpose engobe batch for raw clay is:
> ball clay 70%
> feldspar 20%
> silica 10%

Terra sigillata is something like an engobe, but is never glazed. It is a very fine clay (300 to 600 mesh) that has been ground in creek beds by nature (see ancient Greek red and black decorated vessels), or ground by you in a ball-mill in an excess of water plus 1% sodium hydroxide, then allowed to settle before you can use the middle part. Minus a ball-mill, just let the mixture sit in a glass jar, and siphon off the top layer; the middle layer is sigillata. True sigillata is applied very thin, almost watery, to leather-hard or bone-dry clay, usually sprayed; the surface will be shiny when fired lower than or up to 1950° F (1050° C). The same effect will come from burnishing leather-hard clay or engobes with a smooth stone or with your fingers or the back of a spoon. Sigillata made from white-burning ball clay can be colored with oxides or stains.

Engobe techniques

1. Sgraffito Cover the clay body with one or more colored engobes and draw a design or carve away areas of the engobe through to the clay to a desired depth. Use a variety of tools for different lines.

2. Slip trail Trail the liquid engobe with a syringe, a small bulb, or a small ladle. Try this on the wheel too, allowing the design to go around with different speeds, with your marks.

3. Combing Draw a comb, a fork, a quill, or a needle through one wet engobe to another one. This is a simple method that looks complicated, especially if several colored engobes are used.

4. Marbleizing Pour two or more colored engobes in layers on the piece, pick it up, and rotate it so the colors mingle. **Pattern pour** is similar to marbleizing; pour decoratively using several engobes but don't blend them. Different ladles, pitchers, and other

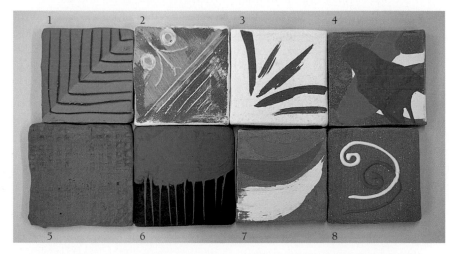

Raw clay, unfired, engobe techniques. Top row, 1. sgraffito; 2. brown engobe brushed, wax covered, carved, white engobe inlaid; 3. wax brushed pattern, white engobe over; 4. engobes poured. Bottom row, 5. mishima; 6. combing; 7. free brush; 8. slip trail

LEFT **Jeanne Otis's** wall sculpture shows a variety of effects achieved with brushed and poured engobes, glazed and overglazed, accented with a thick white crawled glaze. 19½ × 39 × 1½ ins. (50 × 99 × 4 cm)

pouring vessels will give different patterns as you pour, as will different speeds of pouring. **Dipping** a pot into one or more engobes is another way to achieve pattern. Engobes that are too thick may crack off. Experiment: thickness can be one of the beauties of engobes.

5. Brush, pour, dip, and spray engobes Engobe consistency determines the look of the stroke: the thicker the more like oil painting, the thinner the more like watercolor. Spraying with a hand or an electric gun may require the engobe to be thinned to go through the nozzle.

6. Mishima A traditional Oriental technique used especially in Japan and Korea, which involves carving or texturing the clay surface, not too deeply,

then applying an engobe over the whole surface and wiping it away with a cloth or rib tool, leaving the engobe embedded in the carving. The top surface can be wiped clean or some remaining strokes can be left.

7. Wax resist Wax resist technique is most common, but liquid latex, paper or cardboard, commercial labels, masking tapes etc will restrict the application of engobe or glaze. To keep a crisp line, paper and latex should be removed after the design is completed, although they will burn out. Essentially, resist is a stencil.

Wax resist is accomplished with water-soluble waxes, available commercially, or with melted paraffin, to which benzine or turpentine is added to make the wax flow. (Great cau-

tion is needed when using these or any flammable solvents.)

Wax burns out at 300° F (150° C), leaving the blank spaces of the design. Water-soluble waxes are safer to use than paraffin but do not resist as well. Take care not to cover water-soluble wax with liquid engobe or glaze; move fast, as wax really dries quickly. Paraffin cannot be removed from a brush; keep separate brushes for wax and utensils. Always wash brushes with soap.

These techniques can also be used with glaze decoration.

FACING PAGE **Hakeme** is a traditional Korean technique, later brought to Japan (as all ceramic techniques were), in which slip is applied with a huge brush, leaving the texture of the stroke or blob. This pot by **Warren MacKenzie** is reduction fired at high temperature and has an oatmeal glaze over the engobe; 14 ins. (36 cm) high

INSET Heavy engobe, laid on thickly with a big brush, engraved through to the earthenware body and left unglazed; bowl by **Susanne Stephenson**, 20 ins. (51 cm) high

Engobe decoration (pages 120–121) can be left unglazed, which keeps its clay texture and is a handsome finish. Or, covered with a transparent glossy glaze, engobe will show the design exactly and will be shiny; covered with a thinly applied opaque white or lightly colored glaze, the engobe will show through dimly; covered with a translucent matt glaze, it will be diffused and dull in surface.

ENGOBE TECHNIQUES

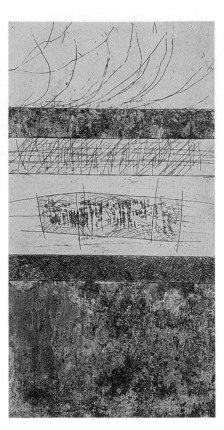

In the **mishima** technique, *raw clay is carved, then brushed over with wet engobe*; the surface is scraped clean, leaving the engobe decoration inlaid. Here the "carving" on the bottle is made by rolling a patterned rope into damp clay covered with engobe. This high-fired stoneware pot by the late **Tzaro Shimaoka** (Japan) shows one of his many famous rope patterns

This stoneware plaque by **Cathy Fleckstein** (Germany) illustrates the fine, crisp line that results from *a sharp tool being drawn through engobe*

Richard Zane Smith's carefully coiled and textured pot is *painted with thin washes of colored engobes*, fired at low temperature without glaze; bamboo handle; 18 ins. (46 cm) wide

Eva Kwong's thrown and assembled *Glimmer Vase*, 7 × 5½ × 5 ins. (18 × 14 × 13 cm), *painted and daubed with colored engobes*, is salt fired at low temperature

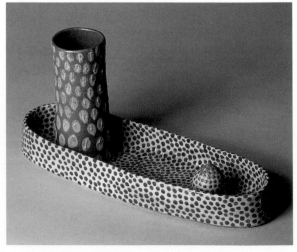

TESTING AND USING GLAZES

Glaze composition

Glazes are made from several basic ingredients added to silica, the essential glass-forming oxide. Because silica requires 3000° F (1650° C) heat before it melts by itself, fluxes must be added to lower the heat to regular glaze-firing temperatures for ceramics. Most glazes contain 50% silica, from various sources. The fluxes that lower the melting point of silica at low temperature—lead, boric oxide, soda, and potassium—and refractory fluxes —those that lower the melting point at higher temperatures, such as calcium, magnesium, barium, lithium, and zinc—are added to the silica in varying amounts according to the temperature to be fired. 10% clay is usually added for bonding. Incidentally, this is the essential difference between a glass and a glaze: glass stands alone, but glaze must bond to something.

The materials for glazes are dry powders, usually 200 mesh, mixed with water to a consistency measured by lifting your hand out of the glaze so that the liquid makes a long drool, then four to seven drops (four for thicker and seven for thinner), and the skin of your hand is still visible through the liquid. Glazes should be compounded in 100% batches to make it easy for experimental materials or colors to be added, or for amounts to be varied. Potter's glaze mixtures are usually weighed on gram scales; 3000 grams dry batch makes one gallon of liquid glaze.

As an artist you want to be in charge of the aesthetic that a glaze can offer, such as color, surface texture (matt or gloss), transparency or opacity, and

Using glaze and glaze decoration techniques is similar to using engobes, but the materials are completely different. Engobe is clay, stays in place, and does not change in the fire; glaze melts to glass in the fire and, except in a matt form, will not hold its line.

more. These qualities can be better implemented and controlled when a more advanced you understands the attributes of raw materials and glaze chemistry.

The late **Shoji Hamada** (Japan) is pictured here in 1970 using a ladle to pour a pattern that will produce black on his famous "kaki" (persimmon-color) glaze; see page 148 for a fired example of kaki glaze

Calculating glaze formulas

Formulas of glazes for specific surfaces and temperatures can be chemically and mathematically calculated from the molecular formulas of all glaze materials, then translated into parts-by-weight batches.

Beginners will probably search books and magazines for glaze "recipes," or buy ready-prepared glazes for all temperatures, which can be purchased commercially in most areas of the world.

Lacking these aids and the will to learn glaze calculation, potters should know that all materials and minerals on the globe will melt at some temperature. Test what you think could make a glaze melt, add a 10% or so portion of white clay to each mixture for the bond, screen the glaze, apply, and fire your tests. Weird and wonderful things may result!

WHY MAKE YOUR OWN GLAZE?

Compounding batches of glazes for yourself is not just fun, it is the beginning of creating your own style, in much the same way as compounding and mixing your own clay body. When you make your own clay and your own glaze, you are in control of your whole ceramic statement. In our view this is part of the process and gives you the utmost command.

However, many clay artists today buy ready-prepared clays and glazes, perhaps adding to them other materials, after making tests, for an

Stains made from metallic oxides are added colorants for engobes, bodies and glazes. Stains can also be used for *under- or overglaze decoration*

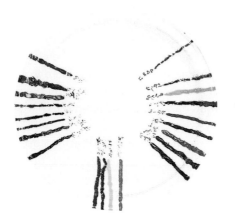

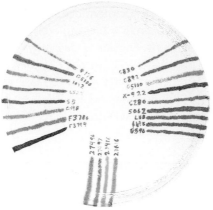

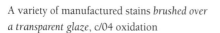

A variety of manufactured stains *brushed over a transparent glaze*, c/04 oxidation

The same stains *brushed under an opaque white glaze*, c/5 oxidation

The same stains *brushed over an opaque white glaze*, c/10 oxidation

The clay body is white. Stains (or metallic oxides) can be applied under or over glazes with varying results, as you see in these tests. Many different companies in the world manufacture glaze stains. Buy samples and make your own tests.

Many ceramic suppliers throughout the world also make and sell their own commercial glazes, wet or dry, in small or larger amounts. The ingredients are secret; shelf life is limited.

Potters buy glazes from color catalog pages, which do not exactly correspond with the actual fired glazes (see p. 142 for catalog vs real sample colored glazes; stains are described but not portrayed in sale catalogs). Stain decorations are usable at all temperatures; the three variations above are for illustration only

individual emphasis. As well, there are hundreds of ways to handle glazes: decorative techniques, thickness of application, means of application, ways of firing, that make hundreds of differences, so that it may not matter where you get your glazes.

On the opposite page you will find a photograph of experimental generic transparent clear and opaque white glazes fired at the three mean temperatures, using the corresponding basic 100% glaze batches. Begin your own experiments by adding various percentages of coloring agents to the basic batches. You may even want to try adding a percentage of some other materials that you think may alter the glaze quality, such as zinc oxide for crystals or rutile (impure titanium dioxide) for streaks (see Compendium).

In the end you choose your own way, but we hope you at least try inventing your own glazes before purchasing commercial ones.

COLORING GLAZES

Glaze stains and oxides

As a start, color any basic glazes, or see page opposite, with metallic oxides such as *2 to 4% copper* for green in oxidation or pink-red in reduction (see Chapter 6); *1 to 2% cobalt* for a strong blue; *1 to 4% chrome* for forest green; *10 to 15% vanadium*

for yellow, best in oxidation; *10% rutile* for burnt orange; *1 to 10% iron* for amber to dark brown in oxidation, celadon to tenmoku in reduction; *2 to 8% manganese* for tan to claret brown.

For a broader range of color, **buy manufactured glaze stains from companies around the world** such as Blythe, Drakenfeld, Ferro, Degussa, Pemco, Mason, and the like. Commercially prepared stains—basic natural coloring oxides combined with other ingredients to widen the palette, fired for stability, and ground again to powder—offer a broad selection of colors at most temperatures. Stains are artificially pigmented raw so you can see the approximate fired color.

Glaze stains are manufactured from combinations of the basic metallic oxides—copper, cobalt, iron, vana-

Basic glaze batches for low, medium, high temperatures

Some basic batches for mixing your own transparent glossy and opaque glazes and tests, to be fired at the three median temperatures: 1900°, 2150°, and 2300° F (1040°, 1180°, and 1260° C), or roughly Orton cones (see page 223) 04, 5, and 10. See below for photos of each glaze.

Color any of these glazes by inserting natural metallic oxides or manufactured glaze stains in 2 to 15% amounts *added to* the basic 100% batch.

Low fire transparent glossy, *c/04*:

> Gerstley borate 55%
> whiting 11%
> soda ash 11%
> china clay 11%
> silica 12%

Low fire opaque white, *c/04*:

> Add 15% zircopax to the 100-part batch of the transparent clear glaze batch *left* for white.

Medium fire opaque white, *c/5*:

> Add 15% zircopax to the 100-part batch *left*.

Medium fire transparent glossy, *c/5*:

> nepheline syenite 50%
> Gerstley borate 25%
> barium carbonate 5%
> whiting 10%
> china clay 5%
> silica 5%

High fire opaque white, *c/10*:

> Add 15% zircopax to the 100-part batch *left*.

High fire transparent glossy, *c/10*:

> nepheline syenite 40%
> whiting 10%
> Gerstley borate 20%
> china clay 10%
> silica 20%

TRANSPARENT GLAZE, SEE BATCHES ABOVE, C/04, C/5, C/10

OPAQUE GLAZE, SEE BATCHES ABOVE RIGHT, C/04, C/5, C/10

All shards are the same beige-colored clay body with a slight iron content. Note that the body color darkens as temperature goes up; clay is darkest at c/10 reduction; glaze is also affected

Fired examples of glaze compositions

C/04 OXIDATION	C/5 OXIDATION	C/10 REDUCTION

C/04	C/5	C/10

dium, chrome, manganese, and a few others—plus added materials that stabilize them and widen the palette. Stains or metallic oxides do not melt by themselves within the ceramic temperature range. **They are the colorants for:**

• clay bodies
• engobes
• decorative techniques such as under- and overglaze
• and glazes.

In addition, they are useful for:

• serigraph printing on ceramics: mix stains with silk-screen medium and hand-roll a design through a silk screen on to a ceramic tile
• photo transfer or emulsion techniques
• glaze stain crayons, made by adding coloring oxides to wax
• decorating slumped glass at very low fire (1300° F, 700° C, or lower); or you can add stains to ground glass and cast it into a bisque mold
• brushing or sponging over bisque to highlight a texture, with or without glaze
• sprinkling dry over sand or grog on a flat surface—you then roll a slab of plastic clay over the sprinkles
• making your own decals.

REDS, YELLOWS, AND ORANGES

Red, meaning fire-engine red, is an exciting color in ceramics but one of the most elusive and difficult to formulate and to fire. Historically, red was not found on ancient Chinese pots—assuming that these are our oldest glazed pots—which were normally coated in browns made with

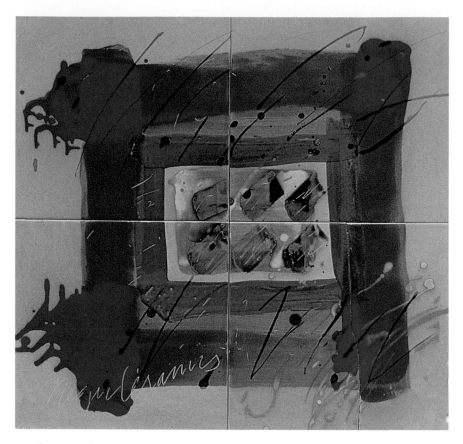

Marylyn Dintenfass's wall piece is a vibrant example of low fire traditional cadmium yellow, orange, and red glazes

iron-bearing earths. The advent of porcelain, high temperature kilns, and the development of oxygen-reduced (a firing called "reduction") copper glazes in the Sung dynasty, about 900 to 1200 CE, brought us so-called oxblood reds. European wares, after the discovery of cobalt in Persia, proliferated with the blue and white glazes those potters saw on Marco Polo's Chinese porcelains. About the same time, the discovery of tin oxide in Persia made possible the popular shiny opaque white of Italian "majolica" backgrounds for overglaze painting using antimony for yellow, chrome for grassy green, and tiny amounts of cobalt for pale blue. The famous Iznik wares from Turkey used a kind of tannish or bluish red made from grinding lead and iron oxide (rust) into an enamel for overglaze; the same

technique was used in Japan after the 16th century for "Kutani" reds. **Yellow was never as much of a problem as red and orange.**

The 19th-century Victorian Age was known for coral and orange reds from 1% cadmium in a high lead glaze at low temperature oxidation and yellow from various sources; even then ceramic cooperatives sold these glazes ready-made. Prior to World War II uranium oxide gave us all three colors, but it was expensive for normal use, and glazes were difficult to formulate and problematic. USA university and chemical company laboratories were surprised when the government confiscated their supplies of uranium during the war, only later to learn of its use in the atom bomb. Except for the discovery of vanadium oxide for yellow, and continued cadmium

RIGHT **Peter Lane** (UK) uses **Amaco Velvets** at porcelain 2300° F (1280° C), adds the underglazes to water, screens with 200 mesh, *airbrushes the colors with and without clear glaze*, producing intricate designs, *unglazed areas polished with fine silicon carbide paper*; 12 ins. (30 cm) diameter, **yellow V308**

LEFT **David Beumée's** thrown porcelain bottle is glazed with reduction fired **copper red inside, outside is Ferro 239416 yellow cadmium inclusion stain**; 13½ × 8 ins. (34 × 20 cm), reduction c/10

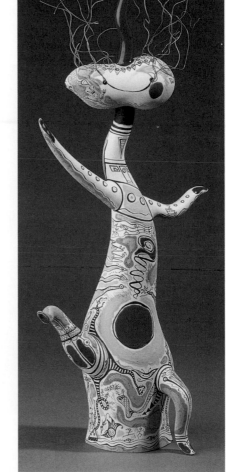

RIGHT **Sylvia Nagy's** dancing figure is coil- and pinch-built stoneware with high temperature red accents, 27 × 9 × 7 ins. (68.5 × 23 × 18 cm)

Anat Shiftan's panel (*right*) is made from several silkscreens **printed on paperclay slab with US Pigment Corp 1352 and 1351** *mixed with water, squeezed on, clear glaze*, fired c/6 oxidation porcelain. Panel (*left*), same underglazes with layers of clear glaze between orange stains to make color more brilliant; *texture of the underglaze pigments builds up by little dots*, fired c/6 oxidation porcelain

Sylvia Fugmann used molds to form some of the shapes of her tall slab-built vase, stoneware c/7, orange underglazes refired c/06, 24 × 13 × 8 ins. (9 × 33 × 20 cm), *pierced, airbrushed*

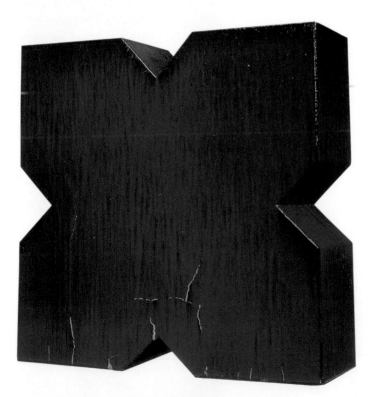

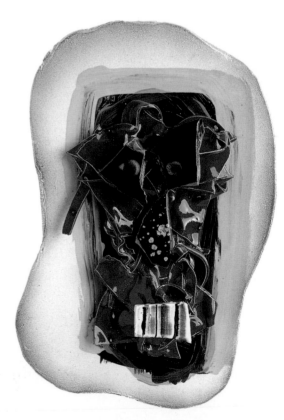

One of **John Mason**'s most famous hand-built sculptures, *Red X* is 73 × 38 × 11 ins. (185 × 96.5 × 28 cm), in the Los Angeles County Museum of Art Collection, 1966. Cadmium red glaze

Ron Gallas's *Red Said Fred* abstract mask wallpiece *layers cut pieces of clay over a mound of dampened paper*; background is glazed **Amaco yellow LG 61 with pieces of red LG 56** (p. 132) laid on top of each other to melt together in the c/05 firing; 22 × 13 × 2 ins. (56 × 33 × 5 cm)

for red and orange, it was nearly impossible to find metals and other minerals that could combine to produce the reds, oranges, and yellows of color-wheel quality in heats above 1800° F (982° C); paints required no elevated temperatures. In the 1950s, when the look of high fire stoneware gained importance, some potters bought glazes and painted red, orange, and yellow in patterns on already high fire glazed wares, and fired them again at low temperature. However, making a liquid color stick to a glazed pot is not fun.

Most artists preferred then, as now, to purchase these glazes commercially rather than going through the complications of developing their own; just learning to use the glazes was daunting. **Application and firing of reds, oranges, and yellows is crucial to develop the brilliance of these colors no matter who makes the glaze, and the kiln atmosphere must be absolutely oxidizing, preferably in a kiln that has never seen a reduction fire (an elephant never forgets…).**

No solution is easy. **High temperature copper reds result from complex reduction firings; yellows from vanadium, praseodymium, or rutile are grayish, orange is almost impossible unless you like pink.** Recently the problem has been partially solved with the invention of patented encapsulated, stabilized cadmium-selenium stains for red, orange, and yellow, incredibly advertised: "for all temperatures and all atmospheres" (don't believe it!). For cadmium stains, Degussa Germany merged with Drakenfeld USA to become Cerdec in America.

We concentrated on testing commercial glazes in the three colors, because **visual information is almost nil. All commercial glaze mixtures are secret, inhibiting the solving of technical problems.** Shelf life of marketed glazes, especially these, is just a few months. If they are dated, check it. **Red, orange, yellow prepared glazes come in tiny jars and catalog pictures are never the same as in real life; you MUST test in your own kiln** (see pages 141–142). It's less expensive to buy Degussa stains and try them in your glazes, use them as stain washes for under- or overglaze decoration, mix them in an engobe, or apply them as solid color under clear glaze. Because of the price even suppliers do not keep many Degussa colors in stock; a much wider range is available direct from Degussa but the minimum quantity they will sell is enormous for the individual studio potter.

We tested representative red, orange, and yellow glazes and underglazes from Amaco, Duncan, Hobby Carrobia (Germany), Mayco, and Spectrum. The samples were fired in an electric kiln to the three mean temperatures c/06–c/05, c/5, and c/10. **We generally used c/05 as the mean low temperature cone, although each glaze specifically advised one low temperature cone on its label. If the label said c/06 we also fired at c/06.** It is surprising how different the results are between c/06 and c/05, with only 32° difference between cones—our test photograph captions are specific. Some brand numbers were usable over the whole range from low to high fire, particularly the engobes that companies call "underglaze." We have gone through the arduous testing procedure: now you figure out how to use these commercial pigments anywhere our tests show that they work in an interesting fashion.

Application is a variable; for smooth, brush four coats in alternating directions; uneven application gives uneven result. Colors can be mixed by applying one over another, or by physically mixing in a container. Our experience shows that it is fine to mix various companies' products on the same piece, and any commercial clear glaze worked over a different company's stains or underglaze. Application method as well as thickness is important and should be recorded in detail; if application is on bisque ware, use the same cone to **bisque every time. Commercial glazes tend to settle; mix them often from the bottom during application. Usually underglazes don't run in the fire; glazes may.** Read the catalog for information.

In general, stack loose in the kiln and fire fast. **Oxygen is essential:** leave the peeps out and perhaps prop the kiln lid or door open slightly for air—an inch is sufficient. Put cone packs frequently on the shelves to ascertain evenness of the firing, place a cone pack (page 163) directly by the sample, use at least one pack with three cones at one peep to watch during firing; do not **ever** rely on the outside "kiln sitter" or the electronic temperature pyrometer—only the cone inside knows what the heat is like inside the kiln. This is absolutely vital for these colors.

A general statement can be made: commercial glazes still on the market with lead bases are the most brilliant colors, if you are willing to use lead frits. Our tests, as far as we know, unless differently noted, are lead free. Although we tested many more glazes over a period of several years, the best results follow.

Amaco glaze tests

David Gamble, potter and glaze chemist, says Amaco is working hard to develop a palette of reds, oranges, and yellows that will be foolproof from low to high fire—we are afraid that

AMACO LG series

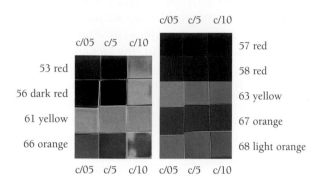

	c/05	c/5	c/10
53 red			
56 dark red			
61 yellow			
66 orange			

c/05 c/5 c/10

	c/05	c/5	c/10
57 red			
58 red			
63 yellow			
67 orange			
68 light orange			

c/05 c/5 c/10

AMACO VELVET series

	c/05	c/5	c/10
382 red			
383 light red			
384 pale orange			
387 red			
388 red			
389 light red			
390 pale orange			
391 yellow			

c/05 c/5 c/10

These colors are engobes and not shiny. Bottom triangle has clear glaze over, which makes them shiny and changes the color slightly

AMACO SS and LUG

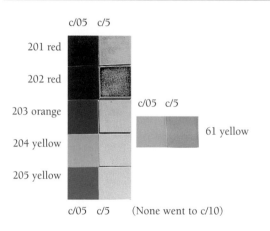

	c/05	c/5
201 red		
202 red		
203 orange		
204 yellow		
205 yellow		

c/05 c/5 (None went to c/10)

	c/05	c/5
61 yellow		

AMACO LM, GDC series, DG, HF

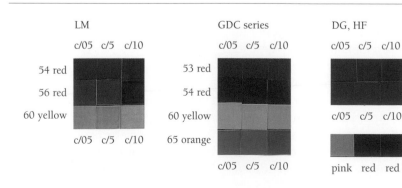

LM

	c/05	c/5	c/10
54 red			
56 red			
60 yellow			

c/05 c/5 c/10

GDC series

	c/05	c/5	c/10
53 red			
54 red			
60 yellow			
65 orange			

c/05 c/5 c/10

DG, HF

	c/05	c/5	c/10
52 red			
53 pale orange			

c/05 c/5 c/10

	pink	red	red
65			

pink red red

is probably too much to ask. However, most companies are always developing new pigments; keep in touch.

LG series: #53, 56, 61, 66 are best at **c/06**, good at c/05 and c/5; #57, 58, 63, 67, 68 are good at c/5 and fine at c/10 but a bit darker in color except that #53, 56, 66 reds burn out at c/10 (#53, called Flame, **must be c/06** for fire-engine color; #56 Christmas Red is darker red). #66 Brilliant Orange is good at c/06, better at c/05, but not good above c/5; #63 is a good yellow at all temperatures to c/10; #61 yellow is a particularly good color at c/06, c/05, and c/5; #67 orange, #68 darker orange are good at c/05, c/5, and c/10; #57 and 58 reds are all good to c/10 oxidation (see our test photo).

Velvet series: these underglazes are excellent colors at all three temperatures, like thin engobes, and give a surface not quite velvet (more gritty than the fabric) but when glazed, as our tests show, with a clear glaze over, they become glossy. These are really unprecedented color tests for all three temperatures but c/05 is a touch more brilliant, and they can be applied on greenware or on bisque; without clear glaze over, these will finger-mark; clear glaze will darken all velvet colors. Use either Amaco or Duncan clear glaze for c/06, c/05, c/04,

and c/5, use any transparent for c/10; we used #16 from Laguna Ceramic Supply (one of the old glazes I made years ago for the former Westwood Ceramic Supply).

SS series: these are lead-based and beautiful at c/05; #201, 202 reds (202 is better than 201), #203, 205 both good orange, #204 good yellow; all burn out at c/5; catalog states "must apply clear glaze over; must be applied on object before firing." We did not apply clear glaze; check our tests.

LUG series: matt #61 yellow is good at c/05, c/5 is better.

Variety: LM matt series: #54, 56 red, #60 yellow; dry matt at c/05, better at c/5 and c/10.

GDC satin matt series: #53, 54 red, #60 yellow, #65 orange, good color through c/10, best color at c/5, very little color variation at all three temperatures; can be used majolica fashion over opaque white glaze at all temperatures, consistent, stable in reduction, **excellent classroom choice**.

DG shiny series: c/05, c/5, c/10 all good, no bubbles, very smooth, #52 red, #53 orange are very good.

HF series: #65 red is really pink matt at c/05; c/5 and c/10 produce good reds. The company says HF #65 series is made for c/4, "firing range

c/04–c/6," but our best tiles are c/10! If you are looking for red at c/10, this is it.

Duncan glaze tests

CN series, left photo without clear-coat glaze over, right photo with clear-coat glaze: good at c/05, c/5, c/10; all similar but best color is c/05; #012 yellow, #073 red, #074 red (both are pink reds), #507 orange, best at c/05; all of our tests look the same with or without clear glaze over (very good color, **much better in our tests than in the catalog pictures**).

GL series: #614 excellent red, #632 orange, #670 yellow are very good at c/05, burn out at c/5 and c/10 (#637 and #135 reds we didn't test, because they are well-known low temperature glazes). All GL series colors were very good, cover well but pull a tiny bit away from edges, and function only at c/05.

SN series: #355 yellow-orange, good color at all three temperatures, unusual smooth satin matt at c/05.

GO series: #134 red, excellent color but only at c/05, burns out at c/5 and c/10, heavy craze.

RC series (see photos page 134): #201, 204, 207 reds give intense color at c/05; color remains at c/5 but sur-

---

DUNCAN CN

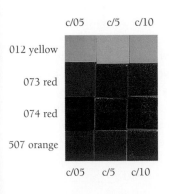

	c/05	c/5	c/10
012 yellow			
073 red			
074 red			
507 orange			

c/05 c/5 c/10

with clear coat over

DUNCAN GL, SN, GO

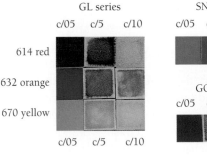

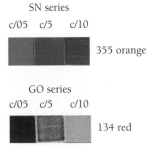

GL series

	c/05	c/5	c/10
614 red			
632 orange			
670 yellow			

c/05 c/5 c/10

SN series

c/05 c/5 c/10   355 orange

GO series

c/05 c/5 c/10   134 red

DUNCAN RC

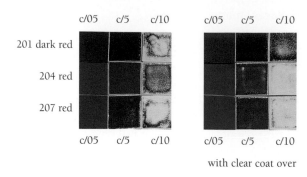

	c/05	c/5	c/10		c/05	c/5	c/10
201 dark red							
204 red							
207 red							
	c/05	c/5	c/10		c/05	c/5	c/10

with clear coat over

HOBBY CARROBIA HC

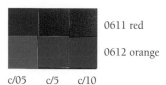

0611 red

0612 orange

c/05 c/5 c/10

MAYCO SC

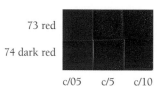

73 red

74 dark red

c/05 c/5 c/10

face is not good; burns out at c/10; so-called "Red Coat" series catalog advises applying clear glaze over, but our tests show that either way is fine but slightly better with clear; RCs act like engobes, do not bleed as glazes do.

Hobby-Carrobia (Germany) glaze tests

#0611 red is dry matt at c/05 and c/5, okay at c/10; #0612 orange is good at all temperatures, but gives a better surface at c/10.

Mayco glaze tests

Originally Mayco was the first to come out with "Stroke and Coat" engobe-glazes with some flux, and made the first reds, then Duncan developed their Concepts series, which is a similar surface, and added Degussa stains; **Mayco SC series 73 and 74** are satin matt

reds at c/05, blister at both c/5 and c/10; this series does not flatten out like glazes do but, conversely, they do not run.

Spectrum glaze tests

700 series: #743, 749 reds satin surface are best at c/05, blistered at c/5; #750 orange and #735 yellow, good at c/05 and c/5.

1100 series: made for high fire, surface excellent at c/5, color okay at c/10 but blistered, not mature at c/05, particularly #1193, 1194 reds, #1195 orange, #1108 yellow.

300 series: c/05 very good for #367 and 368 reds, #369 orange, #306 yellow; except for yellow, which is good at all three temperatures, the other three begin to blister and pockmark at c/5; at c/10 orange burns out, yellow is good, reds blister; #369 orange c/5 has a surface like an orange fruit.

100 series: c/05 and c/5 #120 yellow and #122 red only.

Spectrum multi-color series: We wanted to show a group of colors that function well at all temperatures and chose Spectrum's glazes. See the photo of #325, 326, 327, 328, 329 various greens, #333 light blue, #364 chartreuse, #336, 354 dark blues, #365, 1168, 746 purple, #751, 1196 pinks, #797 white, all nearly the same at each cone except for the pinks—again an indication of how difficult it is to formulate varieties of red; all good at all three temperatures, best surface at c/5, color similar throughout.

The best reds, oranges, yellows: Our ceramic assistant K.C. O'Connell chose the very best of the group. **For red:** c/06, Amaco LG 56; c/05, Duncan RC 204; c/5, Spectrum 1194; c/10, Amaco HF 165. **For orange:** c/05, Amaco LG 66; c/5, Spectrum 1195; c/10, Spectrum 1195. **For yellow:** c/05, Amaco SS 204; c/5, Spectrum 120; c/10, Spectrum 1108.

Our advice, if you are really serious about reds, oranges, yellows: use the ones you like from every company, try layering from different brands, mix them together liquid, be extra careful in firing, and keep copious notes with all details. These colors have judicious use in making art, but in many ways that is another challenge.

Remember, shelf life of commercial glazes is limited, and they are expensive.

Manufacturers of ceramic pigments over the world are working continuously to give us better glazes with more reliable color results in any kind of firing. You potters and artists must keep buying the new samples, and perfect your own working conditions in your own circumstances, for perfect results every time. It is really necessary to keep notes on paper as well as in your head.

SPECTRUM 700, 1100, 300, 100 series

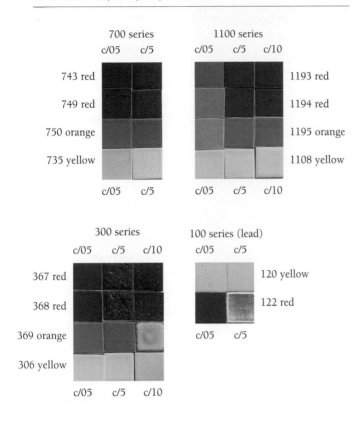

	700 series		1100 series		
	c/05	c/5	c/05	c/5	c/10
743 red						1193 red
749 red						1194 red
750 orange						1195 orange
735 yellow						1108 yellow
	c/05	c/5	c/05	c/5	c/10

	300 series			100 series (lead)	
	c/05	c/5	c/10	c/05	c/5
367 red						120 yellow
368 red						122 red
369 orange				c/05	c/5
306 yellow				
	c/05	c/5	c/10

SPECTRUM

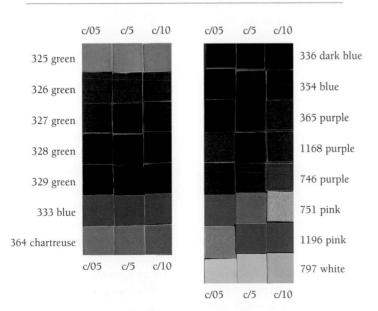

	c/05	c/5	c/10		c/05	c/5	c/10	
325 green								336 dark blue
326 green								354 blue
327 green								365 purple
328 green								1168 purple
329 green								746 purple
333 blue								751 pink
364 chartreuse								1196 pink
	c/05	c/5	c/10					797 white
					c/05	c/5	c/10

MIXING AND STORING GLAZES

Glazes should be written as 100% basic batches of materials **plus** the colorants; think of color as an addition to a base batch. Develop the batch according to your desired results (page 125) or buy a dry glaze. 3000 dry grams (6½ lb) added to water yields one gallon (4.5 litres) of liquid. For larger quantities multiply accordingly.

Mixing glazes Add the dry ingredients to a small amount of water to start with; add more water to make a milky consistency. Screen glaze through a window screen (20 mesh) or finer (60 mesh) if you want even color; if you want uneven color, don't screen the well-mixed dry ingredients.

Store liquid glazes preferably in glass, stoneware, or oak containers, but most of us use plastic (which reacts with the liquid glaze) or metal (galvanized) buckets with lids. If glaze dries out, of course add water to the appropriate consistency. Some glazes tend to settle fast, which can be alleviated by adding 1% magnesium carbonate to any glaze to keep it in suspension, but stir often to the bottom over prolonged use.

GLAZE APPLICATION

Stir glazes with a gloved hand, or a stick, but only the hand can find lumps and feel the general consistency. It is a good idea to screen (strain) glaze every time before using it to avoid lumps. Glazes are not generally haz-

 Stir glaze by hand (wear rubber gloves); adjust the viscosity by adding water until the glaze is as thin as cream and gives a long drool and several drops from your hand

Pots are usually glazed inside first by pouring the glaze in, quickly rotating the vessel and pouring the rest out. Every overlap makes a mark; if you do not want it, scrape it down

After waxing the foot of a stoneware pot, pour glaze on the outside, making a decision whether to keep the overlap pattern

Scrape off the excess glaze to clean the lip; then spray, brush, or dip the lip last

Methods

1. Dipping If the pot is to be all one color, dip it into the glaze container until the pot is covered and remove it quickly. Properly dipped, the piece will be glazed inside and out. Glaze dries almost instantly to a chalky powder. Touch up spots with fingers or a brush. Pots can be dipped in patterns, or dipped in several glazes.

2. Pouring Always glaze the inside of a vessel first, usually by pouring. Fill a cup with glaze, pour it into the pot and roll it round up to the edge; pour the remainder out quickly. Turn the pot over and pour the other glaze over the outside. If the outside pouring is done on a rotating wheel the glaze will coat all round evenly. If you pour in overlapping patterns, generally all variations in application show after the firing.

Clean excess glaze off the lip with a wood knife and dip the lip in glaze, or brush the glaze on.

3. Spraying Using an atomized spray gun is a satisfactory method of applying glaze, but only if the potter sprays evenly. Usually the inside of the vessel is poured even if the outside is sprayed. Spraying different colors can result in highlights and shadows of color. Depending on how dry the glaze is when sprayed or how far away you stand, speckles may develop.

Fill the spray gun with glaze made more liquid than the consistency for dipping or pouring. Standing too close to the vessel while spraying results in runny glaze application—you could like that! Some potters use an air-brush type of sprayer for very controlled application and complicated shadings.

 ardous, but it is sensible to wear a mask, particularly if you suffer from asthma or another respiratory disease.

The method of application, the thickness, the evenness achieved, contribute to variations in the look of the fired glaze and form one of the most important aspects of the ceramic process, often overlooked by beginners. Because each glaze has its own idiosyncrasies regarding application and firing, most professional clayworkers confine themselves to using just a few glazes and combi-

nations of glazes, to be totally knowledgeable and in control of all the subtleties. Be aware, every variation of application will leave its mark after firing.

From thick to thin is one of many of those subtleties in the glazing process: 1/32 in. (0.8 mm) is usual, but to mentally understand what that dimension is, look at it on a ruler. Get into the habit of physically checking the glaze layer with your fingernail or a pin tool, until you can feel thickness in your bones.

4. Brushing Painting is a good idea only when you want brush-strokes to show, because they do. It takes years of practice to learn to apply glaze evenly with a brush. Think of brushing as a means of getting variation and rhythm, according to the size of the brush and the manner of the stroke.

One-of-a-kind handmade brushes: ruff of the Akita dog; horsetail hair; goat, bear, lamb, wolf hair; bamboo and buffalo horn handles. Brushes have sizing—carefully wash stiffness out with soap and water before using; store brush side up with bristles shaped correctly with your clean wet fingers; buy according to desired stroke, try with water. Brushes are available from Zhou Guangzhou ("Po"), Li Jiansheng ("Jackson Lee"), and Luo Xiao Ping: see p. 234 for website addresses

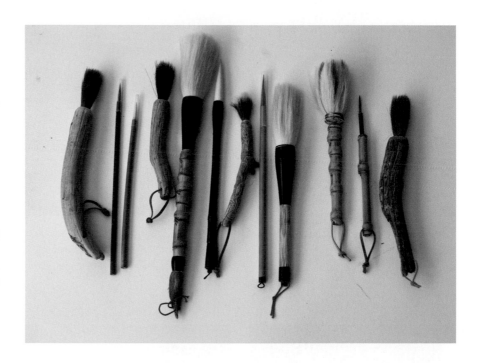

DECORATING WITH GLAZE

Bisque fire
Usually pottery is bisque-fired at least to red heat (1300° F, 700° C), but more usually to a higher temperature such as c/010 to c/06, to make handling of the piece easier during the glazing, and then fired again to the glaze temperature. Some of us fire stoneware or porcelain bisque to high temperatures and glaze for bright color at low temperature. Once-fired ware implies that the work is glazed leather-hard or bone dry and fired to top temperature once only. Depending on which glaze decorating process is used, the results will vary. Drawing through glaze on an unfired vessel offers carving advantages that would not be possible on a bisqued clay piece.

Thickness of glaze
Normal thickness of application of a raw glaze is ½₂ inch (0.8 mm). Thinner than that is very thin, and

Faith Banks Porter double-dips this stoneware vase in tenmoku glaze over her throwing marks, then ladle-pours a white glaze over. Note the color changes with thick and thin applications. 8 ins. (20 cm) high

heavier than that is a thick application. When placing one glaze on top of another, whether pouring, dipping, dropping, or whatever, you must keep in mind the total thickness of all the layers.

Too thick a glaze will crack as it dries and fall off the pot before it reaches the kiln. Test the thickness by placing the point of a needle or pin into the glaze; make a scratch, and estimate the depth. Your needle should feel as if it is going through a slim cushion of glaze; if the tool hits the pot right away the glaze is very thin.

Glaze on glaze effects are usually mottled or striated, with generally pleasing variations in color resulting from one glaze "boiling up" through another in the molten state. If you really want several colors to "run" together in a fluid manner, apply the colored glazes and then apply a coat of clear glaze over all.

1. Dipping or pouring in pattern
Surely this is one of the easiest

Patterns can be created by holding a vessel at different angles and dipping it into glaze

Spraying glaze adds variety of texture or color changes if you desire. Gloves are not necessary when hands do not touch the glaze

Brushing is not a good technique for overall glazing because all the strokes will show in the finished piece. It is better to brush glaze when you want the strokes to remain visible as a pattern

Ladle-pouring one glaze over another is an easy way of achieving decorative effects

Resist pattern with wax. Put your pot up on a bisqued "chuck" or stand so you can see your design. Water-soluble wax or melted paraffin can make patterns over or between glazes, or on the clay before glazing. Here wax over glaze is being scratched . . .

. . . and liquid cobalt oxide is being brushed majolica-fashion over and into the pattern

means of achieving decoration. Try dipping or pouring several colors with or without overlaps; try both matt and gloss surfaces; try leaving some of the clay body exposed. Pour from different containers to make different shapes and widths. Dip into glazes at different angles. If you don't like something you've done, scrape it off and start again. All variations of glaze thickness will show up in the finished fired piece, which is one beauty of this method.

2. Decorative brushing

Stains or glazes can be brushed over or under each other. Brushing is a technique better known in the East and better practiced over and over by us in the West.

3. Spraying one color over another

Colors will blend in this technique, but how depends on the firing, the thickness of application, and the chemistry of the raw glaze; glossy glazes flow, matt glazes stay in place. Keep records of what you do and analyze the results after the glaze firing.

4. Underglaze decoration

Just as this implies, metallic oxides or commercial glaze stains can be mixed with water and applied to

the bisqued surface, then glazed over. As in watercolor painting on paper, the more water the lighter the color will be, the less water the denser. Potters can learn to achieve great subtlety of brush-stroke and nuance with this method. A transparent or translucent glaze should be sprayed—not poured—

over this decorative application. Commercially prepared underglazes have moisture and a bonding medium added in the jar. These colors usually come as liquid in small jars and are very expensive.

Underglaze pencils, crayons, and chalks can be purchased or you can make your own. Even

John Mason's stoneware wall relief with resist patterns shows great surface variety, accomplished by differing thicknesses of brush-stroke and exploiting the fluid quality of glazes that meld with each other during the c/10 reduction fire; 24 ins. (61 cm) diameter

"Majolica," or *brushing oxides over glaze*, is a favorite centuries-old technique. If the glaze is glossy, the brush-stroke moves a lot; if it is matt, the brush-stroke holds, as in this stoneware plate painted by **Seth Cardew** (England), wood-fired at c/10 in his anagama kiln; 14 ins. (35.5 cm) diameter

spray cans with commercially prepared underglazes are sold by ceramic suppliers.

5. Overglaze decoration

Also called **majolica**, this technique is the opposite of underglaze decoration. Metallic oxides or stains mixed with water to watercolor consistency are applied over a dry glazed piece before it is fired. When the decoration is fired in the kiln it melts into the underneath glaze, causing a fuzzy or feathered line. The degree of fusion depends on the kind of glaze—some glazes are more fluid than others during the firing. If the glaze is very stiff, as a matt glaze is, the fusion will be slight. The characteristic melding of the design into the glaze is the trademark of majolica (the term used by Italians of the 13th century for their low fire overglaze).

China paints and enamels are another form of overglaze decoration, but both are applied on top of a fired glaze and refired again at a low temperature, about 1300° F (700° C). Metals, such as gold and platinum, and lusters come in the same category. China paints, metals, and lusters require skill and experience in handling and patience in application. Brushes must be absolutely clean; painting must take place on an

Verne Funk's delightful drawing is achieved with *underglaze pencils on the bisqued clay*, coated with a clear glaze, a technique possible at any temperature; 12 ins. (30 cm) diameter

Liz Quackenbush's press-molded box has traditional Italian-style *majolica painting over the opaque white glaze* on an iron-red clay body, low temperature oxidation firing; 12 ins. (30 cm) high

absolutely clean pot surface; firing is chancy (page 150).

6. Putting texture in glaze

Sand of varying sorts, dirt, tiny particles of grog (bits of ground, previously fired clay shards), or combustible materials, which burn out, such as coffee grounds can be added to glaze, or to engobe. In engobe non-combustible materials stay put and provide texture, in glaze they move around during the firing.

7. Wax or tape resist

Wax on top of one glaze in a pattern, with another glaze applied over, burns out, leaving the second glaze in a design against the first. You can also use metallic oxides or glaze stains mixed with water, brushed or sprayed over the wax, for a harsher look. Various widths of ordinary tape make a sharper resist design; pull the tape off before firing, see photo below.

8. Sgraffito through glaze

Scratch through the raw glaze to the bisque pot (which may have been engobed). If the glaze is matt (matts do not run), it will hold your drawing during firing.

SAMPLE COMMERCIAL GLAZES

Commercial glazes are available from many companies in the United States and the rest of the world. The color quantity, shelf life of the glaze, and cost may vary. Most companies will send samples or sell groups of glazes for your own testing. The c/05 and c/6 samples on the next page, from Georgie's Ceramic Supply, Portland,

Rick Malmgren uses tape against the stoneware pot to make a resist glaze pattern, fired to c/6; 10 ins. (25 cm) high

c/05   c/6

Two catalog pages from "Georgie's Ceramic and Clay Company," Portland, Oregon, USA, showing their prepared c/05 and c/6 glazes

c/05   c/6

Tests of the same glazes (in the same order as the catalog pages) were applied by dipping on bisqued beige-colored clay tiles, fired to c/05 and c/6 oxidation as stated in Georgie's catalog. It is impossible for the catalog to be as accurate as your own tests

Glaze numbers on these tests correspond to numbers on catalog pages above

Oregon, were tested in our electric kilns. Color brochures of glazes from the manufacturer, produced in large quantity, are not usually true to the actual fired glaze surface or color, but you have to buy from the catalog and make your own tests before using.

GLASS IS A CERAMIC MATERIAL

It is important to understand that glass is a large component of the ceramic industry and of the artist's ceramic vocabulary. Glass was probably discovered by the ancient Egyptians, about 5000 BCE, and glaze was probably discovered simultaneously. Glass stands alone; glaze must adhere to something like clay or metal. It follows that glaze is a glass composition with a binder added—usually alumina in the form of clay—to bond the glassy surface to the pot. Simply said, the chemical composition of glass, with clay added, can make glaze.

Slumped glass in a clay mold. On the other hand, a glass object can be "slumped" in a bisqued clay hollow mold that you have made, by the following method:
1. Line the mold with a ½ in. (1.25 cm) layer of parting compound such as powdered red clay, talc, or silica, so the glass will not stick to the mold.
2. Place a sheet of any kind of glass over the open mold.
3. Apply color if desired by brushing or spraying liquid frit mixed with stains or oxides on top of the glass, or by dropping powdered stains or oxides onto a layer of powdered frit on top of the glass. Use Ferro Frit #3124 or any frit you have.

Glen Lukens (1887–1967) was famous for his innovative ceramic and glass techniques. This bowl is a *tour de force* example of a **slumped glass in a clay mold process**, *colored with a turquoise stain brushed over an alkaline frit*, fired at 1500° F (838° C); 16 × 3 ins (41 × 8 cm)

4. Fire, preferably in a small electric kiln, to approximately red heat (1300° F, 704° C); open the kiln door a crack so you can watch as the glass slowly slumps into the mold, maybe at 1500° F (838° C); turn the kiln off when it does and shut the door. Fire slowly because glass tends to thermal shock. Cool slowly for 24 hours, before opening the kiln. Practice will make perfect.

Low shallow shapes work better than deep ones for the "slumped glass" method. The clay mold can be given an interesting texture on its inner surface, which will translate a pattern into the glass when it falls. The late Glen Lukens, former professor at the University of Southern California, was a master of this technique on a large scale; see his bowl, above.

On the other hand, ready-made glass sheets can be layered upright or flat on top of each other in patterns, with frit brushed between the sheets, and perhaps other beads or pieces of glass, to cause them to adhere to each other in the firing. Place the sculpture or tile on a bed of powdered red clay, talc, or silica, layered on top of the kiln shelf. Again, raise the kiln temperature slowly as above, with the door a crack open; watch until the edges of the glass seem slightly wet, or molten, turn off the kiln. Do not open the kiln until it is absolutely cold or your glass piece will crack. Shallow clay molds with no undercuts work best for slumping glass. Alternatively, glass can be blown with a pipe or cast in a mold.

Jun Kaneko, who usually works in clay, recently enlarged his huge ideas vocabulary to encompass cast glass at the Portland, Oregon, Bull's Eye Factory. There he continues his work with an emphasis on scale, using their facilities and materials, and holds exhibitions in their gallery.

Jun Kaneko's layered glass sculpture is made of glass slabs fused together in the kiln at low temperature (watch during fire); usually a low temperature flux such as frit is painted between layers. 9½ × 19½ × 3 ins. (24 × 50 × 7.5 cm)

PUTTING TEXTURE IN GLAZE

Various chemicals (see left) can cause textural changes in glazes during firing. Alternatively, test additions to glaze such as sand, iron filings, dirt, and the like.

"Room-temperature glazes" refers to decorative coatings that are not heat-treated in a kiln. Usually, this implies that the clay piece has been bisque fired. These coatings can be house paint, oil or acrylic paint, poster paint, flock, fabric, crayon, or any other kind of pigment or material, but this may destroy the function of a vessel!

Crawl glazes can be made with excess magnesium carbonate (20% or more), which causes the glaze to mound up during firing, or they can be made by applying a clay slip over a glaze: example above by **Claude Champy** *(France). Lava glazes are made from chemicals that bubble up, such as antimony, trisodium phosphate, silicon carbide, and so on; speak to a chemist and experiment*

LEFT Acrylic paint: **Paul Berube's** stoneware and unglazed bone china is *painted with acrylics*

RIGHT Crayon and paint: **Bill Farrell's** stoneware sculpture is colored with *crayon and brushed pigment*

Keep records

Do your own thing, but keep a record of everything you do. You think you will remember but you won't. Every overlap, every thickness of application, every glaze layer, in short, every nuance should be recorded. After every firing analyze your records and make notes. What you called thin may not appear thin after the firing, or what you thought was thick may not show thick. Perhaps the glaze disappeared because it was very much too thin or it ran all over the kiln because it was too thick.

When you have a number of records and many kiln firings, take the time to make a general analysis of them all, and write this in a separate place to refer to from time to time before you begin to glaze another kiln load. This is the way to teach yourself and to put your experience into intelligent practice.

BELOW "Garbage" glazes. Raw, top row, left to right: green bottle glass, screws and bolts with blue plastic wire, dried lettuce leaf, crushed aluminum soda pop can, copper pennies, string soaked in salt. **Fired**, bottom row, **to c/5 oxidation**. At c/04 some "found objects" will melt, but at higher temperature the effects are more interesting. At c/10 most of the objects' shapes will be obliterated by the melt

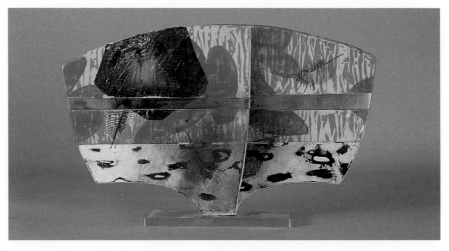

Bennett Bean's press-molded earthenware form is *cut from slabs, "room temperature" (unfired) decorated with Venetian plaster, gold leaf, and digitally printed transfers with colorful inks*; pieces are assembled on aluminum base, 14½ × 9 × 2 ins. (37 × 23 × 5 cm)

GARBAGE GLAZES

Every material on earth will have a residue or a melt when fired to 1300° F (700° C) or above. Naturally, more melt will be achieved at higher temperatures. Among the most interesting materials are hardware and wire of all kinds, fruits and vegetables, broken glass, string, cord, fabric, and coins. One or more of these materials can be used in a sagger with claywork, or they can be scattered around pots in a pitfire, or on the floor of a kiln, or placed in low open forms or on tiles, and fired.

The term "garbage" glazes as used today comes from colonial times when potters would throw their compost into the glaze batches, as they did the wood ash from fires.

See photo below.

Raw,
unfired

ed c/5
lation

COLOR TESTING

These are examples of color line-blend experiments made by students of Jan Peterson at Phoenix College, Phoenix, Arizona. The top members of each test are the same, but each glaze batch varies. See Compendium, page 219, for explanation of how to make a line blend test with percentage additions of colorants to a basic glaze, and the following 50–50 mixtures:

Top member % additions to base glaze: (tiles left to right) **1.** rutile 10%, **2.** copper carbonate 4%, **3.** red iron oxide 5%, **4.** cobalt carbonate 1%, **5.** manganese carbonate 5%

Clay bodies are different but all tests were fired at c/10 reduction. Note that the test in (4) *shows the glaze over four clay bodies on each tile*, indicating the amazing differences made to glazes by different colored clay bodies

◄ Glaze batch 1

potash feldspar	50%
dolomite	22%
whiting	3%
china clay	25%
	100%

Glaze batch 2 ►

potash feldspar	77%
Gerstley borate	11%
whiting	11%
tin oxide	1%
	100%

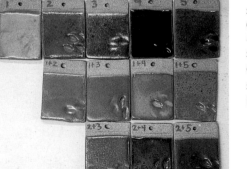

◄ Glaze batch 3

soda feldspar	55%
(preferably nepheline syenite)	
spodumene	23%
Gerstley borate	5%
soda ash	3%
ball clay	14%
	100%

Glaze batch 4 ►

potash feldspar	36%
dolomite	18%
Gerstley borate	4%
whiting	4%
china clay	22%
silica	16%
	100%

Experimentation

You can experiment with percentage or "part" additions to glazes with which you are already familiar, or you can run a line blend with five or more top members (see opposite) and make 50–50 mixtures. Color is always a percentage addition to a given batch. Always use parts of 100, or parts of 10; your base should always add up to 100 or to 10. If you make changes within the batch, keep it adding up to 100 or to 10; if you make additions to the batch, add them in percentage amounts on top.

Fusion button tests can be made of various raw materials by placing a thimble or other tiny container full of the dry material upside down on a fired clay tile which has raised edges to catch the melt if it occurs. After you see the results of the fired buttons you can begin to think of combinations from the visual look of the melts—or non-melts. At the same time you can mix each material with water, paint it on a bisqued test tile, and fire it at the same temperature as the fusion buttons. The buttons work like large amounts of a given material, the painted tiles show the effect of a smaller amount. When you make 50–50 or 33–33–33 combinations, remember those facts.

Beginners especially need to make tests, but all potters experiment some of the time to add variety to their own work.

Line blends

Any known glaze, or any fusion button glaze, or any made-up glaze can be experimented with on a five-member (or more) "line blend," where the five top members are blended 50–50 with each other (see Compendium, pages 219–220). You choose the percentages of colors you want to try,

or you could choose to add percentages of other raw materials, to see how they would change the glaze.

GLAZE IMPROVIZATIONS

Try to think of everything that might melt at the temperature you fire. Or if the material didn't melt, would it be interesting to add it to a glaze or to a single material, such as ground glass, that will melt?

Crushed rocks such as granite, stones such as agate, broken glass bottles, pieces of metal such as copper, should be tested alone on dog-dish-shaped bisque tiles, and in combination with known glazes.

Various plant materials have always been glaze materials in the Orient. The most notable is *wood ash*; the ashes of some woods will melt at 2300° F (1260° C); most ashes will definitely melt when mixed 50–50 with clay, feldspar, soda ash, or borax. In addition, other ashes such as those

IMPROVIZATION: Fired broken glass, c/5; any temperature is possible, but better high than low

of seaweed or flowers, and volcanic ash will give appealing results.

Some flowers and plants will make their mark, if placed in or wrapped round a clay vessel, in a high-temperature firing for stoneware or porcelain. Plants contain at least soda, potassium, calcium, and silica—all glaze ingredients. Such things as seaweed, rice straw, wheat, ferns, and the like will volatilize during firing and will leave the imprint of their shape in a sheen on the clay below.

ASH GLAZES

Ash from any plant, vegetable, or tree material can make a glaze, or ashes can be added to known glazes to change the effect. Ash patina can also be created inside a kiln over a period of days in a wood-fire.

"SLIP" GLAZES AND OVERGLAZE ENAMEL

Most low temperature red clays and certain shales will form glazes when melted at temperatures from c/5 to c/10. One of the most famous "slip" glazes from crushed shale is the so-called kaki, showing rich brown here among the overglaze enamels on the bottle (p. 148) by Shoji Hamada (Japan). The overglaze enamel colors were painted on the already fired kaki and clear glazed stoneware bottle; the pot was refired to a much lower temperature, c/013, just to melt the enamels but not to melt the previously fired glazes.

The late **Shoji Hamada**'s (Japan) "kaki" slip glaze made from local shale ground fine and applied over a clear glaze, wood-fired at c/10 in his noborigama; later his *painted overglaze enamel* decoration was wood-fired to c/013

The metal wire found in copper, stainless steel, and brass kitchen scrub pads can be pulled apart and wound round a clay piece, then glazed over or left bare. Glaze will melt the wire more and will bring out its true color. If left unglazed, the wire will probably melt into a feathered line on the vessel and will have a metallic black color. Alternatively, the wire can be placed over an unfired piece that has been glazed, and in the firing it will melt down into the glaze.

Low fire common surface clays will usually become glazes when fired at 2100° F (1150° C); we call these "slip" glazes. In the United States the most famous clay for this purpose was named Albany Slip and was mined near that city in New York State. The supply has run out, but other similar clays are being mined that give the same result. It is easy to prospect your own surface clay from a creek bed or near a lake, or in the desert in a dry lake or riverbed. You could try clay from a brickyard or from a sewer-pipe or brick plant; fired high enough, a glaze *will* result from a low fire clay.

Shoji Hamada, the famous potter and National Treasure of Japan, used a crushed shale from Mashiko, his pottery village, which when melted at 2300° F (1260° C) was, as he said, the color of ripe persimmons on the 24th day of October. His name for the glaze was Kaki, the Japanese word for persimmon, and he dubbed it the "specialty of the house" from his studio because the color quality and surface luster were so popular.

> It is important to test and keep testing. Artists continue to grow by trying new things.

Karen Koblitz's piece uses commercial underglaze heavily painted under clear glaze; *the gold luster detailing is accomplished in a final, lower temperature fire, 1300° F (690° C), 36 × 24 ins. (91 × 61 cm)*

Crystalline glazes are not exactly for beginners, because of the precision required to grow the crystals and catch them at the proper moment in the fire. Simply stated, add 20% or more zinc oxide to any high temperature glaze; hold the kiln for several hours at c/5 on the cooling side of the firing, and tomorrow you may have crystals. Detail of Sally Resnik Rockriver's crystalline glaze

DECORATION

Commercial pigments, glazes, and china paints can be used alone or in conjunction with your own glaze batches.

BELOW A sculpture by Sandra Taylor (Australia) is painted with *commercial stains, in watercolor technique,* and not glazed, fired c/04; 18 ins. (46 cm) high

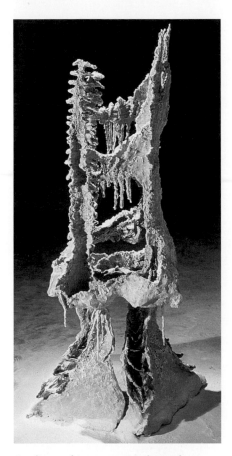

Cryolite can be very reactive during firing, and sometimes continues activity after it has cooled. Sally Resnik Rockriver experiments with a thick application of 50% cryolite and 50% talc, which, after salt-firing at c/4, will continue to grow crystals

Kurt Weiser makes the models himself for the molds into which he casts his porcelain; *glazes, china paints,* and fires his work several times. Commercial china paints and lusters fire from c/019 to c/015 depending on the look desired. 12 × 12 ins. (30 × 30 cm)

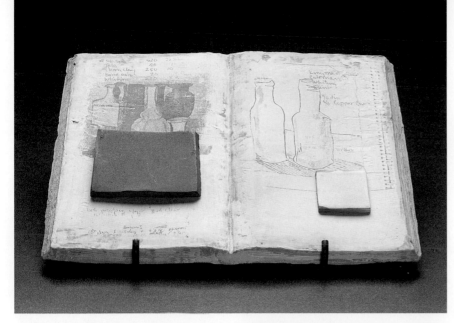

Nancy Selvin's book-sculpture is enhanced by xeroxing images from her own journals on to transparent film. After reversing the film and copying the reversed image on regular xerox paper, she transfers it on to a finished ceramic piece with a non-toxic solvent; the reversed image now reads correctly

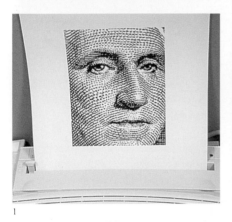

1

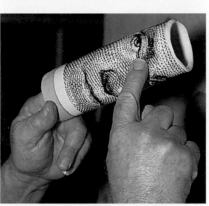

2

TRANSFER PATTERNS

Not for beginners, too difficult really, but interesting to try.

BELOW **Charles Krafft** *silkscreens ceramic pigments* on to flexible decal paper and applies the transfer on to earthenware, as in this plate

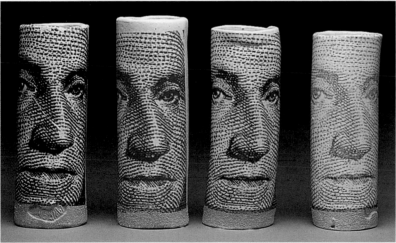

3

ABOVE Two illustrations of *decal overglaze technique* (decal is a commercial process for applying the same decoration to hundreds of pieces):

To make a *ceramic decal* for his sculptures **Les Lawrence: 1.** *uses a magnetic laser printer* with iron oxide in the toner, printing on to decal paper and fixing with a clear lacquer spray. **2.** *The decal design is soaked in water* to loosen the image so that it and its coating can be slid on to the glazed piece. **3.** *The color variation* resulting from different firing temperatures: (left) below c/010 is insufficient for a secure image; at c/04 the decal fuses into the glaze and at c/1 (right) the color bleaches out

ABOVE **Regis Brodie**'s porcelain kaki glazed bottle is refired at c/019 with *resist and platinum luster*

LEFT **Adrian Saxe**'s assembled sculpture includes a porcelain cup with gold luster on a base, *raku fired with a cadmium red glaze*

Elena Karina's hand-built porcelain shell form is bisque fired at c/10 and refired with platinum luster at c/013; 24 ins. (61 cm) wide

Joan Takayama-Ogawa's *Mad Hatter's Tea Party* is thrown and hand-built; fired to c/015 *with engobes, then china painted*, fired to c/013, and gold luster fired to c/019; 12 × 15 × 12 ins. (30 × 38 × 30 cm)

LUSTER GLAZES

Lusters and china paints, which can be painted or sprayed on bisque or on fired glazes, are usually purchased commercially and require a final low fire from c/022 to 013 depending on the desired effect. In fact, you can fire a piece very many times with different glazes, beginning at the top temperature and coming down every cone if you want. Eventually the piece may break from stress.

The late **Ralph Bacerra** makes his own molds, casts porcelain, and fires in high temperature reduction. In this piece the high fired celadon glaze has crazed, perhaps due to the many subsequent low temperature firings for the multicolored and gold lustered surfaces

6

FIRING
CERAMICS

HEAT PRINCIPLES

Firing makes a ceramic body permanent. Ancient peoples fired pottery on the ground, with twigs and other combustible materials between and over the work. In some societies the mound of pots was covered with earth to give some insulation. In China, where huge figures have been excavated in recent years at Xian (see page 208), archaeologists surmise that they were probably bonfired lying horizontally in a pit, or possibly hand-made bricks were piled over the sculptures to retain heat; the bricks would have been removed from round the figure when the firing was over.

Native Americans fire one or a few pots at a time, in an open bonfire fueled with wood, or with organic material such as cow, sheep, squirrel, or deer dung.

Two huge slab-built sculptures by **John Mason** have been loaded into his kiln ready for bisque firing: Figure 60½ × 28 × 25 ins. (154 × 71 × 63.5 cm); Spear 66½ × 29 × 29 ins. (169 × 74 × 74 cm)

RIGHT **In Nepal**, pots are stacked amidst heaps of combustible straw for fuel. This huge mound will be covered over with layers of clay and ash, lit, and allowed to smolder several days

A bonfire reaches red heat, 1300° F (700° C), the lowest temperature at which clay will become chemically hard enough to be somewhat durable. Common surface clays, found everywhere in the world, become more dense at low temperatures than other clays and are the most widely used by tribal peoples.

In most parts of the ancient world, firing was accomplished in caves, or pits in the ground, or in bricked-up cylinders with fire underneath and a lid of some sort on top. In India and Nepal, many "kilns" are piles of bricks or pots interlaced with combustible material

such as twigs and brush, then an overlay of insulating clay is added, with more brush. This is lit to become a large and fast-burning fire, then allowed to smolder for a few days. Astonishingly, such methods of firing are still the norm in many parts of the world. Many contemporary potters enjoy experimenting with these primitive techniques in a quest for unusual effects.

The important point is that clay needs at least red heat to become durable enough to use. Anything that burns can be used as a fuel, but clay needs much hotter than oven temperatures to become practical—we are not baking! Steer clear of that word and call the process "firing."

Various woods are preferable for ceramic firing in countries where trees are plentiful, or where they are planted in a sustainable program. Engineering charts will give you the BTU (British Thermal Unit) rating of different woods, dungs, petroleum fuels, and kinds of electricity; but red heat is the highest temperature that open-fire wood and dungs can yield.

Fossil fuels—such as gas, oil, kerosene, and coal—and electricity produce higher temperatures when contained. Petroleum is sometimes used to fire claywork in pits in the ground, particularly in the Middle East. Most cultures use these fuels today in kilns.

KILNS

When the first "kilns" or enclosures around the ceramic bier were developed, perhaps in about 5000 BCE in China, heat could be contained, reflected, and refracted, making possible the attainment of still higher temperatures. Eventually the Chinese learned to fire at a high enough tem-

Throwing salt into a downdraft outdoor kiln in a night-time firing at USC's Idyllwild School of Music and the Arts, California, where **Susan Peterson** taught for 30 summers. Firing salt or soda at night helps you monitor the flames and see the oxidation. In the same way, glaze firing in the dark of night for a reducing atmosphere helps monitor the color of the flames and the back-pressure

A downdraft car kiln built by **Jun Kaneko** in Los Angeles c. 1965. Note the sprung arch style on this kiln and the catenary arch style on the Turner kiln

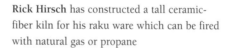

Rick Hirsch has constructed a tall ceramic-fiber kiln for his raku ware which can be fired with natural gas or propane

The late **Robert Turner's** downdraft wood kiln; the wood goes into the large hole at the front, while the smaller holes control the draft; Alfred, New York, c. 1980

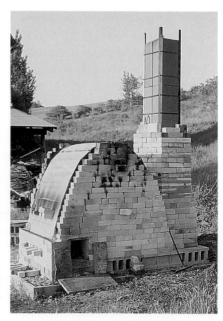

A very tall updraft kiln in Metopec, Mexico, for firing large "trees of life"

The five-chamber wood-fired noborigama kiln that **Shoji Hamada** used to fire; bricks for closing each chamber are piled in front. Mashiko, Japan, c. 1970

Kilns can be built of refractory brick or any other insulating high temperature material, such as the space materials "kaowool" or "fiberfax," or they can be primitive, natural caves or holes in the ground.

perature to turn a china clay body into fine porcelain. Porcelain-making temperatures could not have been attained without the development of kilns—or enclosures—to retain the heat.

Kiln design is ancient but has hardly changed today: there is the single chamber hill-kiln called an anagama, the multi-chamber hill-kiln called a noborigama, and variations; the box or round structure with a side or top-loading door that can have fire under, around, or above the ware; the "tunnel" kiln, through which pottery moves on a firing and cooling temperature curve; the "envelope" kiln that moves over the stationary ware; and shapes and variations of these. Burners under-

neath a firing chamber and an outlet hole at the top constitute an *updraft kiln* for petroleum fuels: burners at the sides and a flue hole at the base of the chamber designate a *downdraft kiln*; atmospheres and temperatures are controlled by the closing or opening of the flue. Electric kilns are boxes with elements all around the stacking chamber. See Fred Olsen's *Kiln Book* (in the Bibliography).

Most kilns that potters use today are fueled with natural gas or propane, or oil. Electricity is also used to fire kilns, although it does not offer the possibility of different atmospheres, as do petroleum fuels. And firing with wood has become very popular for the fun of it—camaraderie builds up in a team that must almost continuously stoke the kiln to top temperature over several days and nights.

The kind of fuel and the way a kiln is designed make quite a difference in the firing. Certain glazes are more affected than others. Oil and coal are "dirtier" fuels than gas or propane; electricity gives only a neu-

Kripal Singh, the well-known potter of Jaipur, India, tending his updraft kiln

tral atmosphere—neither oxidizing nor reducing (see page 165)—which makes certain metallic oxide glaze colorants impossible. Some potters build several types of kilns to exploit the different effects obtainable.

Gas kilns

Many areas of the world do not have access to natural gas; propane or bottled gas is the alternative. Gas is the cleanest, probably the easiest to control, and the fastest-firing fuel. The

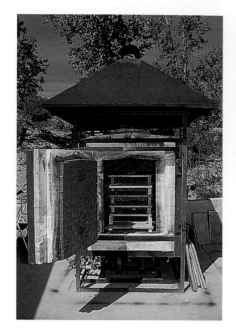

LEFT AND ABOVE **Susan Peterson's** 1955 vintage **updraft gas kiln**, still in use. Twelve burners are under the kiln; center four control bottom of chamber, eight outside control heat at top; excess gas jets to aid reduction are next to inside burners. Today commercial kilns have safety equipment already installed. Mike Kalan, of Advanced Kiln Co. in Los Angeles, and Susan Peterson designed the first commercial high temperature updraft gas kilns in the West for Chouinard Art Institute in 1952. The design has been copied by several other companies

first precautionary rule is always to light a gas kiln with the door or lid open, and with the damper, wherever it is, open. Do not let the fire blow out; if it does, open the kiln again to relight the burners. Gas provides you with complete control of the kiln atmosphere: fully oxidizing, in-between neutral, or partial reduction of oxygen.

Electric kilns

Firing an electric kiln is relatively easy compared with firing wood or petroleum. Electric kilns, as manufactured everywhere in the world, can be purchased with additional gadgets that will turn the kiln on and off, devices that can be programmed to turn it up, or thermostats that hold the heat at a given temperature. Small electric kilns can be installed on regular household current; larger ones require more volts.

Electric kilns are available as top-loading models with a lid, or side-loading with a door, in virtually any size. The simplest and cheapest are built of lightweight refractory brick or ceramic fiber, in a circular design, and with rings that stack for easy load-

Many companies in the world manufacture commercial electric and gas kilns. Today gadgets for computerized firing control are available from simple to complicated and from inexpensive to very expensive.

Electric kilns, such as the Skutt Kiln (Portland, Oregon) pictured here, are particularly useful for artists firing sculptures of varying scale; unlimited rings can be added to increase height

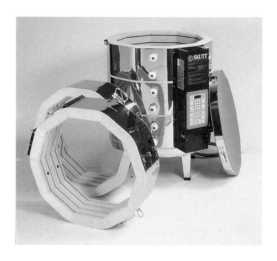

ing and for adding on when extra height is needed. More expensive models are square or rectangular, with hinged or guillotined doors. Today fixtures are available that will vent an electric kiln, which can be a help in gold and luster firings.

In the photograph, a Skutt kiln is shown whole and with the rings removed. Carlton Ball and Susan, teaching at the University of Southern California many years ago, were the first to test the previous generation of kilns and potter's wheels developed by Jim Skutt's father.

COMMERCIAL READY-MADE KILNS

Manufactured kilns are available in most parts of the world. In general the differences are few: gas, wood, or electric; side loading or top loading; round, oval, square, or rectangular; size varying from one to 60 cubic feet or more; refractory brick or ceramic fiber; in sections or one-piece; with pyrometric instrumentation or without; with com-

ELECTRIC VERSUS GAS-PETROLEUM KILNS

Electric	Gas
1. Can be plugged into household current for small kilns up to 8 cu. ft. interior stacking space; needs 220–240v for high temperatures generally above c/04 for any size electric kiln.	1. Gas can be natural gas or "bottled gas," called liquid petroleum or propane; best installed in the open or in an outside building. Optimum requirement for firing: for low pressure, 8 ins. of water-column (½ lb/250 gm. equivalent) on the gauge at the kiln, but 2 or 3 ins. will do; high pressure gas should be reduced to 8 ins. from 5 lb. Pipe diameter depends on distance from meter to kiln; if it's a long way use 3 ins. pipe.
2. Easily moved; doesn't take much room.	2. Not easily moved; gas should be installed by a licensed plumber; generally kiln size is large.
3. Low temperature and high temperature require different elements; specify.	3. Burners can blow out during firing; buy safety features.
4. Initially cheaper but frequent repairs.	4. Costs more but almost never needs repair.
5. Top load is cheapest, easiest to make yourself; hinged lids and doors cost more.	5. Catenary or sprung arch kilns are easily built by you; gas kilns, larger and better insulated than electrics, cool slowly. Ceramic fiber is used now as well as brick but fiber kilns require different firing techniques.
6. Can be made of lightweight "insulating" firebrick, or entirely of ceramic fiber; fiber does not hold heat, kiln cools fast.	6. Updraft, downdraft, crossdraft kilns are variations that can be designed with refractory hard brick or soft brick, or brick lined with fiber.
7. Firing atmosphere is neutral—for more oxygen leave peeps out, and leave lid or door cracked; reduction atmosphere is possible with mothballs or other carbon-releasing materials added during firing. Keep clear, don't inhale.	7. Fires easily any atmosphere, oxidizing or reducing; this perhaps most important difference is easily controlled and easily changed. Note: see *The Kiln Book*, 2nd edition, by Frederick Olsen; Fred says over the world kiln burners are rated in inches of water-column, **never** in centimeters.

puter controllers or without; with "kiln sitter" turn-offs (never to be trusted) or without.

For gas or wood-fired commercial kilns, choose updraft (burners on the bottom, flue at the top), downdraft (burners at front or back, flue opening—damper—at back) or crossdraft (burners on two sides, flue opening at back). We like updraft!

Kilns do not exactly wear out, **but they mellow, and firings may** **change with age.** Bricks do erode after many years of use, or after salt or soda firings, and may need to be repaired or replaced; soft-brick kilns are more fragile than hard-brick, but hard brick takes longer to heat up and cool. The choice of fiber as opposed to brick is controversial. Some potters like a fiber lining over one course of brick; some potters are addicted to ceramic fiber bricks; some potters drape a blanket of fiber over a load of pots and put a burner into the interior. Paperclay kilns (see page 161) provide an experimental toy for some artists.

Electric kilns are more problematic. Europeans, especially Scandinavians, probably have the most experience with them because electricity has been their basic fuel for such a long time. Electric elements give out quickly and

BUILDING A WOOD-FIRED ANAGAMA KILN

1

John Balistreri building an "anagama," Japanese-style single-chamber climbing kiln, in Ohio:

1. **Plywood ribs** make an arch support for the plywood form of the kiln

2. **Brick is laid over the wood form**, which can be burned out in the first firing or can be pulled out after the bricks for the kiln are mortared in place

3. John, the late Ken Ferguson, and a group of students **fire the kiln**

4. **Looking through the door** of the kiln while a log is inserted during firing

5. Decorative slabs made and fired the size and shape of the 60 ft (18.3 m.) long anagama kiln, and pots placed around the huge upright ribs in the **wood firing**, form this gallery exhibition by **John Balistreri**

2

3

4

5

deteriorate over successive firings. Globar and other esoteric elements have a better survival rate, but are costly. Where electricity and natural gas or propane are available, electricity is often more expensive.

For certain kinds of glaze firings—such as colored lusters, gold and plati-num, bright reds, yellows, oranges (these colors need lots of oxygen)—in electric kilns leave out the peeps and the lid or door cracked for air; for

PAPERCLAY KILN

Patty Wouters in Belgium has developed a simple method of constructing a kiln made of paperclay, which is usable at least for temperatures up to c/1, depending on the maturing temperature of the type of clay combined with paper.

1. The clay used in the body for the furnace must be a higher-maturing clay than the clay in the pots it will fire.
2. Such a kiln could fire clay bodies of any kind, but not higher than the temperature of the paperclay used in the furnace.
3. Paperclay bodies have the advantage that they do not burst or blow up from thermal shock during a rapid firing.

Blunging paper and clay with an electric mixer to make a paste. Lay the mixed paperclay for the kiln over an armature of chicken wire and cardboard for any size, whether sculpture or pots

The paperclay kiln, loaded with wares, begins firing at the base stoke-holes, with charcoal first, then wood; or propane or gas burners can be inserted

FIRED HOUSE

Ray Meeker (India) has been building fired houses for the past twenty years in the area of Pondicherry, South India. This staggering feat is accomplished by **building vaults and domes with handmade brick and firing with wood inside the structure for many days.** The house-kiln needs to be full of claywork to hold the heat, so bricks and other clay products are stacked inside. After firing, the house is plastered. Recent tests with coal dust as fuel, mixed into the clay-mud brick, have greatly reduced fuel consumption

Catenary arch form constructed of plywood will support the brick arch for this wood-burning downdraft kiln; exit flues begin the stack on the left; potters **Matt Sleightholm** and **Julie Wills**, Missoula, Montana

After bricking the arch and building up the stack, the wood form is removed. Catenary arch kilns are inefficient for kiln stacking, as this form loses space; a sprung arch style yields a better stacking arrangement but a "cat" is easier to construct

The nearly finished kiln, with door opening, which will be bricked up for firing, shows height of stack and stokeholes for wood fuel. Note: use refractory bricks that will be stable at higher temperatures than you need, such as "K26" (2600°F) bricks for a c/10 (2300°F) kiln. Two courses of brick are necessary for insulation; a fiber blanket could be added over all for more

china paints and crystalline glazes, electric kilns may produce a cleaner, more controllable firing. Any fuel will work for these specialties but results may vary. Lusters, gold, and reds especially need very good ventilation.

You certainly can build your own kiln, in which case you need Fred Olsen's book again (see Bibliography). Fred is the only potter we know

> It is important in stacking a kiln to leave enough spaces everywhere for even heat distribution during the firing.

who makes and sells kiln kits all over the world, along with complete instructions.

Cone and firing charts are on pages 169 and 223.

WHY BUILD YOUR OWN KILN?

Like making your own clay body and concocting your own glaze, to build your own kiln is a similar triumph. Most kilns are built of commercially purchased "soft brick" graded for specific temperatures; hard brick is cheaper, takes longer for heat absorption, withstands wear, and is essential for wood, salt, and soda fires. Books will help you – see the Bibliography.

If natural gas is your fuel choice, the provider will furnish you with the amount of gas you need at the burners for your size of kiln, and will tell you what size line from the meter will deliver that. If the kiln is electric, the type of service you have determines the size and temperature.

In the United States there are no rules about kilns, as there are for water heaters, boilers, stoves, and the like. Safety tells you to install a gas kiln four feet from any existing wall, with plenty of space for you to move about and for ventilation.

Here, potters Matt Sleightholm and Julie Wills build a downdraft kiln in Montana.

FIRING PRINCIPLES

1. Clay bodies shrink as they dry, and in the early stages of firing; they become more dense as the fire gets hotter, and finally warp or melt if the heat is too great for that particular clay.

2. The rate of heating and cooling is determined by the volume of the load in the kiln: the more ware, the longer it will take to fire and cool.

3. How the ware is distributed in the chamber, evenly or not, makes a great difference to the atmosphere and reaction to heat in a kiln. Most potters endure a long series of mistakes before coming to an understanding of the importance of how the kiln is packed.

4. Ceramics fire by heat radiation from the walls of the kiln and from the other surrounding pots.

5. Clay pieces must be properly structured in the first place, to withstand the weight and shrinkage movement that takes place during firing. Every different clay body will react differently.

6. A kiln can be fired fast—one to two hours—up to 1600° F (875° C), then slowed for several hours to top temperature, allowing the last 100° to take half to one hour for glaze to refine, and the whole firing

SET CONES CORRECTLY

WRONG   RIGHT

ABOVE Wrong setting on the left: cones fall against each other. Correct setting on the right: cones fall free to provide accurate temperature measure. Place cone packs away from drafts on broken kiln shelves or refractory pads. Cones may not read accurately in wood, raku, or salt firings

LEFT Cones should be properly set in a pack of clay laced with grog and with holes punched in. Face the cones forward, so that they will fall without touching each other

from five to many hours depending on the size of the ware. How a kiln is fired has many variations and the right degree of control can be discovered only through many trials and much practice. From yellow-white to red heat it can be cooled quickly, then slow down. In general, let the kiln cool before opening it at least as many hours as it took to fire it; open only when 400° F (208° C) registers on your pyrometer or if you can touch the pots; wait to 200° F (100° C) if the air is cold. (See firing curves, page 169.)

TEMPERATURE INDICATORS

The color of the heat changes in a kiln as the temperature goes up. Most of us are familiar with the orange flame of a bonfire, which reaches a maxi-

mum of about 1300° F (700° C). As the temperature rises above that, the color becomes cherry red, then lighter red, until finally at 2300° F (1260° C) the color in the enclosed kiln chamber is nearly white, hence the term white-hot. In China and Japan, where the first stoneware and porcelain products were made, "reading the fire," that is, reading the color of the fire to gauge the corresponding temperatures, became a special profession. Fire readers were hired by potters when it was time to run a kiln.

About one hundred years ago Seger in Germany and Orton in America, more or less simultaneously, devised a system of temperature measurement based on the slumping of certain clay body compositions at certain temperatures. Both men used cone shapes, narrow triangular forms of clay-glaze mixtures, to indicate their temperature scales.

These cones are now commercially manufactured, numbered according to the melting temperatures on the Orton or the Seger scale (see page 223). 2000° F (1095° C) is the mean heat, the melting point of cast iron. C/1 and c/01 are designated immediately on either side of the mean temperature. So above 2000° F the cone numbers have no zero in front; below 2000° there is a zero in front of each number. Below 2000° the numbers run downwards, from 01 (hotter) to 022 (cooler); above 2000° they run up in ascending order. So 022 is cooler than 010; 010 is cooler than 1; 1 is cooler than 10.

Because each cone is made of ingredients similar to the ware and glazes in the kiln, it is the best direct measurement of the heat treatment of the ware during the fire. At least one cone should always be used in every firing—take a new one out of the box each time. Generally potters use three cones, one lower and one higher than the middle cone indicating the desired firing temperature, which act as a warning as well as a check to see if over-firing took place.

Cones should be set in a very small amount of groggy clay and placed opposite the vantage hole inside the kiln, so they can be watched. When a cone has bent to the 3 o'clock position, it has reached its temperature. Cones must not touch each other and must be placed in the cone-pack so that they can fall free as one after the other they slump at the end of the firing.

There are approximately 32° F (18° C) of difference between cones, and about twenty minutes of firing time between cones at the end of a normal cycle; this helps you to know when to keep a constant vigil. If the atmosphere is to be controlled at specific points during the firing, cones for many temperatures can be placed in the kiln. If your kiln has a mechan-

ical thermocouple and pyrometric measuring device – which all potters should own and use for efficient firing – **always** include and watch cones inside the kiln.

Small cones for a "cone sitter," often used to shut off an electric kiln, are not the same as regular-sized cones placed inside the kiln, and will not do as a substitute.

Guide-posts for temperature

It is useful to remember some guide-posts for temperatures and cone numbers for special bodies, glazes, or effects, as follows (Orton scale):

c/10
2350° F (1290° C)
stoneware and porcelain

c/5
2150° F (1175° C)
stoneware

c/1/01
2000° F (1095° C)
melting-point of cast iron

c/04
1922° F (1055° C)
earthenware

c/010
1700° F (930° C)
normal bisque

c/013–022
1300° F (700° C)
lusters, gold

PYROMETRIC TEMPERATURE DEVICES

With energy conservation an issue, as well as the price of fuel per firing, it is important to know exactly at what temperature the kiln is at all times, the length of time it has taken to get wherever it is, and what the settings on the kiln were. Some commercial electric kilns have only numbers of hours that can be set, some have just one or two switches that allow little control; commercial gas kilns usually have no instrumentation, but it should be added.

Inexpensive pyrometers can be purchased, with inexpensive chrome-alumel thermocouples, ordinarily usable only for low temperatures. High fire

Pyrometers gauge temperature during the firing of a kiln. Heat is registered on a two-wire thermocouple in the kiln and is transferred to the pyrometer. Inexpensive thermocouples for low temperature can be used at high temperature if covered with a nickel alloy protection tube as shown here. Today digital pyrometers are also available. A thermocouple for low temperature is nickel-chromium, called "type K," which is still inexpensive; for high fire use the low fire thermocouple with a cover-tube or properly use the more expensive rhodium wires, "type R" or "type S," which won't melt until very high heat but are only as accurate as the calibrating pyrometer. The best pyrometers are very expensive

CELADON IN REDUCTION

The beautiful sea-green or jade green glaze color called **celadon**, developed by the Chinese about 900 CE in the Sung Dynasty, still holds mystery for contemporary potters. One quarter to one per cent iron oxide added to a clear glaze, fired in an atmosphere of reduced oxygen, will yield light to dark celadon. Here **Elaine Coleman** uses a transparent reduction-fired celadon glaze to enhance her design; the glaze flows to puddle in the carvings and break over the smooth surfaces of her thrown porcelain vase.

Celadon glazes can be colored with stains rather than iron oxide, but following the Chinese way, iron is preferred. C/10 is the easiest temperature to yield celadons, but lower temperatures can work. Gas-fueled kilns are easiest for reducing, but electric kiln reduction atmospheres can be achieved by adding reducing agents such as asphaltum, mothballs, and the like, into the kiln through a large port-hole or by opening the kiln door; add the agents when you need reduction, see pages 166–167.

You must monitor your reduction firings and keep good records, to duplicate results

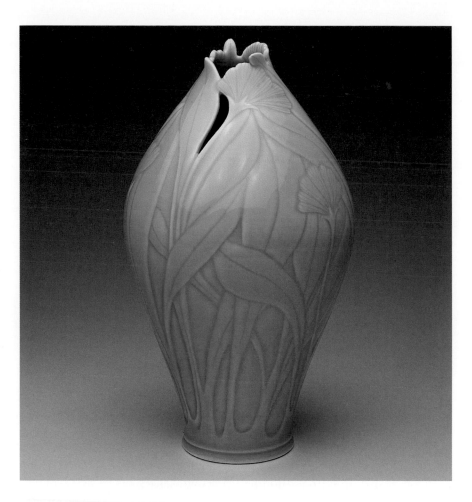

requires a more costly thermocouple, made of platinel or platinum-rhodium. However, the cheap low temperature chrome-alumel thermocouple can be covered with an 8-gauge, 1-in. (2.5 cm) diameter protection tube made of the nickel alloy inconel, which will protect the couple for many years' use at high fire. Any pyrometer must be calibrated to match the type of thermocouple to which it is attached. Instrument companies or ceramic suppliers may help you make a proper purchase. You should definitely use a pyrometric measuring device each time you fire, as well as cones in the kiln. Thermocouples can be repaired by re-welding the ends of the two wires if they show signs of wear.

The intelligent kiln firer always uses a pyrometer-thermocouple, records a temperature curve during the firing cycle, and analyzes each kiln load's firing curve; this enables the potter to duplicate a good firing or change the curve to improve a bad one.

OXIDATION AND REDUCTION ATMOSPHERES

An oxidizing atmosphere is the result of the exact ratio of oxygen to fuel for complete combustion. Or think of it this way: an oxidizing atmosphere is one in which all the molecules of the clay and the glaze have an opportunity to pick up as many oxygen molecules as they need to complete the chemical reaction. Some potters call this a "complete burn." Simply stated, in an organically fueled firing this means a blue rather than an orange flame. Each metallic earth oxide we use for ceramic pigments has an oxidized hue after firing, which can vary according to the oxidized temperature.

Reduction firing means that the amount of oxygen in the atmosphere is reduced. The oxygen supply to the firing chamber must be cut down by:

- inserting more fuel to increase the carbon ratio, or
- cutting down the air supply, thus literally smothering the fire.

Reduction works best from c/5 to c/12, but is possible at low fire too.

In a gas or petroleum-fueled furnace, or in a wood fire, reduction is usually accomplished by cutting down the air supply through means of partially closing a damper on the flue. Increasing the amount of fuel to the chamber will increase the proportion of carbon to oxygen. Primitive potters often smother an open fire with wood ash or animal dung to create a black instead of an oxidized red clay color.

Copper reds

The Chinese discovered that a small amount of copper oxide in a glaze, which customarily yields a grassy green or turquoise color in oxidation, would produce an "ox-blood" red in reduction.

Since the Chinese Sung dynasty (900–1200 CE) potters have continued attempts to achieve orange-reds, pink-reds, purple-reds, in this manner. However, copper oxide is fugitive, that is, flies around in the kiln, and even if once reduced, tends to re-oxidize. It is difficult to capture copper reds, and it is imperative to keep complete firing records for any chance of duplicating good results. If a copper red glaze turns out white it has fired in a neutral atmosphere, if it turns out light turquoise it has fired in an oxidizing atmosphere. Some kilns have uncontrollable spots, try as you might.

COPPER RED
Greg Daly's (Australia) porcelain vase with a brush-stroke of straight copper over the copper-red glaze has been post-reduced on the cooling side at 1300° F (700° C) to achieve this color

A group of stoneware bottles by **Susan Peterson** illustrates tiny variations of percentage amounts of copper carbonate in the high fire reduction base glaze

Iron celadons and tenmokus

The Chinese also discovered that a small amount (¼ to 1%) of iron oxide in a glaze, which usually results in an amber color in oxidation fire, would become jade green in reduction; this color is called celadon (see page 165). A larger amount of iron in a glaze yielded the well-known tenmoku black-brown colors (see page 137), famous from the stoneware and porcelain of the Tang and Sung dynasties. Most other coloring oxides are not affected by a change in atmosphere.

Electric kilns have a neutral atmosphere; no air circulates, causing a not quite oxidizing situation. Reduction is not easily feasible unless a reducing agent is present (such as oil of lavender in commercially manufactured luster glazes), or if the potter adds silicon carbide to the glaze. However, combustible organic materials such as new-mown grass, asphaltum, and mothballs, can be injected into the electric kiln at red heat and above, to burn and therefore reduce what little oxygen is present in the chamber. It isn't easy, but low fire Persian-style lusters and high fire Chinese reds and celadons can be produced this way.

STACKING AND FIRING KILNS

Bisque firing

Bisque or biscuit is the term given to a clay body fired without glaze. It can imply either low or high temperature. Most potters bisque-fire at low temperature—red heat or a bit higher to c/010 or 06—to facilitate

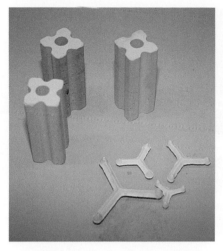

Supports for kiln shelves should be as broad and sturdy as possible; three-point stilts or bar stilts are used for stacking greenware (p. 168) in a fast bisque firing or for stacking low temperature glazed pots (stilts do not withstand high firing)

handling during the glazing process, and glaze at a considerably higher temperature to make the body more durable. Commercial porcelain manufacturers bisque high to support each piece to density, and glaze much lower. Some artists fire high for the body and low for the brighter-colored glazes.

In any case, in a bisque kiln wares can be stacked together, touching, sideways or upside down; yet the weight, volume, and design of the pieces must be thought about for support as well as even distribution of heat. Stack askew, lid sideways on the pot, bowl lip off bowl lip, plate edge off plate edge, so that air can circulate inside the pieces; if such forms are stacked with lids or edges fitting tight, a huge air pocket is formed, which causes probable blow-up of the piece (page 168).

Bisque firing in six to eight hours
Fire carefully, so as not to blow up the ware from the evaporation of the physical and chemically combined moisture content. Go up to a pyrometer reading of 1100° F (600° C), making a gradual temperature rise over about six hours. At this point the clay will have passed through the "water-smoking" period, when the water that made the clay plastic is driven off, and through the "dehydration" period, when the hygroscopic water combined in the clay molecule is driven off. If the ware is large it is a good idea to leave the door or the lid of the kiln open a crack, so that the moisture can escape, and to slow down the heat.

After 1200° F (650° C) close the door if it is still open, and go as fast as the kiln will go to the desired bisque temperature; well-built kilns—electric, gas, oil, or wood—should reach c/010 in another hour or two. Large kilns holding hundreds of pieces will take at least twice as long to fire. Huge hill-style wood kilns can take days and nights of stoking.

When the firing is finished, the kiln should be closed and left untouched until it is cool, for at least as long as it took to fire, but usually for 24 hours. If you have a pyrometer, it should register at or below 400° F (210° C) before the kiln lid or door is opened a crack. Wait until the temperature shows 100° F (38° C), or even room temperature, before removing the ware.

Bisque firing for large wares
If the pots are excessively large or heavy, the bisque firing will take much longer.

Damage in a greenware to bisque firing is almost always caused by improper packing or improper firing. Stacking greenware too tight, packing kiln too full, asks for trouble.

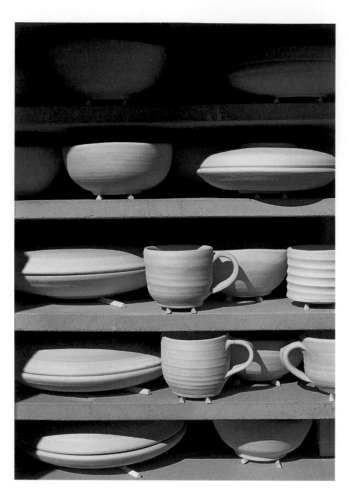

Susan Peterson's bisque fire stacking shows each pot elevated on stilts to allow even heat circulation, and air space between lip-to-lip plate stacking. This method of stacking allows for a relatively **fast bisque firing**, four to six hours, following the curve (see opposite) but shortening the time

Glazed wares fire at the temperature necessary to mature the clay body, or at the temperature necessary for the glaze itself.

Stacking the kiln for a glaze firing is perhaps the most important single act of the firing process. How the kiln is stacked determines the color and surface quality of the glazes as well as how comfortably the kiln will fire.

Glazed wares should be placed about an inch apart. Glaze bubbles like boiling water during the firing and can attach itself to nearby wares, or to the kiln wall or the shelf. Use kiln wash on shelves to prevent glaze sticking if it drips. Large and small pieces should be placed randomly but evenly. Even heat distribution during firing is actually the result of even kiln stacking.

In a gas kiln keep at least a 4 in. (10 cm) open space—called flue space, or combustion space, between the wall and the work—all around the group of wares. In an electric kiln stack wares at least 2 ins. (5 cm) from the elements. Electric atmospheres produce no movement like the turbulence that transpires during firing with wood or gas; leave more room between each piece and each shelf for air circulation in an electric kiln. Only petroleum or organically fired kilns can be fired easily in reduction atmosphere, remember—electric kilns are basically limited to slight oxidation or neutral atmosphere.

The glaze firing starts fast, just the opposite of the bisque firing, and slows as the temperature goes higher. The last 100° F (60° C) of any glaze fire should take one hour to mature and soften the glazes, no matter what the

For instance, for sculpture that may be as tall as the kiln chamber, it is wise to move the firing up a maximum of 50° F (29° C) per hour until past 1200° F (635° C)—this takes at least 24 hours. The pyrometer is measuring the heat at the point the thermocouple reaches into the kiln, not the heat that the pots have actually absorbed, which always lags behind the instrument reading. When the pyrometer registers a certain number of degrees on a kiln full of large pots, you need to allow a bit more time for the interior of the work to become as hot as the pyrometer says.

After reaching 1200° F (635° C) slowly, with vents open, you can close the kiln and proceed as rapidly as your kiln will go under oxidizing conditions,

to the desired bisque temperature. Time and fuel are the costs of firing a kiln; to fire efficiently you must use your watch and a pyrometer and thermocouple, as well as the indicating cones inside the chamber to read the final temperature.

Glaze firing

We have explained the definition of earthenware, stoneware, and porcelain (pages 19–23), the making of which may determine your firing temperature. The body can be bisqued low or high and glazed at some other temperature. Think of maturing the clay body and firing the glaze as two different things, not necessarily linked.

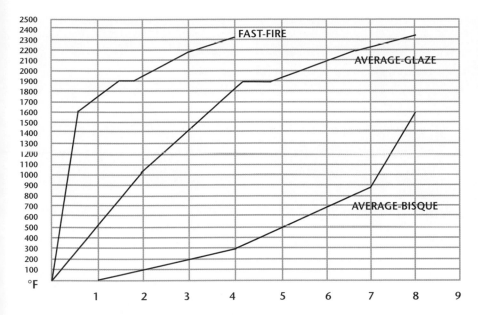

Fast fire and average glaze firing curve for c/10 and average bisque firing curve for c/010 in a gas kiln. Damper, burner settings, and other information such as weather conditions can be written in. Plot your own curve each time you fire with any fuel

temperature. This is an important point often ignored, which produces immature glaze surfaces and undeveloped colors.

A reduction firing requires a proper balance between the fuel and the air to provide the required atmosphere for the desired glazes. Reduction firings are always problematic and frequently yield surprises instead of expected results.

Most glaze firings to stoneware or porcelain temperatures take eight to ten hours, although we fire to c/10 in four to five hours. During this time a complete record should be kept of burner and damper settings in a gas-fired kiln, and of time and temperature. An electric kiln offers fewer options, but keep a record of the switches, time, and temperature. Records should be compared with results every time you fire, and analyses made.

All kilns are individual. Even kilns made by the same manufacturer to the same specifications will not be the same. Kilns built alike sitting next to each other will not fire the same. No matter what, your results will not be the same as ours or anyone else's. Therefore potters can work and learn best with their own kiln. **Firing is an extremely personal matter; if it is recorded and analyzed over and over, doing it satisfactorily will become second nature to the artist.**

ALTERNATIVE FIRINGS
Pit firing

Pit firing has many connotations: an actual pit in the ground, a built-up pit made of brick, a metal garbage can, paperclay formed like a pit, a sand pit, or a sagger. The wares in the pit are usually laced with combustible material such as vegetable garbage, twigs, brush, straw, paper, rags, or sawdust, which will fire and smolder; more fuel can be added to achieve more heat and a longer time, or the firing can be consummated in a few hours.

Low fire glazes or frits can be applied to the raw or bisque pieces for coloration, or chemicals can be sprinkled in the mixture: for example, silver nitrate for silvery luster, potassium bicarbonate for yellows, potassium dichromate for yellow-greens, bismuth subnitrate for goldish color. Experiment with the chlorides and nitrates of all the metallic oxide ceramic coloring agents.

Raku firing

Raku is a special kind of ware, with a good deal of Japanese folklore attached, developed by Zen monks in the 16th century and made famous by a family dynasty named Raku. The firing is akin to the American Indian or any primitive bonfire technique, but not the same. The theoretical idea is to pull a burning glazed pot from the hot fire, at about 1800° F (980° C), and smoke it to develop black lines in the crackles that open up in the thermal-shocked glazed surface. Artists have elaborated on this idea, as have the Japanese tea-ceremony bowlmakers. Some potters use cold water to quench the piece, some thrust the hot pot into combustible materials such as leaves and straw that burn again, some add salt or the chemical salts of metallic coloring oxides to the post-firing for a lustrously fumed surface, some just use smothering of the hot unglazed piece in the combustibles to totally reduce and therefore blacken the work.

Raku is only a decorative technique; the temperature is so low that pots will not hold water, and fear of bacteria in the porous clay body should keep

1

2

SAGGER FIRING

Chuck Hindes's combustibles for **sagger firing** include **1.** corn cobs, straw, woodchips, and leaves, **2.** placed in the container around the pots. **3.** Some saggers can be fired by themselves for low temperature smoldering, but Hindes is placing the sagger in a kiln for high temperature firing. The finished look of saggered claywork at low fire is usually pale and chalky but hard and dense at high fire; either can become gray or black due to the combustibles in the container, or colored if there are pigments in the mix

3

MARIA'S BONFIRE KILN

American Indian bonfiring: Maria Martinez (d. 1980) and her daughter-in-law **Santana** (d. 2002), c. 1975, stack their burnished red pots on a grate over juniper wood, which will be covered by old metal trays and dried cow dung to insulate the bonfire; *the fire is smothered with fresh horse manure and ash to turn the red clay black*

This pot by **Maria** and **Julian Martinez** is an example from a black firing, c. 1920; the surface is achieved by painting a prospected refractory clay over the polished pot, yielding the shiny *avanyu* (rain god) design against the matt background

LUCY FIRES WITH COW CHIPS

Lucy Lewis and her daughters Emma and Dolores set their pots among protective shards surrounded by a mound of dried cow dung, which provides the fuel for the fire, c. 1984

Dung-fired burnished vessel decorated with hematite and red iron oxides by Lucy Lewis, c. 1980

PIT FIRING

Detail of Paula Rice's pinched and slab-built pit-fired figure; the smoking enhances the *iron, rutile, and cobalt engobe* decoration

Jimmy Clark's coil-built, burnished, pit-fired and smoked jar shows the markings from the organic matter he used to fuel the pit

RAKU

1. **Paul Soldner** constructs a wire cradle for holding raku ware, about 1960

2. When the glaze melts on the ware in the 1600° F (870° C) raku firing, he uses iron tongs to grasp the pot…

3. … and pulls pot out. Soldner is probably the most famous exponent of raku technique in the West

LEFT A recent **Paul Soldner** raku sculpture

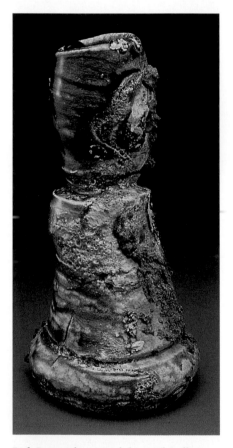

Rick Berman has coined the word "**salku**" for his *wood-firing with salt using the raku technique*

food out of raku containers. The "happening" quality of the firing makes it experimental and joyful, which is a possible meaning of the word *raku* (joy) in Japan.

Salku firing

Salku, or saltku, firing is a combination of salt and raku or salt and higher temperature glaze tumbled firings. Many combinations of all kinds of alternative firings are being coined by potters today, and are highly experimental, often not to be repeated.

Salt firing

Potters experiment with many different types of firings, but usually decide on just one or two for their own work.

Salt, sodium chloride, one of the most important catalysts that can be added to the fire to change the surface of claywork, causes a pock-marked kind of clear glaze on unglazed ware, and was developed in Europe, notably Britain and Germany, during the 16th century. Throwing rock salt (sodium chloride) into the fire **at the maturing**

temperature of the clay body results in an orange-peel, glossy texture, that takes on the color of the clay or engobe decoration underneath. In Europe and later in America this became a relatively inexpensive method of achieving a durable glazed surface on utilitarian wares such as crocks and mugs, and also for roof tiles and water pipes.

Soda firing

Sodium bicarbonate or **soda ash** can be substituted for the usual rock salt used in a salt firing. Soda vapor enhances the color of stains and oxides. Adding soda ash to the fire at any temperature, not necessarily the maturing temperature of the clay body, is a similar treatment to salt glazing, but mainly enhances engobe and clay colors and does not yield the heavily pockmarked glaze quality of salt. Soda ash may be less hazardous than salt to the environment. However, most chemists will state that sodium is not dangerous when volatilized above red heat; potters use soda and salt at much higher temperatures than red heat (1300° F/700° C).

Wood firing

A kiln can be fired with wood purely as a fuel for bisquing and glazing claywares. In contrast, wood and its ashes can become the principal means of coloring and partially glazing the work inside the kiln as it is stoked over long duration—several days and nights—according to the desired build-up of patina on the ware. Wood ashes from firing can be used as actual glaze fluxing ingredients, similar to the mineral feldspar, but with quite different effects. Japanese potters have long been addicted to the look of wood ash firing, mainly in folk-pottery villages such as Shigaraki. A number of other clay artists have adopted wood firing as a principal aesthetic of their work.

BELOW **Marie Woo**'s wall piece was *covered with straw and placed in a soda fire*, leaving markings from the grasses and color from the sodium

LEFT A typical example of **Don Reitz**'s large stoneware vessels glazed with ash in a high temperature **wood fire**, 50 × 19 ins. (127 × 48 cm). Reitz has for many years been one of the foremost exponents of salt glaze and wood fire

BELOW In recent years **Don Reitz** has explored **low fire salt glaze** over vitreous engobes, as in this platter. The effect of salt or soda at low temperatures yields more brilliant colors than when salt is added to the kiln at high temperature

LEFT **Dan Anderson's** covered jar is a combination of **wood and salt firing**

Robert Winokur's local clay hand-built wall piece is *engobe decorated, salt glazed* stoneware, and simulates an aerial view, 18 × 10 × 3 ins. (46 × 25 × 7.6 cm)

Ma Angels Domingo Laplana (Madola) (Spain), *Canal*, colored clays, *slab carved*, **wood fired**, 23½ × 15½ × 19½ ins. (60 × 40 × 50 cm)

LEFT **Jay LaCouture** has improvized a blower system to augment the heavy deposit of **soda ash vapor**, which yields enough sodium during the firing to turn his copper engobe to turquoise color on his thrown and hand-built porcelain teapot

FACING PAGE **Janet Mansfield's** (Australia) vessel, in a blend of local clays and feldspars, is fired in her **wood-burning** anagama kiln for three to four days in alternating oxidation and reduction for *natural ash patina* to c/10; 19 ins. (49 cm) high

Sometimes wood ash reacts on porcelain to give vibrant colors, as in this high temperature **wood-fired** pot by **Don Reitz**

RIGHT Unglazed wares are fired with wood especially for the ash patina, but many potters use wood as the most readily available fuel for glaze firing. **Goro Suzuki** (Japan) uses a traditional copper oxidized green Oribe glaze for his **wood-fired** chair sculpture

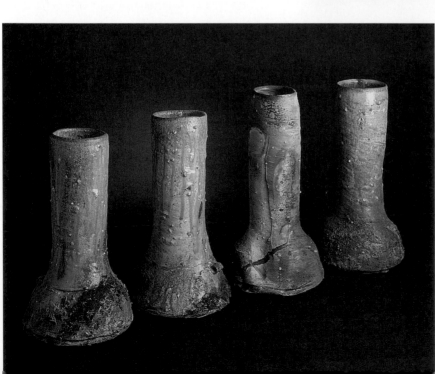

Four long-necked vase forms by **Paul Chaleff** show the colorations of the ash deposits from a six-day **wood firing**

GLAZE AND FIRING PROBLEMS

1. Glaze runs off the pot on to the kiln shelf

• Too much glaze was applied. Remember that the recommended thickness of any glaze application is ⅓₂ inch (0.8 mm). If several layers have been applied, scrape to dry underlayers thinner toward the bottom. Glaze should be the consistency of milk or thin cream in the container; usually studio potters need to add water to glazes that have been standing between uses. Check the thickness of glaze with a needle tool, learn to gauge ⅓₂ in. thickness properly; check several places on the piece.

• Glaze runs too much due to long firing, or firing too slowly as top temperature is reached; remember to take **only** the last 100° F (38° C) in one hour.

Earthenware vessels fired at low temperature can be glazed all over and supported on three-pointed ceramic "stilts" that can be knocked off when the piece is removed from the kiln. Stoneware and porcelain should have no glaze on the foot and for at least ¼ in. (0.6 cm) above it—we call this "dry footing." These wares become so dense in the firing that stilts would warp the piece.

2. Glaze appears bubbled or blistered after firing

• Air was trapped during the glazing application. You can learn to note these bubbles as you work. Glaze dries instantly, so you can rub bubbles down with your fingers before putting the pot in the kiln.

• Specific bubbling material has been added to the glaze.

• The glaze is overfired or underfired; either can cause blisters.

3. Glaze drops off the pot and fuses to the kiln shelf during firing, leaving unglazed areas on the piece

• Probably the glaze application was so thick that bonding could not ensue, hence in the initial stages of firing some glaze fell off.

4. Glaze "crawls" away in spots, revealing unglazed clay in some areas

• The answer can be the same as above, too thick an application. Or the potter may have used hand lotion before glazing and touched the pot—lotion or oil prevents the glaze bonding properly.

5. A glazed piece that has been bisque-fired blows up during the glaze fire

• The kiln was stacked and fired immediately after the pots were glazed. Always let the pieces dry a day after glazing before packing the kiln. Or find a way to fast-dry the glaze, such as putting pots in the oven, in the sun, under a bright lamp. Glazing makes bisqued pots wetter, depending on their size.

6. Several pieces have stuck to each other during the fire

• Ware was placed too close; allow the space of at least two fingers between each work. Be sure the kiln shelf is flat and level, so pots sit straight up. Glaze stuck to a shelf from previous firing must be chipped off or sanded down with an electric sander, and re-kilnwashed. It is better NOT to wash kiln shelves, to keep them always straight, but this does not work with students in classes. The studio potter must glaze properly, as it is too hard to knock dripped glaze off unwashed shelves. Lumps of clay can be put on kiln posts to level them when you are packing the kiln.

7. Pieces fell over during the glaze firing

• Wrong construction, bad support, or improper loading.

8. The fired glaze is harsh and dry to the touch

The glaze can be immature for various reasons:

• the glaze batch could have been improperly mixed, or the formula could be inappropriate for the firing temperature. Sometimes materials from the vendor change, or the batch has omitted an ingredient. Often you must search for the answer

• the firing temperature was wrong or no cone was in the kiln; or something may have happened to prevent the kiln temperature being reached

• the kiln fired in minutes during the last 100° F (38° C) instead of approaching the peak slowly. Each glaze requires different handling, which is one reason potters limit themselves to a few types of glaze in order to learn and appreciate all the nuances.

> Firing is the proof of the pudding. After all the work that has been involved in preparing the claywork for the firing, this is the test. Losses occur during the fire from improper stacking or handling of the kiln and its fuel. The potter should concentrate on the firing during the whole sequence and not do any other tasks.

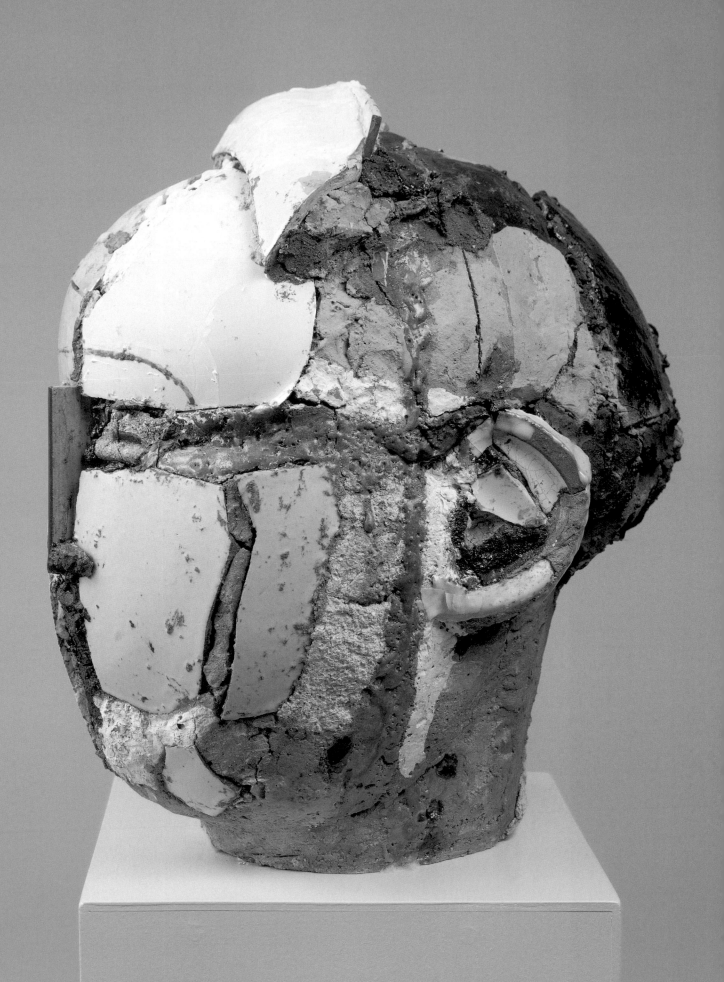

7

THE ART OF
CERAMICS

FROM IDEA TO ART

Having an idea in mind and being able to execute it in clay are two different things until you gain a certain amount of expertise. Knowing what is or isn't art, or if art is craft or craft is art, may not occupy your thinking in the beginning, but later on these questions are of some concern to the clayworker. Philosophically such questions always spark heavy discussions among collectors and purchasers of ceramics. The trick is to know when a piece is good, no matter what it is or how it was made. The artist or the collector tries to develop an eye for what the sense of passion brings.

Learn to see line and space everywhere, in nature, in architecture, in city streets. Practice making decisions intuitively about works that provoke a response in you. Eventually, when working in clay or when buying clay objects, you will see line directions and define shapes and planes automatically. Always be aware of our colorful world; color often supersedes line and even space.

The late **Gertraud Möhwald** (Germany), *Head with Orange Earring.* Stoneware, glaze and added broken bits, 15 ins. (39 cm) high

Make judgments alone, so that they are personal and meaningful to you. No one can tell you what design is or what art is. You tell yourself through constant observation and silent pro and con discussions with yourself, refining your judgment as you go.

The remarkable assets clay has—surface, color, scale, unlimited shape—have been incredibly exploited in the last 50 years. Clayworks overlap with sculpture in all media, with shaped canvas and off the wall painting, and functional ceramics in many cases become objects of art. As well, we are looking at historical ceramic objects with a new realization of the remarkable contributions of all cultures to the art of today.

Peter Voulkos (1924–2002) is generally considered to be the clay artist exerting the single most revolutionary change in ceramic art, moving as he did from functional wares into large thrown, cut, and altered shapes that became sought-after sculptures. His bravado, innovations, and personal magnetism will live on and continue to be a beacon.

The stunning international portfolio that follows will give you a small understanding of the larger ceramic picture, from all areas of representation to installation and conceptual art. Use the work of these clay artists as a springboard for your own discoveries.

POTS AND PLATES

There is no limit to form and design in clay.

Juan Quesada (Mexico), *Double Vessel*. Earthenware, bonfired, 12 × 5 ins. (30 × 13 cm)

Betsy Rosenmiller, *Soup Tureen*. Porcelain, cast with hand-built additions, 11 × 15 × 12 ins. (28 × 38 × 30 cm)

Tom Hubert, *Tea and other Pots*. Earthenware, thrown, hand-built, and cast, multi-layered sprayed pigments under clear glaze, 27 ins. (68.5 cm) high

Dennis Parks's large thrown stoneware charger with *sprayed engobe resist décor* is high fired in his oil-drip kiln; 24 ins. (61 cm) wide

Luo Xiaoping (China), *Teapot Ramifications.*
Vitreous YiXing clay and porcelain, slab-built,
34 × 16½ × 31 ins. (86 × 42 × 79 cm)

Peter Voulkos, *Untitled.* Thrown and altered
stoneware, wood-fired, 24 × 24 ins. (60 × 60 cm)

Ron Nagle, *Cup Metaphor.* Earthenware, cast
and mounted, 12 ins. (30 cm) square

BIRDS AND ANIMALS

Hollow-building ceramic sculpture with reference to birds and animals is currently very popular.

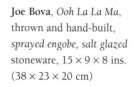

Ria Ovans's delicate moose painting is *cobalt oxide under clear-glazed* porcelain bowl, 12 × 4 ins. (30 × 20 cm)

Ann Adair Voulkos, *Pope-Alligator*. Earthenware, slab-built, 18 ins. (46 cm) high

Joe Bova, *Ooh La La Ma*, thrown and hand-built, *sprayed engobe, salt glazed* stoneware, 15 × 9 × 8 ins. (38 × 23 × 20 cm)

Tom Supensky, *Where is the Water?* Stoneware, press-molded, hand-built, 24 ins. (60 cm) high

David Smith's bird sculpture, thrown and hand-built, *engobe decorated*, glazed stoneware, 23 × 11 × 10 ins. (58 × 28 × 25 cm)

Marlene Ferrell Parillo's global animal *Totem Pole* is hand-built stoneware, c/6 oxidation, 22 × 14 × 14 ins. (56 × 35.5 × 35.5 cm)

Etta Winigrad, *The Guardian*. Earthenware, smoke-fired with newspapers, hand-built, 30 × 14 × 5 ins. (76 × 35.5 × 13 cm)

FIGURES AND HEADS

Large-scale sculpture is hollow-built in a similar manner to coil, pinched, or slab vessels, or it is cast, or a combination. Some of the most exciting work being done in ceramics today is figurative.

Patti Warashina, *China Crisis*, hand-built and slip-cast, *engobes, underglazes, glaze*, fired in sections, reassembled; stoneware, 64 × 22 × 19 ins. (163 × 56 × 48 cm)

BELOW **Cara Moczygemba**, *Princess*. Stoneware and porcelain, cast and hand-built, smoke-fired

Jean Cappadonna Nichols, *In Front of Every Woman*. Earthenware, coil-built on a slab base, *multi-firings, underglaze, overglaze, luster, and enamel paint*; 39 × 25 × 13 ins. (99 × 63 × 33 cm)

Michael Lucero, *Snow-capped Mountain*. Multiple *shards of stain-colored earthenware* strung on fuzzy wires with added appendages, life-size

Jeff Schlanger, *Three Tenors*. Stoneware, thrown and altered from live concert sketches, glazed c/10; 36 × 42 ins. (91 × 106 cm)

Claire Clark, *Lila Sitting*. Stoneware sculpted solid, stains, 12 ins. (30 cm) high

Ingrid Jacobsen (Germany), *Ein Mann sucht was* (A man seeks something). Stoneware hollow-built figures, with stains, unglazed, life-size

Akio Takamori, *Dwarf and Girl with Ball*, stoneware thrown and hand-built, *underglaze and oxide decoration*,
27 × 19 × 14 ins. (68.5 × 48 × 35.5 cm), 34 × 13 × 8 ins. (86 × 33 × 20 cm)

Imre Schrammel (Hungary), *Lifesize Figure*

E. Jane Pleak, *The Fine Art of Conversation*. Pinched and slab-built figures, c/5 stoneware

LEFT **Richard Slee** (UK), *Young Toby*. Cast porcelain, glazed at lower temperature, 10 ins. (25 cm) high

BELOW **Stephen Braun**, *Out of Gas*. Hand-built stoneware, *stains and paint*

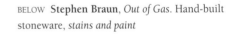

WALLS

RIGHT **John Mason**, *Blue Wall*. Mason was one of the few ceramic artists in the 1960s to fabricate and install large wall constructions. This 21 ft × 7ft × 6 ins. (6.4 × 2.13 m × 15 cm) wall is one of his best-known

Henry Pim (Ireland), *Grid Piece 2000*. Stoneware and paperclay hand-fabricated tiles make a wall unit, 45 × 45 ins. (114 × 114 cm)

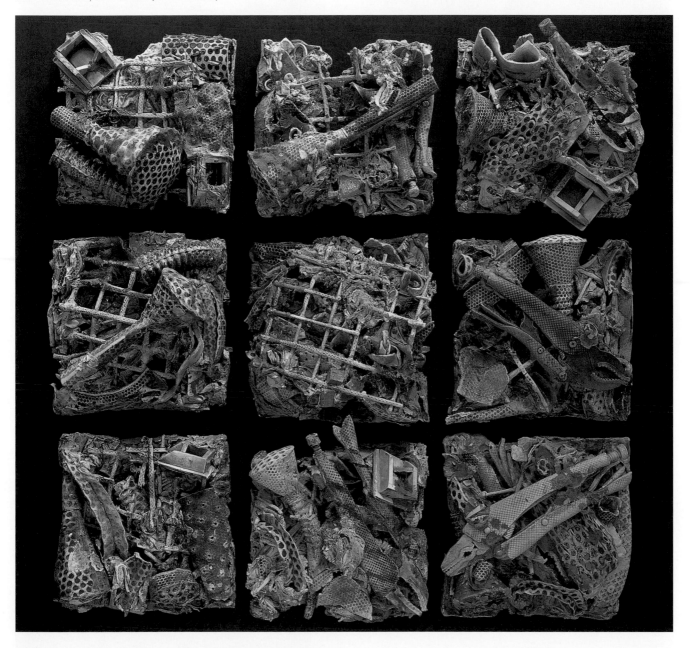

Vaslav Serak (Czech Republic), *Wall Piece*. Porcelain, thrown and altered forms, 24 × 24 ins. (60 × 60 cm)

Carol Aoki, *Pod Collage No.1*. Paperclay body wall collage, 28 × 30 ins. (71 × 76 cm)

ABOVE **Anthony Rubino**, *Ovid's Threshold*. Room-sized stoneware door with arch and ornaments, multi-glazed, c/10

RIGHT **Marit Tingleff** (Norway), *Wall*. Porcelain and stoneware, 8 ft (2.4 m.) high

ABOVE **Jim Melchert**, section of 220-ft (67 m.) long *Mural*, made of hundreds of hand-decorated and glazed tiles

RIGHT **Dale Zheutlin**, *Archisites*. Earthenware and stoneware tile pictographs mounted on lobby walls

Yule Yilmambaşa (Turkey), *Eyes*. Hand-built, building-sized earthenware wall installed in Istanbul

Ole Lislerud (Norway), Oslo Supreme Court Building. Detail of staircase with cast porcelain wall panels with symbolic calligraphy and writing as metaphor for this public site

John Glick, *Mantel Diptych*. Engobes, stoneware and porcelain, soda-fired, c/10 reduction, 3 ft (91 cm) long

Paula Winokur, *Entry III*, *Boulder Field*. Room-sized porcelain portal, slab-built with pinched-out accessories

Wayne Higby, *Intangible Notch*. Thousands of raku fired shards augment the glazed earthenware tiles in this wall-sized installation

MIXED MEDIA

Ceramic materials are often combined with one or a variety of other materials, for aesthetic or structural reasons.

Elisabeth Langsch (Switzerland), *Garden Balls*. Concrete, clay, glaze, largest 36 ins. (91 cm) diameter

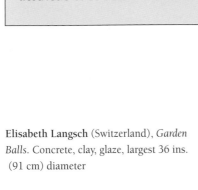

Rick Hirsch, *Altar Bowl with Weapon*. Raku fired with forged steel base, 18 × 9 ins. (46 × 23 cm)

Nina Hole (Denmark), *Firer*, thickly applied textured, colored glaze, *wood-fired at low temperature*; 12½ × 2¾ × 10½ ins. (32 × 7 × 27 cm)

Juan Granados, *Growth*. Earthenware, copper, and glaze, 29 × 23 × 20 ins. (74 × 58 × 51 cm)

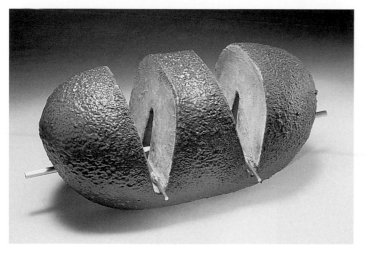

John Stephenson, *Isolator*. Wooden dowels and stoneware clay, 18 × 7 ins. (46 × 18 cm)

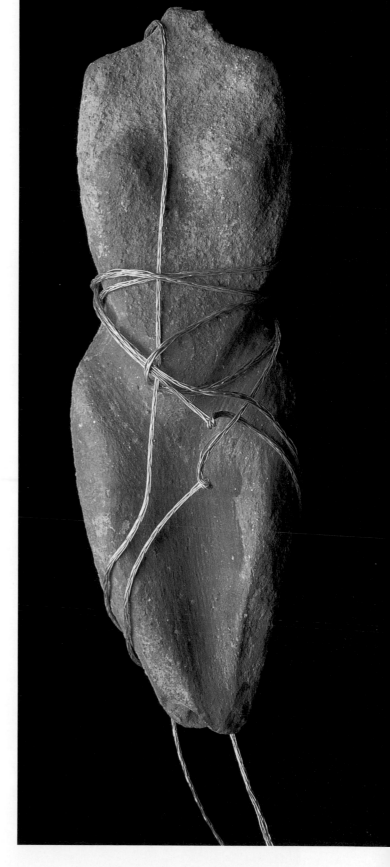

Nora Naranjo-Morse, *Mother*. Hand-built micaceous local clay from Santa Clara Pueblo, New Mexico, wood-fired with cedar, wire wrap, 4 × 12 ins. (10 × 30 cm)

SCULPTURE

Sculpture is a nebulous term. Often it applies to abstract work with no realistic meaning. Sometimes sculpture is allegorical or metaphorical, or even humorous. Recognizing that all three-dimensional pieces can be called sculpture, we have chosen a few representative images here.

Bill Stewart, *Doodad*. Earthenware, wheel-thrown, pinch and slab; *engobes and glaze*, 72 ins. (182 cm) high

Sylvia Hyman, *Still Life no.5*. Stoneware and porcelain, 8 × 17 × 6 ins. (20 × 43 × 15 cm)

Richard Shaw, *Dark Temple*. A master at trompe l'oeil, Richard slab-builds stories for high temperature; *decals, glazes, paints*, 12 × 12 × 8 ins. (30 × 30 × 20 cm)

LEFT **Steven Montgomery**, *Quadrus*. Stoneware, wheel-thrown, press-molded, hand-built; 36 × 36 ins. (91 × 91 cm)

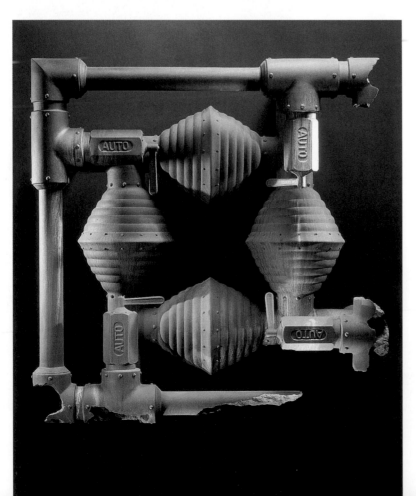

FACING PAGE **Øyvind Suul** (Norway), *Dive*. Stoneware, cast and hand-built sections, wall size, unglazed

INSET **Angel Garraza** (Spain), *Casket*. Stoneware, hand-built of vari-colored clays, height 72 ins. (182 cm)

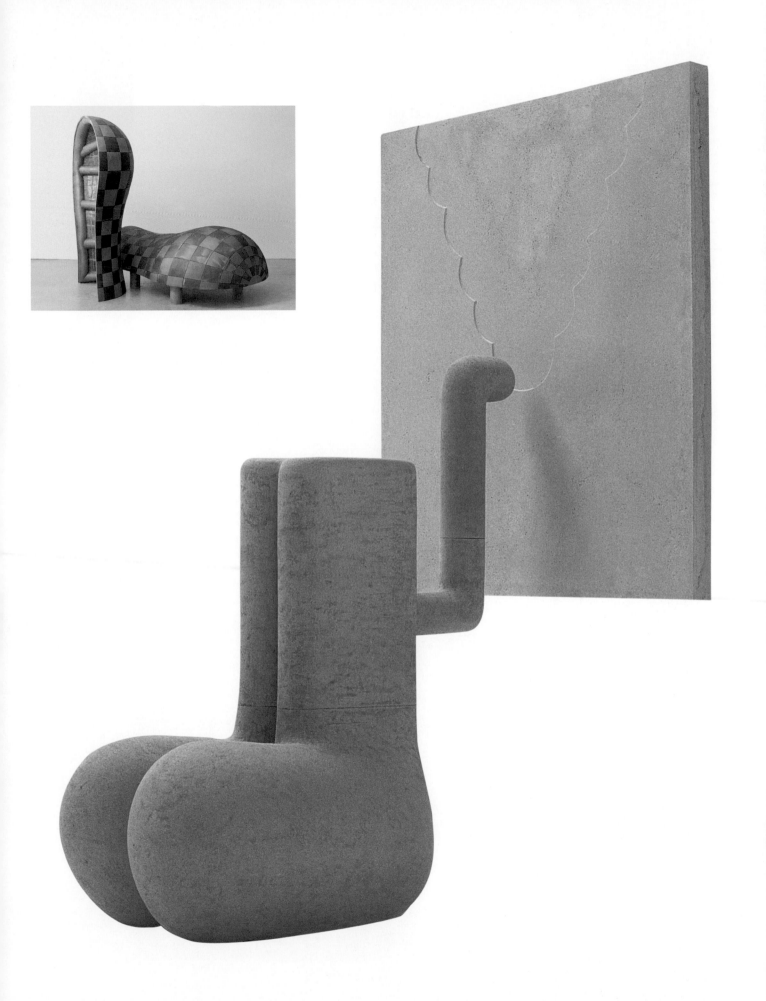

Lynda Benglis, *Warm Spring Band Knot Hat*, solid-built sophisticated organic forms, stoneware, *engobes and glazes*, 12 × 16 × 12½ ins. (30 × 41 × 32 cm)

Jerry Rothman, famous years ago for his huge monolithic works, his "sky pots," 0% shrinkage clay body (see p. 101), his glazed sculptural soup tureens, and realistic but abstracted figures of mythological origin, has changed direction lately to a lyrical trend, as in *Leda And*, unglazed stoneware, 26 × 24 × 20 ins. (66 × 61 × 57 cm)

FACING PAGE **Lu Pin-chang** (China), *View of Relic No.1*. Stoneware, hand-built, smoke-fired in wood kiln, c/10, unglazed; 16 × 14 × 67 ins. (40 × 36 × 170 cm)

Xavier Toubes, *'Namorados da Lua*. Hollow-built stoneware, *gold luster glaze* c/013, 6 ft (182 cm) high

INSTALLATIONS

Ceramic installations are increasingly important as outdoor public art statements, as accessories to architecture, and in large public spaces such as lobbies, subways, hospitals, stations, and so on.

Edoardo Vega (Ecuador), *Los Totems* (detail)

BELOW **Patricia Lay**, *Mythoi. Black clay with colored inlay*, steel pole installation, 10 ft. (300 cm) high, installed in Denmark

ABOVE **Mary Jo Bole**,
Odd Luck. Black
porcelain, bone china,
decals, hand-built hollow
with additions and
photo silkscreen,
12 ft × 8 ft × 16 ins.
(3.6 × 2.4 m. × 41 cm)

RIGHT **Berry Matthews**,
White Space. Installation
of metal and ceramic tiles
coated with wax to be set
on fire; room-size

Deborah Horrell, *Hell and In Between*. Multiple arches fabricated at Otsuka Factory, Shigaraki, Japan; room-size

Nan Smith, *Beyond Illusions*. Life-size figures constructed with latex and plaster molds plus modeling and carving; steel gate; *commercial stains and glazes airbrushed* over stencil decoration, c/04; 92 × 72 × 192 ins. (2.33 × 1.83 × 4.88 m.)

Many artists have websites. Look up your favorites.

Organizations, museums, galleries, ceramic suppliers, have websites promoting artists and materials.

Most cities have clay clubs you can join.

Many cities have municipal classes in ceramics. Universities and community colleges offer courses.

Get going on your own.

ABOVE **Bernard Kerr** (Australia), *Throne*. Earthenware, stoneware, and porcelain, exhibition installation, thrown, cast, and hand-built, unglazed; 10 × 8 × 4 ft (3 × 2.4 × 1.2 m.)

RIGHT **Nedda Guidi** (Italy), *Limerick*. Terracotta-colored earthenware slab construction, 8 × 8 ft (2.4 × 2.4 m.)

Marilyn Lysohir, *Tattooed Ladies*. Hollow-built stoneware, *sprayed and brushed stains and oxides*, oxidation fired; each figure 26 × 11 × 9 ins. (66 × 28 × 23 cm)

Sadashi Inuzuka, Wall-mounted installation; *dried clay slurry on the floor, glazed pieces mounted*

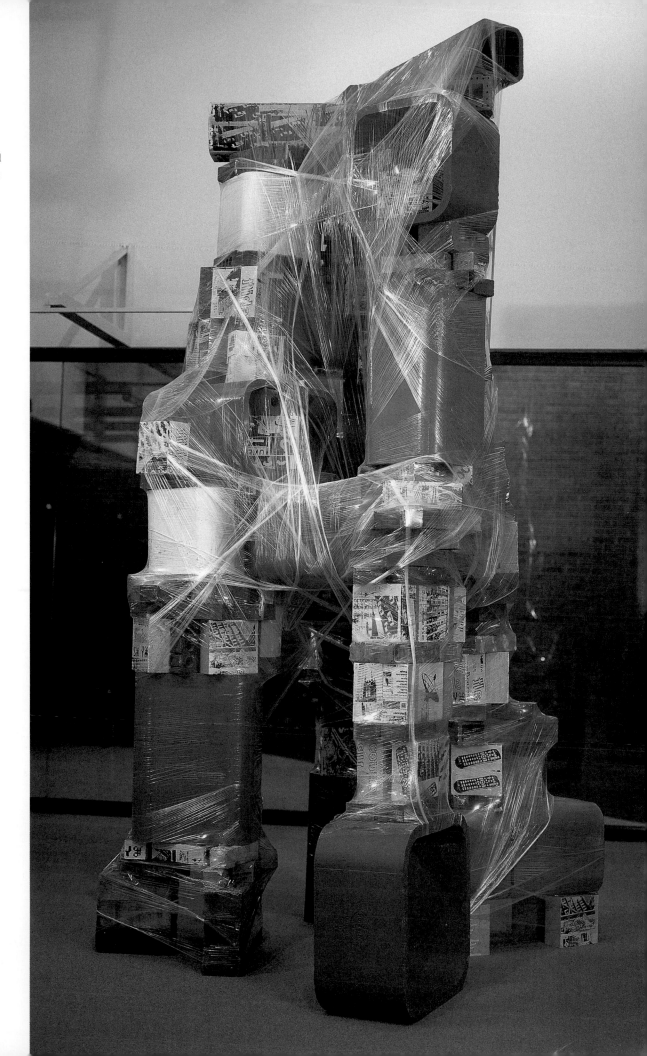

Fred Spaulding, Brick sculpture. Arbitrarily arranged manufactured brick, shrink-wrapped; decoration involves *silk-screened engobes, home-made decals, and overglazed majolica* techniques; 10 ft (3 m.) high

8

THE TIMELESS WORLD HISTORY OF CERAMIC ART

Jomon ("cord pattern") large jar, coil-built, with characteristic impressed surface decoration, from prehistoric Japan; 10,000 BCE

Prehistoric Chinese pot, one of the earliest examples from the long tradition of Chinese pottery unbroken until the "cultural revolution" in the 20th century; c. 5000 BCE

What seem to be the earliest glazes were discovered in Egypt, dating from about 5000 BCE. At the same time, the Egyptians mixed clay and glaze into "Egyptian paste," a self-glazing clay body, to make small "ushabti" figures to be buried with the dead

Fragments of clay vessels and objects have been the chief and sometimes the only remnants left from prehistoric human activities. Ancient peoples are studied mainly through the clay artifacts that remain in tombs and excavations all over the world. From the ceramic fragments that survive we draw inferences about cross-cultural borrowing, trade, migration, lifestyles, and the degree of sophistication of various societies according to their art forms. Clay was such a universal, easily obtained and moldable material that—more than rock art or marble sculpture—its remains supply countless ways to determine an intimate picture of ancient life, albeit without language.

Decorative motifs often seem to be similar and timeless. Perhaps the motifs that we see repeated time and again, simultaneously in different cultures or progressively through the ages, occur because processes are parallel and because the universal forms demand certain kinds of graphics. Or perhaps, as some leaders of surviving tribal groups maintain, there were long-term, long-distance migrations, exchanges, and communications of all sorts among distant peoples.

Tradition prevails in ceramics more than in other arts, because there are so many variables to be controlled in the materials and firing. Potters tend not to change anything for fear of having to change everything. Families and dynasties continued secret processes for generations and knowledge was refused to outsiders. All the same, new ways developed and some traditions were lost.

It is interesting to speculate why certain cultures were ceramic pioneers and others were not. For instance, why did only the Chinese develop porcelain, when the natural china clay plus flux and filler combination existed in the ground in Japan and Korea as well? Why did it take several thousand years for Europeans to develop porcelain, when they had the same ingredients but deposited separately? Why did North and South American societies burnish clay and never discover glaze? Why was the wheel used historically by potters only in the Orient, Middle East, and Europe, never in the so-called West? The answer probably lies in the fact that, if the societies did not invent or pick up from each other, their attention was focused elsewhere. Strangely enough, through the ages, warfare has been one of the main mediums of cultural exchange.

The art of ceramics has the longest and most varied history of any of the arts. Neanderthal hunting and gathering groups roamed across Eurasia 70,000 to 35,000 years ago at least. Those early people had fire and probably made clay pots.

The first evidence of carving and the artistic employment of clay for

The early Minoan culture on the island of Crete made very sophisticated pottery, thrown on the wheel, unglazed and decorated with various clays; 2500 BCE

Yokes of press-molded Egyptian paste ornaments, as depicted in hieroglyphs, were used to hold up women's garments; c. 2000 BCE

Amlash stylized animal, burnished and bonfired, from Luristan, Persia (Iran); 1500 BCE

The Etruscans, ancient pre-Roman people of Italy, buried their dead in clay sarcophagi of vast scale topped with representational life-sized figures; 700 BCE, placed in underground tombs

A black on red terra sigillata jar from Attica, mainland Greece, produced during the so-called Golden Age of ceramics, 500 BCE

Xian soldier, one of 6,000 life-size figures buried with the Chinese Emperor Ch'in Shih Huang-ti; 200 BCE

ritual and functional use occurs about 35,000 years ago, during the Ice Age; clay animals and figures emerge, modeled in the round as well as carved in clay floors and walls. Ruins of prehistoric kilns have also been found dating from early periods. Native American Indians were burning clay pots in bonfires 25,000 years ago, according to the late Carl Denzel, founder of the Southwest Museum of the American Indian, Los Angeles, California, USA; to this day they do not use kilns. This long and varied history of ceramic art changed directions many times, dropped out of sight, moved forward, or stood still, then cropped up again in other pockets of time and space

Wonderful, spirited engobe decoration characterized Chinese Tz'u-chou dynasty pots; 600–1100 CE

The mysterious Mimbres North American Indians (900–1300 CE) disappeared inexplicably, but left us with exquisite stylized designs on ceremonial pots. When used as a funerary vessel and placed over the face the hole allowed the dead person's spirit to be released

Pottery in the Chinese Tang dynasty was noted for its lead-based polychrome glazes—grass-green, amber yellow, and indigo blue—and for its technically masterful hollow-built horses, camels, and warriors; 600–900 CE

During the Han dynasty in China, seemingly thousands of figures and dwellings were created, depicting with wonderful movement and grace the daily life of the people; 200 BCE–200 CE

The Chinese Sung (Song) dynasty is thought of as the greatest age in ceramics. It combined the highest technical ability with simplicity of form. The outstanding contribution was the discovery of reduction atmosphere, which produced celadons and ox-blood red glazes. Porcelain, celadon-glazed ewer, 900–1200 CE

The slick sheen characteristic of Roman pots was accomplished by the use of iron-colored terra sigillata, often over relief designs; 100–200 CE

Stylized hollow-built Haniwa figures of warriors and animals were set into the ground around Japanese tombs; 400 CE

as civilization progressed; it is still continuing.

Although new ways have been adopted by whole cultures, evolutionary stages of clay art have more often originated with individuals. In contrast to the large body of anonymous folk artists, these innovative individuals have often been known by name. Some even reached a stage where they created economic gain for their societies.

In modern culture the break with tradition initiated by contemporary clay artists in their search for new ways

has liberated claywork, sending it storming into the art world, and allowing not only space-age applications but also such non-traditional uses of clay as unfired clay art and site-specific installations.

In the pictorial time-line that comprises this chapter we indicate some of the highlights in the lengthy development of ceramics. The dates given are approximate. This overview is based on our own observations in museums and at archaeological digs in various parts of the world. In the 19th and 20th centuries some of the greatest

The Persians developed a scintillating luster technique, achieved by painting copper sulfate over a glaze and reducing it on the cooling cycle of a firing at 1300° F (700° C). They had to judge the exact point of red heat by eye; 900–1300 CE

Pre-Columbian pottery from South America is represented by this Zapotec figure of a god, 900 CE

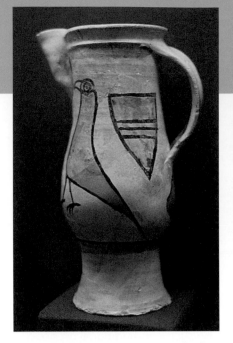

This medieval French jug is an example of the exuberant functional wares that were being produced all over Europe; c. 1100 CE

An unglazed Persian burial pot with an effigy; c. 1150 CE

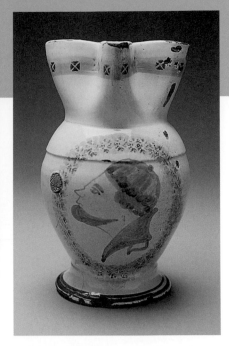

Early Italian majolica overglaze decoration on a tin opacified glazed pitcher; c. 1400 CE

painters and sculptors of our time have been enamored of the plastic qualities of clay and have chosen to experiment seriously with the medium. **We all need to be aware of the magnetism that history holds for our own involvement with clay.**

The famous Persian blue was produced by copper in a high-alkaline glaze. This ewer is decorated with engobe under the transparent turquoise glaze; c. 1600 CE

The long history of Turkish ceramics culminated in the 15th and 16th centuries in the beautifully overglazed Iznik vessels and tiles

The important Imari porcelain factory in Arita, Japan, produced spectacular overglaze enameled and gold lustered wares such as this platter; c. 1600 CE

The luster technique that the Persians developed spread across Europe, but was perfected in Valencia, Spain, which was a center of lusterware production in the 1500s CE

For several generations the **Della Robbia** family in Italy produced architectural ceramics for interiors and exteriors, usually in carved and added white clay body with colorful majolica brushings; c. 1480 CE

In France, King Louis XV instituted a state porcelain factory at Sèvres, where unusually fine overglaze painting was practiced on rather extravagant forms. Floor vase, c. 1750 CE

In China, potters of the Ming dynasty imported cobalt from Persia for blue-painted decorations on their clear-glazed white porcelain bodies. The dynasty also gave us the Ming colors of yellow, apple-green, and lavender that have never been duplicated; c. 1500 CE

The Dutch settlers, originally from German-speaking Switzerland, who came to Pennsylvania, USA in the 1700s brought the peasant style of engobes on redware under clear glaze

Early in the 18th century, a porcelain body was developed at Meissen, Germany; porcelain centerpiece, c. 1750 CE

Besides functional porcelain dinnerware, large portrait sculptures were produced all over Europe, such as this one from the 18th-century St-Cloud factory in France

In Switzerland and northern Europe, clay was used exuberantly to fashion sculptural stoves as room-warmers; c. 1800 CE

Josiah Wedgwood developed a porcelain clay body at Stoke-on-Trent, England, in 1760. The white porcelain body was colored with cobalt blue, chrome green, or basalt black, with added relief carvings in white porcelain superimposed; teapot, unglazed, c. 1800 CE

Adelaide Robineau made elaborate porcelain carvings early in the 20th century and founded the Ceramic Museum in Syracuse, New York

Maija Grotell was a Finn who worked in the USA at about the same time as Adelaide Robineau; both women were influential. The work Grotell did in the 40s and 50s initiated an early modern style in ceramics

Platter by Joan Miró (1893–1983); famous painters tried clay

European ceramists who had worked in the state-subsidized porcelain factories settled in Ohio, USA, where there were good clay deposits, and founded the Rookwood factory, which closed in 1900. This subtly colored vase was one of this firm's many individually produced designs

European painters who were inspired by the vigor of folk pottery began to use ceramics as an art medium; most notably, **Pablo Picasso** (1881–1973) carried clay into museum sophistication, as exemplified in this vase. The contribution of many of these artists—Braque, Giacometti, Chagall, Miró, Léger, Rouault, Matisse, Gauguin, Renoir, among others— elevated the status of clay as an art form

Bust by **Pierre-Auguste Renoir** (1841–1919)

Fine French china from the Limoges factory, overglaze hand-painted in contemporary designs, 1990s

Mai Järmut (Estonia), *Hopeful*, 2000

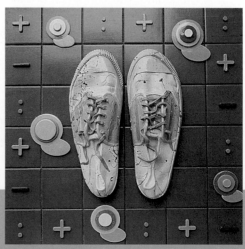

9

COMPENDIUM

The technical options for all the suggestions in this chapter can be found in the previous chapters

1. SUGGESTED PROJECTS FOR INDIVIDUAL WORK

Decide on general procedure

Clayworkers can use these Compendium suggestions to "teach themselves" in a class of one, or teachers can use these ideas in their groups. In most cases the suggested order in each category is arranged from the simplest to the most advanced ways to learn. Some generalizations pertain to all ceramic work and should be thought about each time. Now, choose an abstract or functional piece to begin.

1. Determine method of production to be used: hand-building; throwing; coil or slab or both; casting in a mold, or other.
2. Always consider size, proportion, shape, and color in relation to function.
3. Design in terms of the characteristics of your production method.
4. Remember shrinkage and limitations of your clay.
5. Structure of the shape is implicit in the design.
6. Color, textures, type of glaze or clay surface, must relate to the shape and function.
7. What temperature do you usually fire at? If your kiln provides a choice, determine what temperature will be best for the proposed idea, for whatever reasons.
8. Where the piece will be used or shown may make a difference to method of building, size and form, clay and glazes, and whether there is pattern or decoration.
9. Drawings may help to crystallize your decisions.

Basically functional

General thoughts for any style of fabrication.

I. OVEN OR SERVING CONTAINERS FOR HOT FOODS

a. *Casserole*—Design container for particular foods. What shape? What type lid? Handles necessary? Slant of sides? Easy to clean? Can it be used at table? What volume? Is color pleasing? Easy to store?
b. *Individual casseroles*—Same as above.
c. *Soup tureen*—How big? How carried? Does ladle rest in tureen? Designed to keep soup hot? Appropriate glaze surface and color?
d. *Chafing dish*—Size? Handle? Where and how does it get heat?

II. BEVERAGE CONTAINER OR DISPENSER

a. *Pitcher*—Do size and shape correspond to contents? Hot or cold liquid? Easy to grasp or hold? Pleasant and easily cleaned surfaces? Is handle attached near maximum weight? Is handle close to pot for leverage? Does spout provide guide to the liquid? Is spout edge sharp enough and parallel to base to prevent drip? Does the pitcher have a substantial base?

b. *Mugs*—Large enough? Hot or cold liquids? Easy to grasp or hold, especially if hot? Pleasant lip to drink from?
   If members of a set, do they hold correct amount in proportion to size of pitcher?

c. *Teapot*—Size? Spout pours well? Balance of handle? Is lid secure when teapot is tilted? Lid easy to grasp? Relationship of teapot body, handle, spout, and lid? Is there means of straining tea? Spout placed high enough so pot can be filled up?

d. *Cups and saucers*—Cup easy to hold and drink from? Does shape retain heat? Does saucer need a "well"? Relation of cup to saucer?

e. *Wine or liqueur bottle or pitcher*—Size? Shape? How picked up? Will it pour? Visual appeal for this type of liquid?

f. *Coffee pot*—Large enough? Pouring facility? Lift? Will it keep coffee hot?

g. *Creamer and sugar*—Size? Pouring facility? Pouring lip? Handles or not? Lid for sugar?

h. *Punch bowl*—Size? Room for ice? Ladle? Cups?

i. *Water cooler or party keg*—Size and shape? How is liquid dispensed?

III. KITCHEN AND TABLEWARE

a. *Mixing bowls*—Different sizes? Can they be measuring bowls? Are they substantial? Reinforced lip? Really designed for mixing?

b. *Canisters*—Sized for contents? Shaped for storage? Type of lid? Rugged construction?

c. *Butter dish*—For both serving and storage? Size and shape?

d. *Salt and pepper*—Easy to load? What shape and size? Difference between salt and pepper? Easily cleaned?

e. *Salad bowl*—Shape? Size? Color? Smaller serving bowls, matching or totally separate?

f. *Jello/jelly molds*—Shaped for easy release of contents?

g. *Soufflé dish*—Size? Straight sides?

h. *Fruit bowl*—To hold what kind of fruit? What shape best? Can it have a tall foot?

i. *Cookie/biscuit jar*—How much does it hold? Will it keep contents dry/moist? Loose or tight-fitting lid? Large enough opening for hand to go in easily?

j. *Miscellaneous*—Cake plate, condiment trays, snack servers, cruets, tile hot-pads or trivets, batter bowl, jam pot, garlic pot, herb jars, colanders.

IV. LAMP BASE

Size? Shape? For reading or purely decoration—think of how these two differ? Type of shade? Fixture? What happens to cord? Proportion of base to size of shade to light fixture? Simplicity, good substantial form, or outrageous?

V. PLANT AND FLOWER CONTAINERS

a. What type plant, as to size, color, culture? Should pot be porous? Must it provide drainage? Does it need a stand? Is there enough root area?

b. Cut flowers, what kind? Short or long stems, graceful or stiff? Design container for maximum water at base of stem.

c. Florist-type flower container, possible for mass production, low cost.

d. Should it be glazed either inside or out?

VI. OUTDOOR ACCESSORIES

a. *Brazier*—Size? Depth? Stand? Type and placement of grill? Porous clay body essential.

b. *Planter or decorative garden pot*—Glazed or not? Textured? Root room? Drainage?

c. *Space divider*—Such as could be made from ovals cut from thrown cylinder shapes, or slab constructions, etc.; or from many assembled clay shapes.

d. *Garden sculpture*—Withstand the elements? Where will it be used—among plants, on brick, free-standing? Interesting clay body important asset.

e. *Barbecue cooking accessories*—Large salt and pepper, basting pot, oversized salad container, condiment jars, etc.

VII. INTERIOR ACCESSORIES

a. *Wall decoration*—Flat tiles, relief sculpture, etc. How will it hang? Does it retain clay quality? Movable or permanent?

b. *Pipe tobacco humidor*—Size? Shape? Lid? Means of retaining moisture, such as a place to hold an apple chip inside the lid?

c. *Tile table-top or tile trays*—How are tiles mounted? Spaces between? Continuity? Decorative or functional?

d. *Miscellaneous*—Door knobs, bells, tree or patio decorations, table centerpiece, clock, candle-holders, boxes, mirror frames, branch vases, hanging lights, porch lights, thrown or hand-built sculptures for interior or exterior spaces.

Basically sculptural

Think of a *metaphor* (dictionary: the application of a word or phrase to an object or concept it does not literally denote), or a *concept* (dictionary: an idea of something formed by mentally combining all its characteristics or particulars), or an *idea* (dictionary: any conception existing in the mind). Realize one or all of these in clay; see if a friend can understand your sculpture in one of these terms; if not, add text, or something else.

VIII. INDOOR SCULPTURE

a. *Wall hanging*—Mounted on board, with metal armature, or substantial by itself? Size? Change clay body to reduce fired weight? Finishing texture, colored engobe, or glaze? How to hang?
b. *Over-size abstract or realistic sculpture*—Free-standing? Monolithic or made in pieces and reassembled leather-hard? Made in pieces and reassembled after firing? Texture? Finish?
c. *Figure*—Abstract or realistic? Size? Pedestal? Type of clay and finish?
d. *Installation*—Scale? Mounted or not? How many pieces? What kind of togetherness? Do the pieces stay in place or are they movable? How related or not related? Probable placement?
e. *How to*—Plan how to move sculpture into kiln, decide a firing schedule.

IX. OUTDOOR SCULPTURE

Most of the same possibilities exist for OUTDOOR as for INDOOR sculpture, but:

a. *All sculptures*—Climate, especially extreme cold, requires a clay body that is flexible between degrees of change. How to adapt? What finish withstands rain, ice, heat? Test fired clay body under water, in icebox or refrigerator, in oven slowly to 500°F/260°C.
b. *Placement*—Low or high vantage point; area surrounding placement will affect look of the sculpture(s); consider various options.

Note: All sculpture projects can be executed by hand or wheel or from plaster; see glazed and fired options in Chapter 4.

X. PROJECTS IN PLASTER

It is possible to begin all forms in claywork in plaster, but plaster techniques may be too involved for beginners; experiment with:

a. Make a one-piece mold; use a "found object" for the model or make a clay or a plaster model by hand or on the wheel.
b. Make a two-piece mold; same as above, from a found object or from a model.
c. Develop or buy a casting slip, cast the mold(s); try the one-piece mold also as a press mold for plastic clay.
d. Carve a plaster stamp for your signature or logo.
e. Carve plaster texture stamps for pressing into clay.
f. Make a free-form plaster model by filling a plastic bag (different sizes) with liquid plaster, tie the bag, then put the soft plaster in the bag into a bucket of water and manipulate a form with your hands; make a mold of this model or drape clay over this model; if it breaks on removing, paste it together with clay or more plaster.
g. Make a textured or patterned plaster tile mold for pressing clay.
h. Try putting several forms together in the same mold for simultaneous casting.

2. SUGGESTED PROJECTS FOR BEGINNING HAND-BUILDING

TEXTURE Experiment with objects pushed into clay to make patterns: tools, nails, bolts, buttons, seed pods, bark, etc. Glaze or stain to emphasize the texture.

COIL Round form with coils exposed and textured, or round form with coil-building method concealed by smoothing the clay inside and out.

SLAB   Build box or rectangular form with slab bottoms and sides, or cut *two* patterns and put them together in an asymmetrical shape. Glaze to enhance the main directional line.

HUMP OR SLING

Hump: rock or clay form.

Sling: hammock, draped in box or between four table legs, made of cloth. This is a good method for making simple, flat, low open forms. You can add a foot or feet, or a top, or spouts, or put two humps or slings together, etc.

HISTORICAL POT OR FIGURE

Not copy, but grasp the same "flavor" as something from ceramic history. Suggestions: Tang, Sung, Haniwa, Jomon, Harappa, Syrian, medieval English, pre-Columbian, Native American, Egyptian, early Greek, Pennsylvania Dutch, etc. (See Bibliography for help in finding historical illustrations.)

POT OR CONTAINER FOR DRIED BRANCHES

Find the grasses, stalks, or branches, then design the pot. This can be designed to hang free, hang against, stand alone, or be a group. Glaze only partially so the vegetation will relate to some "natural" clay surface.

PATIO LAMP

Light, lantern, or candle container, for outdoor use. Most important: light pattern, cut holes designed for shadows. Does it stand or hang?

---

3. PROGRESSION OF INDIVIDUAL STEPS IN THROWING PROJECTS

1. Learn to *center* ball of clay. Try progressively larger balls, up to 10 or 15 lb (5 or 7.5 kg).
2. *Pull cylinder* with even cross-section. Get clay *up* from bat. Cylinder walls should be slightly heavier at base, gradually thinner toward the top.
3. Throw *bowl* shape, low and wide.
4. Pull *tall* cylinder, work up to 13 ins. (33 cm) high, even wall-thickness.
5. *Collar* in small neck of cylinder, for bottle.
6. Throw *pitcher* and pull lip. Sharpen pitcher lip-edge so it will not drip. Pull and attach handle.
7. Throw *mug* and add handle.
8. *Pot with lid* to fit. Practice making flange on either pot or lid.
9. *Teapot*, watch size, proportion, balance, height of spout, type of handle.
10. *Set* of four or six *all alike*.
11. *Set*, one large container and several small ones, according to size and volume. Make enough small ones to hold the contents of large pot, no more, no less.
    • *Watch structure*, learn to prevent warping, slumping. Engineer cross-section and profile for greatest support.
    • *Watch foot shape* and size: should relate appropriately to profile-line of pot, and be similar thickness to the lip of the pot.
    • *Signature of potter* should finish design, not hurt it.
    • *Lip of pot* should end the shape. Try different ways of making and finishing feet and lips—bevels, sharp edges, soft rolls, beads, etc.
    • *Try larger scale*; try progressively larger lumps, do again these beginning steps and forms, but larger.

If you master the steps above, try these with more sculptural intent:

1. Combine wheel-thrown shapes into larger pots or sculptural forms, putting them together wet, squashing or paddling the thrown pieces, adding texture, etc.
2. Large decorative plates for table or wall.
3. Planters.
4. Lamps or lights.
5. Hanging units: bells, mobiles, planters.
6. Teapots and coffee pots.
7. Sets, not alike but two or more relating in some way.
8. Closed hollow forms with a pinhole for air escape.
9. Footed compote.

4. SUGGESTED PROJECTS FOR CLAY, GLAZE, AND DECORATION EXPERIMENTS

Body and glaze development

1. Learn properties of raw materials by experimental testing; think of various ways to test such as % additions or subtractions, compare materials against each other, etc.
2. Set up standards for a particular type of clay body, color, firing properties, working qualities. Fit composition together, mix a batch, and run tests.
3. Set up standards for developing glazes to fit this clay body. Determine composition of raw materials, mix a batch, test, make necessary correction, try colorants.
4. Set up standards for any specific type of glaze—surface texture, temperature, color. Make a composition, mix, and test.
5. Develop casting slip for specific temperature, type, color.

This can go on indefinitely!

Decoration

1. **Engobe:** brush, trail, dip, sgraffito; add flux to make engobe more vitreous; add more color to make it bleed through glaze.
2. **Underglaze:** decoration with stains or oxides on bisque. Practice varieties of brush-strokes. Vary shading by spraying.
3. **Majolica:** decoration with stains or oxides over an unfired opaque glaze. Lines will fuse and feather. Freer than underglaze technique; use "washes" and other watercolor techniques.
4. **Glaze on glaze:** learn characteristics of various types of glazes. Watch color combinations. Spray, dip, over-dip, brush.
5. **Sgraffito:** draw lines through engobe or glaze or scrape away areas. Glaze should be non-fluid so lines will remain clear-cut in firing.
6. **Wax resist:** brush decoration with paraffin or wax emulsion on bisque, engobe or glaze over, or wax between two glazes.
7. **Stencil:** spray colored areas through stencil with underglaze, majolica, or over-spray techniques; or brush or sponge color using stencil pattern.

Exploit characteristic effects by analyzing your results, and making more tests.

Design standards to keep in mind

1. Proportion, size relationship, weight, balance, volume.
2. Placement of appendages.
3. Function and utility of shape.
4. Definite changes of plane make more vital form.
5. Keep character and freedom of the clay and its production process.

5. EXPERIMENTING WITH MATERIAL ADDITIONS TO A BASE GLAZE

Bisque a number of tiles for making tests:

(a) test individual glaze materials mixed with water and applied to tiles; fire at c/04, 5, and 10 to see the separate melts.

(b) Batch glaze for testing—one you already know or want to try. Mix it dry, well. Divide it into 100-gram amounts and add the proper material additions (see below). Mix each one wet and apply to tile with spatula, or by pouring or dipping. Fire.

Note: It is interesting to try the test at each of the above temperatures to see how it varies, but if you can't do that, just use the one temperature (cone) at which you usually fire.

Code back of each test-tile with cobalt, or black stain, and water, or use a commercial ceramic pencil; better still, mark code on back of each tile before applying glaze.

TEST TILES: BASE GLAZE PLUS IMPROVIZATIONS. Take a known glaze and test it with additions:

Flint 20%	Flint 30%	Kaolin 20%	Kaolin 30%	Talc 20%
Dolomite 20%	Nephelene syenite 20%	Barium carbonate 20%	Zinc oxide 20%	Whiting 20%
Magnesium carbonate 20%	Calcium borate 20%	Rutile 20%	Wood ash 20%	Base glaze 100%

Make a second test, replacing the 20% with 30% additions and 30% with 40%, to see the limits.
Make color tests with oxide additions.

6. GLAZE IMPROVIZATIONS

Everybody, even children of elementary school-age, enjoys doing individual raw material experiments. Always use parts of 100, or parts of 10, that is, keep the "base" adding up to 100 or to 10. Add test materials to the base in percentage amounts to make changes. **See above diagram.** For example:

MAKE
- 10%–20% additions of all the raw materials on your shelves to many base glazes, your own batches or taken from books.
- Or additions of natural raw organic plant materials (wood ash, flowers, volcanic ash, seaweed, etc.) to a base glaze.
- Or additions of low temperature common surface clay (found in the desert or near creek beds).
- Or organic ash 50–50 with a glaze, or to glaze batches starting with 10%.
- Or crushed, pulverized, ground rock used by itself, or added to other base glazes.

Test these sample experimental glazes on tiles or pots and fire at the temperature you normally use.

Seeing the results of standard glaze materials or of additions such as wood ash, etc., *as they melt by themselves (or don't melt) at various temperatures* can be a fascinating experience for students, and an absolute necessity for the potter; then, make more compositions from these results.

7. GLAZE "LINE-BLEND" TEST (diagram page 220)

This involves making all possible 50–50 combinations of some basic colors on your favorite glaze, at your favorite temperature. Mix ingredients dry, then add measured amount of water for application.

1. Make 15 tiles for one test. (If you want more tests, add more top-members to the test.)
2. Mix 100 grams glaze for every top-member—in

this case there are five, so measure 500 dry grams of glaze, mix well, and divide equally into five sandwich bags or plastic cups.

3. Add appropriate colorant to each sack and mix well. For instance:
   sack #1 = 2% cobalt carbonate
   sack #2 = 4% copper carbonate
   sack #3 = 10% rutile
   sack #4 = 5% iron oxide
   sack #5 = 10% zircopax
   —or make your own top-member list.

4. The line blend looks like this:

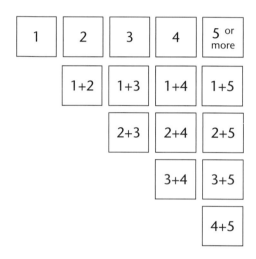

Mix with water in a cup or on a plate: Take a measuring spoon of dry glaze from each of the five sacks, mix it with water and apply each color to the first five tiles. Then each successive tile is a 50–50 blend of the top-members. Take a measuring spoon of dry glaze from each of two sacks, mix together with water and apply to tiles (e.g., ½ #1 & ½ #2; ½ #1 & ½ #3, etc.). You can mix dry with water on a plate, pick up the liquid with a spatula and apply directly on the vertically-held tile, or mix in a cup and brush on test-tile. Mark back of tile with code number and fire.

On these tiles, try to use the application method that you generally use for applying glazes. Using a spatula (akin to pouring) allows you to apply glaze on the tile halfway down; then overlap the next spatula-pour so that you will see a double thickness of glaze after firing. Brushing glaze often leaves strokes showing after firing, especially with matt glazes.

5. *Most commercial low fire white clay bodies are talc/clay combinations that become glazes at c/10. Buy the body dry or grind your dry low fire commercial clay scrap, add colors, apply as glazes, test at c/10.*

8. SPECIAL LOW FIRE INFORMATION

Egyptian paste

White Batch Formula (Self-glazing clay/glaze composition similar to that used several thousand years ago by the Egyptians).

Fire c/010 to c/04
(1800° to 1900° F, 980° to 1040° C)

Nepheline syenite	342 grams
Silica	342 grams
Ball clay	133 grams
Soda ash	53 grams
Baking soda	<u>53 grams</u>
Total	923 grams

(makes about 2 lb/1 kg)

Keep wet batch wrapped in damp cloth and stored in airtight container, or keep dry to use when needed.

Colors for Egyptian paste

(Try adding one of these to the base batch above)

Turquoise—copper carbonate			3% (light)
		or	4% (darker)
		or	6% (black)
Dark blue—cobalt oxide	1–2%		
Yellow-green—yellow-green stain	5%		
Purple—manganese dioxide	2%		
Yellow—yellow stain	8%		
Dark green—chrome oxide	5%		

Experiment with other metallic oxides and stains for color; 12% color addition is maximum.

Use Egyptian paste for beads, pins, buttons, jewelry. Fire on ni-chrome (nickel-chrome) wire in regular bisque firing, or bonfire as the Egyptians would have (see pages 206, 207).

Mosaic cement

Use for setting ceramic or glass mosaic pieces for table tops, walls or wall hangings, on sculpture, etc. Mix: magnasite and magnesium chloride together into paste form, 50–50.

Low fire engobe

For c/04: use the dry white commercial low fire clay body for adding colorants, or mix all-purpose engobe (page 121) up to c/10, or batch 50% ball clay–50% talc up to c/5; apply white plus color mixture to wet or leather-hard clay, fire to c/04 or lower (this will be a glaze at c/10).

Add colors:

Blue—cobalt blue	20%
Orange—rutile	40%
Green—chrome oxide	40%
Violet brown—manganese dioxide	6–12%
White—zircopax	15%
Black—black stain	10%, plus
iron oxide	10%, plus
manganese dioxide	10%

(for black start with a red clay, if possible, rather than white)

or mix your own low fire base white engobe as follows:

Talc	70%
Ball clay	30%

(See "Engobes," pages 120–121, for example of a high fire engobe.)

9. SOME SUGGESTIONS FOR TAKING PHOTOGRAPHS OF YOUR ARTWORK

When you look through the viewfinder of your camera, digital or film, some of the things you need to consider are: keeping an uncluttered frame—a single art-work is best, and take it up close, close enough to fill the frame with the object; if you are photographing a set try to keep the picture simple, and use as few in the set as possible or create an interesting composition with the pieces in the set; if you are taking the picture outside in daylight, it is best to do it in the afternoon, approximately 4 p.m. or so in the summer, when the sunlight is not as intense as at noon. Keep the photograph simple by using a white or gray paper background. If you are taking the picture inside create a box with bottom and sides of white or gray paper, use two photo-lights at 45°, one on each side facing toward the artwork; the lights will cancel out the shadows. Good luck in creating beautiful photographs of your artwork.

10. EXAMPLE OF A POTTERY STUDIO

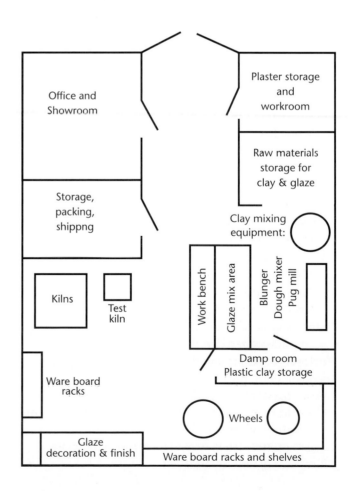

11. TERMS EASILY MIXED UP

Some terms are confusing because they have several meanings. The list below gives them all or their alternatives.

Bat—wheel head; movable work surface of any shape, usually plaster but also wood or fiberboard.

Bisque—biscuit; any *unglazed* ware at any temperature; an initial firing without glaze.

Calcium spar—Cornwall stone, or any spar high in calcium oxide.

China—any white ceramic ware; term for any tableware, usually porcelain.

China clay—kaolin.

China paint—enamel; luster; very low fire glaze applied over a fired glaze.

Crackle—craze; fine line matrix decoration; fault of glaze chemistry.

Deflocculant—Darvan; sodium silicate; soda ash; tea.

Enamel—room-temperature paint; fired-on paint at 300° F (150° C); porcelain enamel on metal signs or refrigerators, etc.; low fire glaze.

Ferric oxide—iron oxide, usually red but can be black.

Flux—anything that lowers the temperature of a material or a mixture, or that melts at low temperature by itself.

Frit—ground glass; pre-melted chemical mixture you make yourself or buy, numbered according to composition.

Gum—gum tragacanth; gum arabic; synthetic gum (CMC, methyl cellulose).

Model—maquette; something to work from; to work clay with fingers or a tool.

Plastic, plasticity—workability of clay; material to cover ware to keep it damp.

Potash spar—Kingman; Custer; G-200, or any spar higher in potassium oxide than in sodium oxide.

Pottery—ceramic; low-fired claywork; any claywork.

Raw—unfired, greenware (green as in "fresh").

Refractory—anything that resists heat or raises the temperature of another material, or that fires at high temperature by itself.

Resist—stencil; latex; wax; paper; metal template.

Silica—sand; flint; quartz.

Slip—engobe (liquid clay for decoration); casting slip; slip glaze.

Slurry—slurpy-wet clay; any liquid mess; plaster not yet hard.

Soda spar—nepheline syenite; Kona A4, or any spar higher in sodium oxide than in potassium oxide.

Spar—short for feldspar, the mineral.

Stain—metallic coloring oxide and other chemicals in stable combinations; wash; commercially sold or home-made pigment mixture; waterbased room-temperature paint thinly applied.

Suspension agent—bentonite; epsom salts; magnesium carbonate; CMC gum.

Terracotta—a color; low fire red clay; art historian's term for redware of all kinds.

Volcanic ash—pumice, found in lumber yards; pumice is purer than volcanic ash, and both are natural materials.

Wax—water-soluble commercial product such as "Ceremul A"; melted paraffin; crayon.

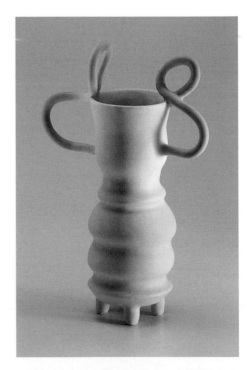

Jill Bonovitz, porcelain (sometimes called china) vessel, 6 ins. (15 cm) high

TEMPERATURE EQUIVALENTS OF ORTON CONES

The cone number on each chart is equivalent to the melting point of each cone on the Fahrenheit and Centigrade scales on each chart. United States potters usually use the Orton cones, the rest of the world mainly Seger cones. Remember that cone temperatures are approximate—it is always best to watch the cones inside the kiln, even if you are using a "kiln sitter" outside the kiln, and a cone pack can always be kept for reference.

CONE NO.			CONE NO.		
022	1085	585	10	2300	1260
021	1103	595	11	2345	1285
020	1157	625	12	2390	1310
019	1166	630	13	2462	1350
018	1238	670	14	2534	1390
017	1328	720	15	2570	1410
016	1355	735	16	2642	1450
015	1418	770	17	2669	1465
014	1463	795	18	2705	1485
013	1517	825	19	2759	1515
012	1544	840	20	2768	1520
011	1607	875	23	2876	1580
010	1634	890	26	2903	1595
09	1706	930	27	2921	1605
08	1733	945	28	2939	1615
07	1787	975	29	2984	1640
06	1841	1005	30	3002	1650
05	1886	1030	31	3056	1680
04	1922	1050	32	3092	1700
03	1976	1080	32½	3137	1725
02	2003	1095	33	3173	1745
01	2030	1110	34	3200	1760
1	2057	1125	35	3245	1785
2	2075	1135	36	3290	1810
3	2093	1145	37	3308	1820
4	2129	1165	38	3335	1835
5	2156	1180	39	3389	1865
6	2174	1190	40	3425	1885
7	2210	1210	41	3578	1970
8	2237	1225	42	3659	2015
9	2282	1250			

TEMPERATURE EQUIVALENTS OF SEGER CONES

The cone number on each chart is equivalent to the melting point of each cone on the Fahrenheit and Centigrade scales on each chart. United States potters usually use the Orton cones, the rest of the world mainly Seger cones

CONE NO.	MELTING POINT		CONE NO.	MELTING POINT		CONE NO.	MELTING POINT	
	°F	°C		°F	°C		°F	°C
021	1202	650	01a	1976	1080	20	2786	1530
020	1238	670	1a	2012	1100	*26	2876	1580
019	1274	690	2a	2048	1120	27	2930	1610
018	1310	710	3a	2084	1140	28	2966	1630
017	1346	730	4a	2120	1160	29	3002	1650
016	1382	750	5a	2156	1180	30	3038	1670
015a	1454	790	6a	2192	1200	31	3074	1690
014a	1499	815	7	2246	1230	32	3110	1710
013a	1535	835	8	2282	1250	33	3146	1730
012a	1590	866	9	2336	1280	34	3182	1750
011a	1616	880	10	2372	1300	35	3218	1770
010a	1652	900	11	2408	1320	36	3254	1790
09a	1688	920	12	2462	1350	37	3317	1825
08a	1724	940	13	2516	1380	38	3362	1850
07a	1760	960	14	2570	1410	39	3416	1880
06a	1796	980	15	2615	1435	40	3488	1920
05a	1832	1000	16	2660	1460	41	3560	1960
04a	1868	1020	17	2696	1480	42	3632	2000
03a	1904	1040	18	2732	1500	* Numbers 21 to 25 are obsolete		
02a	1940	1060	19	2768	1520			

GLOSSARY

Anagama Tube-like single chamber hill kiln; predecessor of *noborigama*, a multi-chambered hill kiln of Oriental style.

Armature Any structure of clay tubes, wire, cardboard, etc., to be removed before firing or left in to support the piece.

Ash The residue made by burning tree, plant, or vegetable material; can be used alone or with other materials for glaze; volcanic ash can also be used.

Ball clay Highly plastic refractory clay that fires off-white; workable, fine-grained sedimentary clay used in white bodies, engobes, and glazes.

Bat Any slab used as a base for throwing or hand-building clay; also applies to a trough used to dry slurry clay to the plastic state; usually made of plaster, press board, plywood, or other porous material.

Batch A mixture of glaze or engobe ingredients calculated by parts or weight.

Bisque, Biscuit Unglazed, but fired ware, usually accomplished in a low temperature firing prior to a glaze fire; also applies to unglazed ware fired high, as in porcelain bisque.

Blender A mechanical mixing machine, kitchen or commercial factory style, for mixing small quantities of materials for clay or glaze testing.

Blistering Bubbles formed in the glaze during the firing due to liberation of gases caused by firing that is too fast; or caused deliberately by putting into the glaze a material such as trisodium phosphate, which will promote decorative bloats.

Blunger A mechanical machine for mixing liquid or slurry clay.

Body A combination of natural clays and non-plastics, especially formulated to have certain workability and firing characteristics.

Bone china Porcelain of high translucency made with bone ash as the flux, produced mainly in England and Japan.

Bonfire An open fire on the ground fueled with wood sticks, brush, dried combustible organic material.

Burnishing Polishing with a smooth stone or tool on leather-hard clay or slip to make a surface sheen; the surface will not stay shiny at temperatures above 2000° F (1100° C).

Casting Process of forming shapes by pouring deflocculated liquid clay slip into plaster molds for repetitive production.

Celadon glaze Sea-green glaze with a small percentage of iron as the colorant; fired in a reduced oxygen atmosphere, usually a stoneware or porcelain glaze, first used in the Orient.

Centering Pushing a mass of clay toward the center with the centrifugal motion of a potter's wheel.

Ceramics Art and science of forming objects from earth materials containing or combined with silica, produced with the aid of heat treatment at 1300° F (700° C) or more.

China (1) A porcelain clay body, with up to 1% absorption, usually translucent. (2) Whiteware, vitreous and hard, sometimes translucent. (3) A general term used in trade when discussing any kind of tableware.

China clay Primary or secondary kaolin, refractory, not very plastic, white-burning, rare in the world; used in the blending of all whiteware and porcelain bodies.

Clay Theoretically $Al_2O_3-2SiO_2-6H_2O$; earth materials formed by the decomposition of igneous rock; when combined with water, clay is plastic enough to be shaped; when subject to red heat or above, it becomes dense and rock-like.

Coiling, Coil-building Age-old method of constructing hollow forms by rolling and attaching ropes of soft clay.

Cones Pyrometric cones, Orton or Seger brand; pyramids made of clay and glaze constituents that bend at specific temperature. Cones are placed in the kiln during firing to indicate the final heat; they are classified by numbers coded to their softening point.

Core The interior of a piece, or a framing or the stuffing on or over which work can be supported; combustible core materials burn out in the kiln; rigid cores should be removed before the clay shrinks.

Crackle Decorative and intentional fissures netting the surface of a glaze due to a variation of expansion and contraction of the glaze and the clay body.

Crawling Glaze that has separated into mounds on the clay surface during firing, generally caused by fluffy or high-shrink materials in raw glazes.

Crystalline glazes Large crystals grown on the glaze surface during firing and cooling, primarily induced by high zinc oxide and low alumina content in glazes.

Damper Adjustable shutter to control draft at the kiln flue.

Decal Ceramic pigments photo-screened or pattern-screened onto flexible decal paper for transfer to bisque or over glaze; can be bought or made.

Deflocculation The addition of a catalyst to a clay and water slip to reduce the amount of water required to make a liquid, usually for casting in molds; water is about 40% by weight.

Design All parts of a two-dimensional (2-D) or three-dimensional (3-D) plan for the composition of a work of art containing the classic five principles and seven elements of design. **Principles:** asymmetric or symmetrical balance, consistency with variety, dominance or focal point, proportion, rhythm. **Elements:** color, contrast, light, line, shape, texture, value.

Downdraft kiln Kiln with fire entering at the side or base, where heat is forced around, up, and down through the ware, and exits via a flue at the back of the chamber.

Dry foot No glaze on the foot rim; used for stoneware and porcelain, rather than the stilt method used for earthenware; stilts would warp the piece when fired to these higher densities.

Earthenware All ware with a permeable or porous body after firing; by definition earthenware has 10% to 15% absorption.

Enamel (1) Applied to pottery: low-temperature glazes applied over other glazes. (2) Applied to metals: glaze that melts lower than steel, copper, silver, or gold, on which enamel is used, fired about 1300° F (700° C). (3) A term for paint.

Engobe [*pronounced on-gobe*] A liquid clay slip colored with metallic earth oxides or glaze stains applied to wet or leather-hard ware for decoration. Engobe can be covered by glaze or used alone.

Extrusion Forcing plastic clay through an auger or form, mechanically or by hand, to change its shape; can be solid or hollow.

Faience A general art-historian's word covering low fire colored clay bodies, such as Egyptian paste.

Feldspar Mineral found in granite which melts around 2300° F (1260° C), used as a flux in clay bodies and glazes.

Fire box The chamber of certain kilns into which the fuel is fed and in which the initial combustion takes place.

Fire clay Secondary clay that withstands high temperature and has a varying amount of free silica in addition to the clay molecule.

Firing (1) Heating in a kiln to the required temperature for clay or glaze, at least to red heat, 1300° F (700° C). (2) Bonfiring in a pit or on the ground.

Firing curve The track made by firing points on a graph, showing the relationship between change in temperature and firing time.

Flue (1) The passageway for flames in kilns—essentially the combustion space; the flue is the area around the stacking space. (2) The place of escape for the products of combustion from the kiln chamber.

Flux A material or mixture having a low melting point or lowering the melting point of other materials. One of the three main components of glaze; also used to increase density in clay bodies; examples include lead, borax, lime, feldspar, and frit.

Foot Base or bottom of a piece.

Frit Mixture melted at high temperature, quenched, and ground to a fine powder. Fritting renders soluble glaze ingredients, such as soda ash, insoluble, and poisonous materials, such as lead, non-poisonous.

Glaze Glassy melted coating developed by chemicals and heat on a clay or metal surface. Glaze provides decoration and color, prevents some penetration of liquids or acids, and yields a matt or glossy, functional surface.

Glaze stains Fabricated ceramic colorants from metallic oxides mixed in combination with other elements to widen the glaze decorating palette; sold by code number, color, and company.

Greenware Finished leather-hard or bone-dry clay pieces not yet fired; raw ware.

Grog Crushed or ground-up fired clay, purchased commercially or made by the potter; used to reduce shrinkage, it yields texture; aids in even drying and firing.

Hollow casting Pouring liquid clay slip into a hollow plaster mold to create a shell of a specific shape; can be repeated.

Intaglio Depressed surface decoration, the reverse of bas-relief.

Jiggering A mechanical method of producing many of the same shapes with a plaster mold and a metal template.

Kaki glaze Traditional glaze from the village of Mashiko, Japan. Created by grinding local rock; according to Shoji Hamada it was named for the color that a persimmon is on October 24.

Kaolin Anglicized form of the Chinese word for china clay. Pure kaolin is a white-burning, high-firing natural clay that is the essential component of porcelain bodies and an ingredient in many glazes.

Kick wheel A potter's machine for working clay with a centrifugal motion propelled by kicking.

Kiln Furnace for firing clay, slumping glass, or melting enamels; studio kilns can achieve temperatures up to 2500° F (1370° C). They can be fueled carbonaceously, organically, or electrically.

Kiln furniture Refractory slabs, posts, supports (called setters) for holding ware in the kiln, handmade or purchased.

Kiln wash Half clay, half silica, mixed with water to coat kiln shelves.

Leather-hard Cheese-hard stage which clay reaches before being bone-dry; stiff enough to support itself, but still can be altered.

Local reduction A means of removing oxygen from glazes for "reduction firing" without changing the kiln fuel; material is added such as 1% or more 600 mesh silicon carbide to a glaze, particularly for electric kilns, yielding reduction-style color change.

Luster A brilliant, iridescent metallic film on glaze, formed from certain metallic salts at a specific temperature in a reduced atmosphere, usually on the cooling side of the firing cycle.

Luting A method of putting together coils, slabs, or other clay forms in the wet or leather-hard stage by cross-hatching and moistening; the same as scoring.

Majolica The decorative application of coloring oxides and stains over an unfired glaze that fuses into the base glaze during the firing, leaving fuzzy edges. The term comes from the Balearic island of Majorca.

Majolica glaze An opaque glaze with a glossy surface, usually white, generally opacified by tin oxide; a base for colored stain or overglaze decoration.

Matt Dull, non-reflective surface; in the case of glaze, due to deliberate composition or immature firing.

Mesh Holes per square inch in any screen, used for screening clay or glaze.

Millefiore A traditional technique in glass and clay where several, or many, slabs of color are combined in patterns, and cut through in cross-section to make other forms.

Mishima Carved decoration in leather-hard clay, covered with engobe and rubbed off when drier, leaving engobe inlaid in the carving.

Mold Usually a plaster form, single or multi-pieced, which will be used to reproduce any number of accurate copies of the original model in clay or plaster.

Neutral atmosphere An atmosphere in a kiln that is neither completely oxidizing nor completely reducing.

Off-the-hump Method of throwing small forms consecutively from one large mound of clay.

Once-firing Glazing leather-hard or bone-dry ware and firing to maturing temperature (this skips the first bisquing); frequently used in commercial production; often the method in salt or wood firing.

Oxidation, Oxidizing fire Opposite of a reducing fire; the firing of a kiln where combustion of the fuel is complete.

Paint To apply anything with a brush; a term for colored or white pigment for decorating pots without kiln firing.

Peephole A view or observation hole in the wall or door of a kiln; it should be large enough to see into the kiln easily during the firing; also used for pulling draw trials and tests during the firing.

Pinching Moving and shaping clay with the fingers.

Pitfire A hole in the ground for firing primitive-style, or a pit built up on the ground with bricks, ceramic fiber, or other, and filled with any flammable material.

Plaster The mineral gypsum, with the chemical composition of calcium sulfate, used for clay/mold reproduction and as a work surface.

Plasticity Workability; clay is the only mineral having real plasticity, meaning the ability to form into any shape, and to get progressively harder in the same shape on being fired to 1300° F (700° C) and above. Other materials, such as talc, can be said to have claylike plasticity.

Porcelain Mechanically strong, hard, frequently translucent, fired clay body with 0% absorption; the strongest of all clay bodies unless very thin.

Pottery A loosely used term; often means earthenware or just any clay piece that has been fired.

Pressing Forming plastic clay in a plaster mold or other form, by laying it against the mold face.

Profile line Outside or inside line; the line formed when shape bisects space.

Pyrometer A calibrating instrument on the outside of a kiln, used with a thermocouple inside the kiln to measure temperature during the firing.

Raku A firing or a type of ware; porous, groggy ware, with or without a glaze, put into and pulled out of a hot fire and sometimes smoked. Developed in Japan in the 1600s.

Raw glaze Unfired glaze.

Reduction, Reducing fire Opposite of an oxidation fire; the firing of a kiln with an atmosphere of reduced oxygen, where combustion of the fuel is incomplete. Copper in reduction is ox-blood red, in oxidation green; iron in reduction is celadon, in oxidation amber yellow, or brown. See also **Local reduction**

Refractory Resistant to melting or fusion; a substance that raises the melting point of another material. Refractory materials are the basis of high temperature ceramics.

Resist Wax, varnish, latex, or other substance applied in pattern on a clay or glaze surface to cover an area while the background is treated by another material or color.

Sagger An enclosure for firing pots to achieve various effects.

Salt firing Rock salt is thrown into the fire at the maturing temperature of the clay until an "orange-peel" clear glaze appears on the ware.

Sawdust firing Firing with sawdust to reduce oxygen and blacken the ware.

Scoring A cross-hatch and moistening method of putting together coils and slabs in the wet or leather-hard; the same as luting.

Sgraffito A design scratched through one surface to another.

Shards Fragments of pottery; the state in which many clay works are found.

Shrinkage Contraction of clays or bodies in drying and firing, caused by the loss of physical and chemical water and the achieving of molecular density.

Silica Oxide of silicon, SiO_2; found abundantly in nature as quartz, sand, and flint; the most essential oxide in ceramics; the glass-forming oxide.

Silicon carbide Used in kiln furniture for high temperatures; ground fine, it can be added to glaze to produce a reduction of oxygen in an oxidizing fire, causing color change of metallic oxides such as copper and iron.

Slab Flat piece of clay from which shapes can be fabricated.

Slip A suspension of ceramic materials in water; generally refers to casting slip for molds; can mean a liquid clay engobe for decorating or a glaze slip.

Slurry Thick suspension of one or more ceramic materials in water; usually refers to slushy clay.

Spiral wedging Kneading clay with a pivoting motion to remove air pockets and make the clay mix homogeneous, ready to work.

Stain Watercolor wash on bisque with metallic coloring oxides or commercial glaze stains; also a term referring to "stain" colors.

Stoneware Hard, dense, and durable ware generally fired to 2150° F (1180° C) or above; a body with 0 to 5% absorption, regardless of firing temperature.

Tenmoku Japanese name for a type of glaze used especially by the Chinese during the Sung Dynasty; glaze whose rich black appearance is caused by an overabundance of iron oxide.

Terracotta Term used to describe rust-red clays; an art historian's term for low fired, unglazed, generally red-colored ware; a color.

Terra sigillata Low-fired clay work with sheen resulting from burnishing; an extraordinarily fine-ground clay suspension in water that shines when applied as a coating. It is always fired at low temperature to preserve the shine. It is also the surface on Attic Greek wares.

Thermocouple A pair of wires of different metals (platinum and rhodium or, for low temperature, chrome-alumel) twisted together and sealed at one end. The sealed end registers the temperature; the reading is transmitted through the wires to a connector and thence via insulated wiring to the pyrometer, where the reading is measured in degrees.

Throwing The process of forming pieces on a revolving potter's wheel from solid lumps of clay into hollow forms.

Trailing A method of decorating with engobe or glaze squeezed out of a bulb from a small orifice or poured from a narrow lip.

Translucency Ability to transmit scattered light, not quite transparent.

Transparent Clear, like window glass; can be colored or colorless. Texture or decoration instantly shows through a transparent glaze.

Underglaze or G.S. Pigments designated as underglaze stains, overglaze stains, and body stains, according to usage. Also a name used by commercial manufacturers for a glaze product that stays put and does not melt.

Updraft kiln Kiln in which the fire is underneath or at the low end of the tube or chamber; heat moves up through the ware and out of a flue at the top.

Viscosity Property of a flow; a highly viscous glaze is "stiff" and does not flow much during firing. A glaze of low viscosity is fluid, and can cause running or glaze decoration to become fluid in firing.

Vitreous Glass-like, hard, dense.

Wax Melted paraffin wax (which is not water-soluble), mixed with kerosene or benzine for ease of application, used for resist techniques; also commercially produced water-soluble waxes such as Ceremul A.

Wedging Kneading clay to expel air and make the mass homogeneous for hand processes.

Whiteware All ware with a white or ivory clay body after firing; industrial term.

LIST OF ARTISTS

Living artists; deceased artists are listed at end

Ann Agee 4
Teaching: Princeton University, New Jersey
Studio: Princeton, New Jersey

Beate Andersen 194
Studio: Copenhagen, Denmark

Dan Anderson 174
Teaching: Southern Illinois University
   at Edwardsville
Studio: Edwardsville, Illinois

Carol Aoki 190
Studio: New York City

Linda Arbuckle 88
Teaching: University of Florida at Gainsville
Studio: Micanophy, Florida

Doug Baldwin 49
Retired: Maryland Institute of Art,
   Baltimore, Maryland
Studio: Missoula, Montana

John Balistreri 160
Teaching: Bowling Green State University,
   Bowling Green, Ohio
Studio: Bowling Green, Ohio

Bennett Bean 145
Studio: Blairstown, New Jersey

Lynda Benglis 199
Studio: Santa Fe, New Mexico

Juris Bergins 90
Studio: Latvia, Lithuania

Rick Berman 172
Teaching: Pace Academy, Georgia
Studio: Atlanta, Georgia

Paul Berube 144
Teaching: University of Massachusetts
Studio: Amherst, Massachusetts

David Beumée front cover, 129
Studio: Lafayette, Colorado

Karin Bjorquist 60
Studio: Gustavsberg, Sweden

Sandra Black 40
Studio: Perth, Australia

Mary Jo Bole 201
Teaching: Ohio State University
Studio: Columbus, Ohio

Jill Bonovitz 222
Studio: Philadelphia, Pennsylvania

Ruth Borgenicht 103
Studio: Glen Ridge, New Jersey

Joe Bova 182
Teaching: Ohio University, Athens
Studio: Guysville, Ohio

George Bowes 77
Studio: Davis, California

Robert Brady 4
Teaching: California State University, Sacramento
Studio: Berkeley, California

Stephen Braun 188
Studio: Williams, Oregon

Regis Brodie 152
Teaching: Skidmore College
Studio: Saratoga Springs, New York

Seth Cardew 140
Studio: Wenford Bridge, Cornwall, UK

Nino Caruso 14
Studio: Rome, Italy

Claudi Casanovas 21
Studio: Girona, Spain

Paul Chaleff 176
Studio: Pine Plains, New York

Ruth Chambers 104
Teaching: University of Regina,
   Saskatchewan, Canada
Studio: Saskatchewan, Canada

Claude Champy 144
Studio: Plaisir, France

Claire Clark 186
Retired, New York City Public Schools
Studio: New York City

Jimmy Clark 171
Studio: Peters Valley, New Jersey

Elaine Coleman 165
Studio: Henderson, Nevada

Greg Daly 166
Studio: Cowra, Australia

P.R. Daroz 63, 100
Studio: New Delhi, India

Don Davis 93
Studio: Asheville, North Carolina

Tim De Rose 95
Studio: Wilton Pottery, Ontario, Canada

Stephen De Staebler 97
Teaching: California State University,
   San Francisco
Studio: San Francisco, California

Josh DeWeese 95
Studio: Archie Bray, Helena, Montana

Richard DeVore 43, 112
Studio: Fort Collins, Colorado

Jane Dillon 74
Studio: Niwot, Colorado

Marylyn Dintenfass 15, 128
Studio: New York City

Joanne Emelock 46
Studio: Tempe, Arizona

Bill Farrell 144
Teaching: Chicago Art Institute
Studio: Galena, Illinois

Cathy Fleckstein 124
Studio: Kiel, Germany

Ron Fondaw 25
Teaching: Webster University
Studio: St. Louis, Missouri

Michael Frimkess 18, 77
Studio: Venice, California

Sylvia Fugmann 130
Studio: Phoenix, Arizona

Verne Funk 140
Studio: San Antonio, Texas

Ron Gallas 130
Teaching: St. Olaf College, Northfield, Minnesota
Studio: Northfield, Minnesota

Dolores Lewis Garcia 171
Studio: San Fidel, New Mexico

Angel Garraza 196
Teaching: University of País Vasco, Bilbao
Studio: Mungia-Vizcaya, Spain

Marea Gazzard 44
Studio: Sydney, Australia

John Glick back cover, 193
Studio: Farmington Hills, Michigan

Juan Granados 195
Teaching: School of Art at Texas Tech
   University, Lubbock, Texas
Studio: Lubbock, Texas

Gerit Grimm 106
Studio: Halle an der Saale, Germany

Nedda Guidi 203
Studio: Rome, Italy

Shinsaku Hamada 75
Studio: Mashiko, Japan

Ernst Häusermann 4
Studio: Lenzburg, Switzerland

Graham Hay 27, 28, 29
Studio: Perth, Australia

Peter Hayes 35, 64
Studio: Bath, UK

Otto Heino 76
Studio: Ojai, California

Wayne Higby 193
Teaching: New York State College of Ceramics
Studio: Alfred, New York

Chuck Hindes 170
Teaching: University of Iowa
Studio: Iowa City, Iowa

Rick Hirsch 156, 194
Teaching: School for American Craftsmen, RIT
Studio: Churchville, New York

Bryan Hiveley 26
Teaching: International Fine Arts College, Miami, Florida
Studio: Miami, Florida

Curtis Hoard 95
Retired, University of Minnesota
Studio: Tetonia, Idaho

Nina Hole 194
Studio: Skaelskør, Denmark

Deborah Horrell 202
Studio: Portland, Oregon

Bruce Howdle 42
Studio: Mineral Point, Wisconsin

Tom Hubert 180
Teaching: Mercyhurst College, Erie
Studio: Erie, Pennsylvania

Woody Hughes 94
Studio: Wading River, New York

Hwang Jeng-Daw 92
Studio: Tainan, Taiwan

Sylvia Hyman 196
Studio: Nashville, Tennessee

Sadashi Inuzuka 204
Teaching: University of Michigan
Studio: Ann Arbor, Michigan

Jeff Irwin 102
Teaching: Grossmont College, Grossmont, California
Studio: San Diego, California

Ingrid Jacobsen 186
Studio: Berlin, Germany

Nidhi Jalan 104
Studio: Brooklyn, New York

Mai Järmut 213
Studio: Tallinn, Estonia

Nick Joerling 90
Studio: Penland, North Carolina

Randy J. Johnston 92
Retired, University of Wisconsin, River Falls
Studio: River Falls, Wisconsin

Nancy Jurs 113
Studio: Scottsville, New York

Jun Kaneko 25, 98, 110, 117, 143, 156
Studio: Omaha, Nebraska

Elena Karina 152
Studio: Los Angeles, California

Elaine Katzer 112
Studio: San Pedro, California

Katie Kazan 119
Studio: Madison, Wisconsin

Pat Kenny Lopez 65
Studio: Santa Barbara, California

Bernard Kerr 203
Studio: Perth, Western Australia

Bob Kinzie 86, 87
Studio: Aptos, California

Gudrun Klix 119
Teaching: University of Sydney, Australia
Studio: Balmain, Australia

Karen Koblitz 148
Teaching: University of Southern California
Studio: Los Angeles, California

Ron Kovatch 41
Teaching: University of Illinois
Studio: Urbana, Illinois

Charles Krafft 151
Studio: Seattle, Washington

Elisabeth van Krogh 34
Studio: Bornheim, Norway

Eva Kwong 124
Studio: Kent, Ohio

Jay LaCouture 174
Teaching: Salve Regina University
Studio: Carolina, Rhode Island

Peter Lane 129
Studio: Hampshire, UK

Elisabeth Langsch 194
Studio: Zurich, Switzerland

Dora De Larios 4
Studio: Santa Monica, California

Bruno Lavadiere 15
Studio: Hadley, New York

Les Lawrence 151
Teaching: Grossmont College
Studio: El Cajon, California

Patricia Lay 200
Teaching: Montclair State College
Studio: Jersey City, New Jersey

Jennifer Lee 46
Studio: London, UK

Jim Leedy 107
Teaching: Kansas City Art Institute
Studio: Kansas City, Missouri

Enid Legros-Wise 23
Studio: Quebec, Canada

Ah Leon 118
Studio: Taipei, Taiwan

Marc Leuthold 119
Teaching: State University of New York at Potsdam
Studio: Potsdam, New York

Li Jiansheng ("Jackson Lee") 106, 234
Studio: Toronto, Canada, and San Bao, Jingdezhen, China

Ole Lislerud 192
Teaching: National Academy of Art and Design, Oslo, Norway
Studio: Alesund, Norway

Lu Pin-chang 199
Teaching: Central Academy of Fine Arts, Beijing, China
Studio: Beijing, China

Michael Lucero 185
Studio: New York City

Luo Xiao-Ping 113, 181, 234
Teaching: YiXing Ceramic Art Institute, China
Studio: Mesa, Arizona; Yi Xing and Shanghai, China

Val Lyle 112
Studio: Bristol, Tennessee

Marilyn Lysohir 204
Studio: Moscow, Idaho

Warren MacKenzie 122
Retired, University of Minnesota
Studio: Stillwater, Minnesota

Ma Angels Domingo Laplana (Madola) 174
Sudio: Barcelona, Spain

James Makins 120
Teaching: Philadelphia College of Art
Studio: Tokoname, Japan

Rick Malmgren 89, 141
Studio: Lothian, Maryland

Nina Malterud 94
Studio: Bergen, Norway

Kirk Mangus 4, 14
Teaching: Kent State University
Studio: Kent, Ohio

Janet Mansfield 174
Studio: Gulgong, NSW, Australia

Bodil Manz 23
Studio: Horve, Denmark

Susan Margin 104
Studio: Santa Fe, New Mexico

John Mason 17, 18, 37, 50, 103, 110, 111, 114, 130, 139, 153, 189
Retired, Hunter College, City University of New York
Studio: Los Angeles, California

Karen Massaro 61
Studio: Santa Cruz, California

Patriciu Mateiescu 61
Studio: Dayton, New Jersey

Frank Matranga 109
Studio: Manhattan Beach, California

Berry Matthews 201
Teaching: State University of New York
at Plattsburgh
Studio: Plattsburgh, New York

John McCuistion 56
Teaching: University of Puget Sound,
Tacoma, Washington
Studio: University Place, Washington

Harrison McIntosh 91
Studio: Claremont, California

Ray Meeker 91, 161
Studio: Pondicherry, South India

Jim Melchert 191
Studio: Oakland, California

David Middlebrook 50
Teaching: California State University at San Jose
Studio: San Jose, California

Greg Miller 88
Studio: Hirtshals, Denmark

Sequoia Miller 229
Studio: Olympia, Washington

Keisuke Mizuno 115
Teaching: St. Cloud State University,
Minnesota
Studio: St. Cloud, Minnesota

Emma Lewis Mitchell 55, 171
Studio: San Fidel, New Mexico

Cara Moczygemba 184
Studio: Vista, California

Steven Montgomery 196
Studio: New York City

Ron Nagle 181
Teaching: Mills College, Oakland
Studio: Oakland, California

Màrta Nagy 48
Studio: Pecs, Hungary

Sylvia Nagy 48, 129
Studio: New York City

Charles Nalle 64
Studio: Melbourne, Florida

Barbara Nanning Frontispiece
Studio: Amsterdam, The Netherlands

Nora Naranjo-Morse 195
Studio: Santa Clara Pueblo, New Mexico

Andy Nasisse 77
Teaching: University of Georgia
Studio: Athens, Georgia

Farraday Newsome 92
Studio: Mesa, Arizona

Jean Cappadonna Nichols 185
Studio: Fort Myers, Florida

Nobuhito Nishigawara 23
Teaching: California State University
at Fullerton
Studio: Fullerton, California

Richard Notkin 62
Studio: Helena, Montana

Magdalene Odundo 21
Studio: Hampshire, UK

Gilda Oliver 59
Studio: Baltimore, Maryland

Fred Olsen 77
Studio: Mountain Center, California

Judy Onofrio 108
Studio: Rochester, Minnesota

Jeanne Otis 122
Retired, Arizona State University
Studio: Tempe, Arizona

Ria Ovans 182
Studio: Laguna, California

Marlene Ferrell Parillo 182
Studio: Lincolndale, New York

Dennis Parks 180
Studio: Tuscarora, Nevada

Rina Peleg 15
Studio: New York City

Jan Peterson 52, 53, 60
Studio: Scottsdale, Arizona

Susan Peterson 76, 102, 119, 158, 166, 168
Retired, Hunter College, City University
of New York
Studio: Scottsdale, Arizona

Taäg Peterson 87
Studio: Arlee, Montana

Henry Pim 189
Studio: Dublin, Ireland

E. Jane Pleak 137
Teaching: Georgia Southern University
Studio: Statesboro, Georgia

Faith Banks Porter 137
Studio: Los Angeles, California

Carla Potter 44
Studio: Anchorage, Alaska

Ken Price 17, 18
Retired, University of Southern California
Studio: Taos, New Mexico, and
Venice, California

Liz Quackenbush 141
Teaching: Penn State University
Studio: Pleasant Gap, Pennsylvania

Juan Quesada 180
Studio: Mata Ortiz, Casas Grande, Mexico

Elsa Rady 67
Studio: Venice, California

Brian Ransom 14
Studio: St. Petersburg, Florida

Don Reitz 90, 173, 176
Retired, University of Wisconsin
Studio: Clarkdale, Arizona

Paula Rice 111, 171
Teaching: Northern Arizona State University
Studio: Flagstaff, Arizona

Sally Resnik Rockriver 149
Studio: Chapel Hill, North Carolina

Annabeth Rosen 21
Teaching: University of California at Davis
Studio: Davis, California

Betsy Rosenmiller 180
Studio: Tempe, Arizona

Carol Rossman 19
Studio: Dundas, Canada

Jerry Rothman 18, 101, 110, 199
Retired, California State University at
Fullerton
Studio: San Miguel d'Alende, Mexico

Anthony Rubino 190
Teaching: New York City Public Schools
Studio: Jamaica, New York

Adrian Saxe 152
Teaching: University of California at
Los Angeles
Studio: Los Angeles, California

Jeff Schlanger 186
Studio: New Rochelle, New York

Imre Schrammel 188
Studio: Budapest, Hungary

Virginia Scotchie 58
Teaching: University of South Carolina
Studio: Columbus, South Carolina

Nancy Selvin 151
Teaching: Laney College
Studio: Berkeley, California

Vaslav Serak 190
Studio: Prague, Czech Republic

Shao Junya 51
Studio: Mesa, Arizona, and Jingdezhen,
China

Richard Shaw 196
Teaching: University of California, Berkeley
Studio: Fairfax, California

Anat Shiftan 130
Teaching: State University of New York,
New Paltz
Studio: New Paltz, New York

Linda Sikora 91
Teaching: Alfred University, New York
Studio: Houston, Minnesota

Sandy Simon 92
Studio: Berkeley, California

Kripal Singh 14, 157
Studio: Jaipur, India

Richard Slee 188
Teaching: Camberwell College of Arts, London
Studio: Brighton, UK

Matt Sleightholm 162
Studio: Gunnison, Colorado

David Smith 182
Teaching: Edgewood College, Madison, Wisconsin
Studio: Stoughton, Wisconsin

Deborah Smith 91
Studio: Pondicherry, South India

Nan Smith 203
Teaching: University of Florida at Gainsville
Studio: Gainsville, Florida

Richard Zane Smith 124
Studio: Glorieta, New Mexico

Conrad Snider 111, 234
Studio: Newton, Kansas

Paul Soldner 18, 133, 172
Retired, Scripps College, Claremont
Studio: Aspen, Colorado

Barbara Sorensen 38
Studio: Winter Park, Florida/Snowmass Village, Colorado

Fred Spaulding 205
Teaching: Victoria College, Victoria, Texas
Studio: Victoria, Texas

Linda Speranza 57
Teaching: Mesa Community College
Studio: Mesa, Arizona

Victor Spinski 61
Teaching: University of Delaware
Studio: Newark, Delaware

Chris Staley 94
Teaching: Penn State University
Studio: State College, Pennsylvania

John Stephenson 195
Retired, University of Michigan
Studio: Ann Arbor, Michigan

Susanne Stephenson 122
Retired, Eastern Michigan University
Studio: Ann Arbor, Michigan

Bill Stewart 196
Studio: Hamlin, New York

DongHee Suh 98
Teaching: Kon Kuk University, Seoul, Korea
Studio: Seoul, Korea

Tom Supensky 182
Retired, Towson State University
Studio: Baltimore, Maryland

Øyvind Suul 196
Studio: Oslo, Norway

Goro Suzuki 176
Studio: Aichi, Japan

Toshiko Takaezu 21, 76, 85
Retired, Princeton University
Studio: Quakertown, New Jersey

Akio Takamori 187
Teaching: University of Washington
Studio: Seattle, Washington

Joan Takayama-Ogawa 153
Studio: Pasadena, California

Hirotsune Tashima 99
Teaching: Pima Community College, Tucson
Studio: Tucson, Arizona

Sandra Taylor 149
Studio: Buccarumbi, NSW, Australia

Neil Tetkowski 87
Studio: New York City

Marit Tingleff 190
Studio: Honefoss, Norway

Xavier Toubes 199
Teaching: The School Art Institute of Chicago
Studio: Chicago, Illinois

Jack Troy 88
Teaching: Juniata College, Huntingdon, Pennsylvania
Studio: Huntingdon, Pennsylvania

Edoardo Vega 200
Studio: Cuenca, Ecuador

Ann Adair Voulkos 182
Studio: Oakland, California

Patti Warashina 184
Teaching: University of Washington
Studio: Seattle, Washington

Kurt Weiser 150
Teaching: Arizona State University
Studio: Tempe, Arizona

Julie Wills 162
Studio: Gunnison, Colorado

Matthew Wilt 95
Studio: Philadelphia, Pennsylvania

Etta Winigrad 183
Studio: Paoli, Pennsylvania

Paula Winokur 48, 193
Teaching: Beaver College, Glenside, Pennsylvania
Studio: Horsham, Pennsylvania

Robert Winokur 174
Teaching: Tyler School of Art
Studio: Horsham, Pennsylvania

Lisa Wolkow 114
Studio: Madison, Connecticut

Marie Woo 173
Studio: N. Bloomfield, Michigan

Betty Woodman 13, 105
Studio: New York City and Antella, Italy

Patty Wouters 161
Studio: Brasschaat, Belgium

Mutsuo Yanagihara 23
Studio: Kyoto, Japan

Yule Yilmambaşar 191
Studio: Istanbul, Turkey

Sun-Koo Yuh 106
Teaching: University of Georgia, Athens, Georgia
Studio: Athens, Georgia

Zhang Wanxin 110
Teaching: San Francisco Academy of Art University
Studio: San Francisco, California

Dale Zheutlin 191
Studio: New Rochelle, New York

Zhou Ding-Fang 26
Studio: YiXing, China

Guangzhou "Po" Zhou 39, 234
Studio: San Jose, California

Some artists whose work is represented in this book are now deceased and do not feature in the preceding list:

Ralph Bacerra, Eagle Rock, California 153

Christine Federighi, Miami, Florida 102

Ken Ferguson, Shawnee Mission, Kansas 160

Shoji Hamada, Mashiko, Japan 17, 18, 125, 148, 157

Viveka Heino, Ojai, California 76

Bernard Leach, St Ives, Cornwall, UK 17, 18, 40

Marilyn Levine, Oakland, California 48

Lucy M. Lewis, Acoma Pueblo, New Mexico 4, 45, 55, 171

Glen Lukens, Los Angeles, California 143

Maria Martinez, San Ildefonso Pueblo, New Mexico 44, 170

Gertraud Möhwald, Halle, Germany 179

Tzaro Shimaoka, Mashiko, Japan 124

Henry Takamoto, 18

Robert Turner, Sandy Springs, Maryland 156

Peter Voulkos, Berkeley, California 10, 17, 18, 111, 179, 181

Artists' countries are indicated in the captions, except for American artists which are the majority.

RESIDENCIES

When you have learned quite a lot about ceramics and are ready to work on your own, perhaps before establishing your own studio, assisting someone else, working in industry, or teaching, you may want the opportunity of a residency for several months. Typically the host provides housing, studio space, materials, firing, perhaps exhibition, perhaps monetary subsidy. Well-known artists are often invited and subsidized to do residencies (send your portfolio) or less known ones can pay to work. Additional benefits to you are: publicity, networking, comradeship. Some of the best known in the USA and international follow; more listings can be found using the online resources included below.

USA
Anderson Center
163 Tower View Drive
P.O. Box 406
Red Wing, Minnesota 55066 ??
TEL 651 388 2009
http://www.andersoncenter.org

Anderson Ranch Arts Center
PO Box 5598
Snowmass Village, Colorado 81615
TEL 970 923 3181
FAX 970 923 3871
http://www.andersonranch.org

Archie Bray Foundation for the Ceramic
   Arts
2915 Country Club Ave
Helena, Montana 59602
TEL 406 443 3502
FAX 406 443 0934
http://www.archiebray.org

Arrowmont School of Arts and Crafts
556 Parkway
PO Box 567
Gatlinburg, TN 37738
TEL 865 436 5860
http://www.arrowmont.org

Clay Art Center
40 Beech Street
Port Chester, NY 10573
TEL 914 937 2047
FAX 914 935 1205
http://www.clayartcenter.org

The Clay Studio
139 N. 2nd St
Philadelphia, PA 19106
TEL 215 925 3453
FAX 215 925 7774

Genesee Center for the Arts and Education
713 Monroe Avenue
Rochester, NY 14607
TEL 585 244 1730
http://www.geneseearts.org

Hambidge Center for Creative Arts and
   Sciences
PO Box 339
Rabun Gap, GA 30568
TEL 706 746 5718
FAX 706 746 9933
http://www.hambidge.org

Haystack Mountain School of Crafts
PO Box 518
Deer Isle, Maine 04627
TEL 207 348 2306
FAX 207 348 2307
http://www.haystack-mtn.org

Joe L. Evins Appalachian Center for Craft
Tennessee Tech University
1560 Craft Center Drive
Smithville TN 37166
TEL 931 372 3051
FAX 615 597 6803
http://www.tntech.edu/craftcenter

John Michael Kohler Arts Center
608 New York Avenue
Sheboygan, WI 53081
TEL 920 458 6144
FAX 920 458 4473
http://www.jmkac.org

Lawrence Art Center
940 New Hampshire St.
Lawrence, Kansas 66044
TEL 785 843 2787
http://www.lawrenceartscenter.com

Northern Clay Center
2424 Franklin Avenue East
Minneapolis MN 55406
TEL 612 339 8007
FAX 612 339 0592
http://www.northernclaycenter.org

Nottingham Center for the Arts
P.O. Box 460
San Marcos, CA 92079
http://www.nottinghamarts.org

Oregon College of Art and Craft
8245 S.W. Barnes Road
Portland, OR 97225
TEL 503 297 5544
FAX 503 297 3155
http://www.ocac.edu

Penland School of Crafts
Post Office Box 37
Penland NC 28765-0037
TEL 828 765 2359
FAX 828 765 7389
http://www.penland.org

Peters Valley Craft Center
19 Kuhn Rd.
Layton, NJ 07851
TEL 973 948 5200
FAX 973 948 0011
http://www.pvcrafts.org

Red Lodge Clay Center
PO Box 1527
Red Lodge, Montana 59068
TEL 406 446 3993
http://redlodgeclaycenter.com

Watershed Center for the Ceramic Arts
19 Brick Hill Rd.
Newcastle, ME 04553
TEL 207 882 6075
FAX 207 882 6045
http://www.watershedceramics.org

INTERNATIONAL
A.I.R.- Vallauris
Place Lisnard
1 Boulevard des Deux Vallons
06220 Vallauris
France
TEL +33(0) 493 646 550
http://www.air-vallauris.org

Artigas Foundation
Cami del Raco s/n
Gallifa 08146
Barcelona
Spain
TEL +34 93 866 2434
FAX +34 93 866 2434

Banff Centre
Box 1020
Banff, Alberta
Canada T1L 1H5
TEL: 403 762 6100
http://www.banffcentre.ca

Europees Keramisch Werkcentrum (The European Ceramic Work Center)
Zuid-Willemsvaart 215
5211 SG's-Hertogenbosch
The Netherlands
TEL 011 31 0 73124500
http://www.ekwc.nl

Guldagergaard
International Ceramic Research Center—Denmark
Heilmannsvej 31A
DK-4230 Skælskør
TEL +455 819 0016
FAX +455 819 0037
http://www.ceramic.dk

International Ceramics Studio
H6000 Kecskemét
Kdpolna u, IT
Hungary
TEL + 36 76 486867
FAX + 36 76 482223
http://www.icshu.org

The Pottery Workshop
Artists in Residency Program
2nd Floor, 220 Taikang Lu
Shanghai, 200025
P.R. China
TEL 8621 6445 0902
FAX 8621 6445 0937
http://www.potteryworkshop.com.cn

Rufford Craft Centre
Rufford Country Park
Ollerton, Newark
Nottinghamshire, UK
NG22 9DF
TEL 01623 822944
FAX 01623 825919
http://www.ruffordceramiccentre.org.uk

Sanbao Ceramic Art Institute at Jingdezhen
PO Box 1000
Jingdezhen, Jiangxi Province, 333001
P.R. China
TEL 86 798 8483665
FAX 86 798 8496513

or

Sanbao Ceramic Art Institute at Jingdezhen
Ceramic Art Residency
14 Courtwright Rd.
Etobicoke
Ontario 49C 4B4
Canada
TEL/FAX 416 695 3607
http://www.chinaclayart.com

The Foundation of Shigaraki Ceramic Cultural Park
2188-7 Shigarakicho-Chokushi
Koka City Shiga Pref.
Japan 529-1804
TEL +81 748 83 0909
FAX +81 748 83 1193
http://sccp.main.jp

MORE RESIDENCIES USA AND INTERNATIONAL can be found on the internet by accessing various cities, countries, and other titles. Interestingly, new residencies, or ones we have not yet heard of, are cropping up all the time. Let us know if you have been to or heard of one we have not listed here.

The International Academy of Ceramics (FAC) is a juried organization of ceramic artists, writers, curators, and the like. Inquire regarding the biennial conference somewhere in the world. In 2008 it was held in Xian, China. The usual attendance is several hundred.

NCECA, the National Ceramic Education Council of America, can supply all kinds of international ceramic data such as phone numbers and email addresses; inquire about the annual conference. Conference registration can be 6,000 members.

SEE ALSO
Alliance of Artists Communities
http://www.artistcommunities.org

Ceramics Monthly
http://www.ceramicsmonthly.com

Worldwide Network of Artists Residencies
http://www.resartis.org

INFORMATION SOURCES

Most countries have a Craft Council or similar organization; some have a museum or gallery associated with the organization, such as the American Craft Council on Spring Street and the Museum of Arts & Design at Columbus Circle in New York City, USA. The British Crafts Council is in Pentonville Road, London, with a gallery in the V&A Museum. Also in London is the Craft Potters' Association and its shop and gallery in Marshall Street. Generally these craft organizations provide resource materials such as slides, movies, videos, and publications. Ceramics galleries feature in almost every corner of the world.

The International Academy of Ceramics (IAC) headquarters are in Geneva, Switzerland, at the Ariana Museum.

Suppliers of ceramic materials and companies that manufacture ceramic equipment are fixtures in most countries. Their catalogs and data books give necessary information about their products. Clay mines, frit and stain manufacturers provide important technical brochures. Finally, commercially prepared clay bodies, under- and overglaze pigments, and ready-to-use glazes, as well as helpful information bulletins, are supplied universally by these commercial corporations.

A wealth of ceramic information is available online. Search for ceramic suppliers in your area or for specialty items from around the globe. Glaze databases and exhibit opportunities can also be easily found via a simple web search. All major ceramic organizations, as well as many potters' groups and university departments, have websites and newsletters. Current discussions, along with over ten years of archives from the clay art discussion group, can be found at potters.org. Here you will find an abundance of technical and aesthetic information. Check the website of your favorite ceramic magazine for additional resources.

Ceramics magazines around the world include:

AUSTRALIA
Ceramics: Art and Perception and *Ceramics Technical*
120 Glenmore Rd.
Paddington, Sydney
NSW 2021
www.ceramicart.com.au

Craft Art International
P.O. Box 363
Neutral Bay Junction
NSW 2089
www.craftarts.com.au

Australian Ceramics
P.O. Box 274
Waverly NSW 2024
www.potteryinaustralia.com
www.australianceramics.com

CANADA
Fusion
The Ontario Clay and Glass Association
1444 Queen Street East
Toronto, Ontario M4L 1E1
TEL 416 438 8946
FAX 416 438 0192
http://www.clayandglass.on.ca

CHINA
China Ceramic Artist
Yuhuili No. 3
Chaoyang District, Beijing

Chinese Potters' Newsletter
Box 100600-9025
International Post Office
Beijing
TEL 8610 6438 331
FAX 8610 6437 5405
www.chinesepotters.com

CZECH REPUBLIC
Ceramic Art
P.O. Box 732
1121 Prague
TEL 420 2 663 11438

FRANCE
La Céramique Moderne
22 rue Le Brun
75013 Paris

La Revue de la Céramique et du Verre
61 rue Marconi
62880 Vendin-le-Vieil
www.revue-ceramique-verre.com

GERMANY
Keramik Magazin Europa
(editorial) Bensheimer Strasse 4a
D-64653 Lorsch (distribution)
Verlagsgesellschaft Ritterbach mbH
Rudolf-Diesel-Strasse 5-7
D-50226 Frechen
www.keramikmagazin.de

Neue Keramik
Steinreuschweg 2
56203 Höhr-Grenzhausen
www.neue-keramik.de

IRELAND
Ceramics Ireland
10 Down's Industrial Estate
Delgany, Co. Wicklow
http://ceramicsireland.org

ITALY
Ceramica Italiana Nell'Edilizia
Via Firenze 276
48018 Faenza

JAPAN
Honoho Geijutsu
Abe Publishing
4-30-12 Kamimeguro
Meguro-ku
Tokyo 153-0051

KOREA
Ceramic Art Monthly
1502-12 Seocho 3dong
Seocho-ku
Seoul, KOREA
TEL 02 597 8621
FAX 02 597 8039

NETHERLANDS
Keramiek
Zoutlaan 33
4731 MH Oudenbosch
www.nvk-keramiek.nl

Klei
Marterlaan 13
6705 CK Wageningen
www.klei.nl

NEW ZEALAND
New Zealand Potter
P.O. Box 881
Auckland

SPAIN
Bulleti Informatiu de Ceramica
Sant Honorat 7
Barcelona 08002

Ceramica
Apartado de Correos 7008
Passeo de las Acacias 9
Madrid 5

Revista Cerámica
Calle Guadiana, 38
28864 Ajalvir, Madrid
www.revistaceramica.com

TAIWAN
Ceramic Art
P.O. Box 47-74
Taipei

UK
Ceramic Review
25 Foubert's Place
London W1F 7QF
www.ceramicreview.com

Crafts
44a Pentonville Road
London N1 9BY
TEL 0 20 7806 2542
FAX 0 20 7837 0858
http://www.craftscouncil.org.uk

USA
American Ceramics
9 East 45 Street
New York, NY 10017-2403
TEL 212 661 4397
FAX 212 661 2389
www.americanceramics.org

American Ceramic Society Bulletin and *The Journal of the American Ceramic Society*
757 Brooksedge Plaza Drive
Westerville, OH 43081-6136
www.ceramics.org

American Craft Magazine
72 Spring Street
New York, NY 10012
www.craftcouncil.org

Ceramic Industry
5900 Harper Road, Suite 109
Solon, OH 44139
www.ceramicindustry.com

Ceramics Monthly
735 Ceramic Place
P.O. Box 6012
Westerville, OH 43086
www.ceramicsmonthly.com

Clay Times
15481 Second Street
P.O. Box 365
Waterford, VA 20197-0365
www.claytimes.com

Pottery Making Illustrated
735 Ceramic Place, Suite 100
Westerville, Ohio 43081
TEL 614 794 5890
FAX 614 794 5892
www.potterymaking.org

Studio Potter
P.O. Box 65
Goffstown, NH 03045
www.studiopotter.org

SPECIALIST SUPPLIES

Li Jiansheng ("Jackson Lee"): sanbaostudio.com

Luo Xiao Ping: xiaostudio.com

Zhou Guangzhou ("Po"):
chineseclayart.com

Soldner Clay Mixer: sold by Conrad Snider, Newton, Kansas

Soldner Potter's Wheel: sold by Stephanie Soldner, Claremont, California

Skutt Kilns: sold by Jim Skutt, Portland, Oregon

BIBLIOGRAPHY

Public libraries, museum libraries, university and college libraries are filled with books on ceramic art, history, and technology. Please make yourself aware of these great repositories at some point in your study. New treatises are continuously being added to the long list of in and out of print ceramic books—visit your local book stores often.

The following books will serve as a basic introduction to the general subject. We have tried to recommend only books that are currently in print; libraries will give you access to previously well known volumes.

Books of general interest

Atasoy, Nurhan and Raby, Julian. *Iznik, The Pottery of Ottoman Turkey*.
London: Laurence King, 1994

Bai, Ming. *Ceramic Art (8 vols.)*, with forewords by Janet Mansfield, Tony Franks, Wayne Higby, Susan Peterson, Judith Schwartz, Ole Lislerud.
China: Hebei Fine Arts Publishing House, 2005

Barley, Nigel. *Smashing Pots, Works of Clay from Africa*.
Washington, D.C.: Smithsonian Institution Press, 1994

Brown, Charlotte. *The Remarkable Potters of Seagrove*.
Asheville, North Carolina: Lark Books, 2005

Camusso, Lorenzo and Bortone, Sandra. *Ceramics of the World*.
New York: Harry N. Abrams, 1992

Cardew, Michael. *Pioneer Pottery*, revised edition.
New York: Oxford University Press, 1989

Charleston, Robert J. *World Ceramics*.
London: Hamlyn, 1968

Chinese Ceramics, a New Survey by the Asian Art Museum of San Francisco.
New York: Rizzoli International, 1996

Clark, Garth. *American Ceramics: 1876 to the Present*, revised edition.
New York: Abbeville Press, 1990

Clark, Garth. *The Potter's Art, A Complete History of Pottery in Britain*.
London: Phaidon, 1995

Del Vecchio, Mark. *Postmodern Ceramics*.
New York: Thames & Hudson, 2001

Ferrin, Leslie. *Teapots Transformed*.
Madison, WI: Guild Publishing, 2000

Fournier, Robert. *Illustrated Dictionary of Practical Pottery*, revised edition.
London: A. & C. Black, 1992

Frankel, Cyril. *Modern Pots, the Lisa Sainsbury Collection*.
London: Thames & Hudson, 2000

Lane, Peter. *Contemporary Studio Porcelain*, second edition.
Philadelphia: University of Pennsylvania Press, 2003

Lauria, Jo, et al. (Susan Peterson, Garth Clark, Peter Selz, Gretchen Adkins). *Color and Fire: Defining Moments in Studio Ceramics, 1950–2000*.
Los Angeles: LACMA; New York: Rizzoli International, 2000

Levin, Elaine. *The History of American Ceramics*.
New York: Harry N. Abrams, 1988

Mansfield, Janet. *Ceramics in the Environment*.
London: A. & C. Black; Westerville, OH: American Ceramic Society, 2005

McCready, Karen. *Art Deco and Modernist Ceramics*.
London: Thames & Hudson, 1995

Osterman, Matthias. *The Ceramic Narrative*.
London: A. & C. Black; Philadelphia: University of Pennsylvania Press, 2005

Perryman, Jane. *Traditional Pottery of India* (foreword by Susan Peterson).
London: A. & C. Black, 2000

Peterson, Susan. *The Craft and Art of Clay*, fourth edition.
New Jersey: Prentice Hall; New York: Overlook Press; London: Laurence King, 2002

Robison, Jim. *Large Scale Ceramics*, second edition.
London: A. & C. Black, 2005

Soetsu, Yanagi and Leach, Bernard. *The Unknown Craftsman: A Japanese Insight into Beauty*, revised edition.
New York and Tokyo: Kodansha International, 1997

Staubach, Suzanne. *Clay: the History and Evolution of Humankind's Relationship with Earth's Most Primal Element*.
New York: Penguin Group, 2005

Sweet, Marvin. *The Yixing Effect, Echoes of the Chinese Scholar*.
Beijing: Foreign Languages Press, 2006

Veronika, Alice Gunter, ed. *500 Figures in Clay: Ceramic Artists Celebrate the Human Form*.
Asheville, North Carolina: Lark Books, 2004

Zug, Charles. *Turners and Burners, The Folk Potters of North Carolina*.
Raleigh-Durham: University of North Carolina Press, 1986

Monographs

Beyond YiXing, the Ceramic Art of Ah Leon.
Taiwan: Purple Sands Publishers, 1998

Birks, Tony and Wingfield, Cornelia. *Bernard Leach, Hamada, and Their Circle*.
London: Phaidon, 1990

Birks, Tony. *Hans Coper*.
New York: Icon Editions, Harper & Row, 1983

Birks, Tony. *Lucie Rie*.
Radnor, PA: Chilton, 1989

Bischofberger, Bruno. *Ettore Sottsass, Ceramics*.
London: Thames & Hudson

Clark, Garth. *Gilded Vessel: The Lustrous Life and Art of Beatrice Wood*.
Madison, Wisconsin: Guild Publishing Company, 2001

Clark, Garth. *The Mad Potter of Biloxi: The Art and Life of George Ohr*.
New York: Abbeville Press, 1989

Cooper, Emmanuel. *Bernard Leach: Life and Work*.
London: Paul Mellon Centre, 2003

Cooper, Emmanuel. *Janet Leach— A Potter's Life*.
London: Ceramic Review Publishing, 2006

Failing, Patricia. *Howard Kottler*.
Seattle: University of Washington Press, 1995

Lewis, David. *Warren MacKenzie*.
New York: Kodansha International, 1991

Miro, Martha and Hepburn, Tony. *Robert Turner: Shaping Silence: A Life in Clay*.
Tokyo: Kodansha International, 2003

Peterson, Susan. *Feat of Clay: Five Decades of Jerry Rothman*.
California: Laguna Art Museum, 2003

Peterson, Susan. *Jun Kaneko*.
London: Laurence King, 2001

Peterson, Susan. *The Living Tradition of Maria Martinez*, revised edition.
New York: Kodansha International, 1996

Peterson, Susan. *Lucy M. Lewis, American Indian Potter.*
New York: Kodansha International, 1984
Peterson, Susan. *Pottery by American Indian Women: The Legacy of Generations.*
New York: Abbeville Press, 1997
Peterson, Susan. *Shoji Hamada, A Potter's Way and Work,* new edition.
London: A. & C. Black, 2004
Schlanger, Jeff and Takaezu, Toshiko. *Maija Grotell.*
Seattle: University of Washington Press, 1995
Slivka, Rose and Tsujimoto, Karen. *The Art of Peter Voulkos.*
New York: Kodansha International, 1995
Wood, Beatrice. *I Shock Myself.*
San Francisco: Chronicle Books, 2006

Technical books
Berensohn, Paulus. *Finding One's Way with Clay,* revised edition.
New York: Simon & Schuster, 1997
Braunfman, Steve. *Raku, A Practical Approach.*
Radnor, PA: Chilton, 1991

Cager-Smith, Alan. *Luster-ware.*
London: Faber & Faber, 1985
Creber, Diane. *Crystalline Glazes.*
London: A. & C. Black; Philadelphia: University of Pennsylvania Press, 2004
Daly, Greg. *Glazes and Glazing Techniques.*
Sydney, Australia: Kangaroo Press, 1995
Finch, Joe. *Kiln Construction, A Brick by Brick Approach.*
Philadelphia: University of Pennsylvania Press, 2006
Frith, Donald. *Mold Making for Ceramics.*
Radnor, PA: Chilton, 1985
Hamer, Frank and Janet. *A Potter's Dictionary of Materials and Techniques,* fifth edition.
Pittman/Watson-Guptill; London, A. & C. Black, 2004
Hopper, Robin. *The Ceramic Spectrum,* second edition.
Iola, WI: Krause Publications, 2001
Kingery, W. David and Vandiver, Pamela B. *Ceramic Masterpieces, Art, Structure, Technology.*
New York: The Free Press/Macmillan Inc., 1986

Martin, Andrew. *The Essential Guide to Mold Making and Slip Casting.*
Ashville, NC: Lark Books, 2007
Obstler, Mimi. *Out of the Earth into the Fire.*
Westerville, OH: The American Ceramic Society, 1996
Olsen, Frederick L. *The Kiln Book.*
London: A. & C. Black; Iola, WI: Krause Publications, 2001
Parmelee, C.W. and Harmon, C.G. *Ceramic Glazes,* second edition.
Boston: Cahners Books, 1973
Perryman, Jane. *Smoke Fired Pottery.*
London: A. & C. Black, 1995
Peterson, Susan. *Smashing Glazes.*
Guild Publishing, 2000
Rhodes, Daniel, revised by Hopper, Robin. *Clay and Glazes for the Potter.*
Iola, WI: Krause Publications, 2000
Rogers, Phil. *Ash Glazes.*
London: A. & C. Black, 2003
Troy, Jack. *Wood-Fired Stoneware and Porcelain.*
Pennsylvania: Chilton Publishing, 1995

PHOTO CREDITS

A considerable number of the photographs in this book were taken by the authors. They are specially grateful to Craig Smith, Phoenix, AZ, who took the process photographs and others. Among other photographers, to whom the authors and the publishers would like to express sincere thanks, are:

Vanessa Adams, Ole Akhos, Noel Allum, Chris Arend, Anders Bergersen, Glen Blakley, R. de la Cruz, John Cummings, Anthony Cuñha, Susan Einstein, Donald Felting, V. France, Howard Goodman, Don Hall, Takashi Hatakeyama, Ole Haupt (Denmark), Toby Hollander, Tom Holt, Paula Jansen, Kelley Kirkpatrick, Vineet Kacker, Bernd Kuhnert (Berlin), Peter Lee, Mahatta, Gail Reynolds Matzler, Lee Milne, Hiromu Narita, Richard Nicol, Steven Ogawa, Brian Oglesbee, Joseph Painter, Rick Paulson, Eli Ping (courtesy Betty Woodman and Max Protetch Gallery, New York), Renwick/Smithsonian, Nina Rizzo, Hugh Sainsbury, Joshua Schreier, Bill Scott, Mike Short, Bernd Sinterhauf (Berlin), Vada Snider, Gakuji Tanaka, John Tsantes, Van Tuil, Olga L. Valle, Malcolm Varon, Paul Warchol, Neil Winter, Ron Zijlstra (Museum voor Moderne Kunst, Arnhem).

Galleries and other institutions which kindly supplied photographs are listed below:

Anita Besson, London; Garth Clark, New York City, NY; Charles Cowles, New York City, NY; Habitat, Minneapolis, MN; Materia Gallery, Scottsdale, AZ; Paul Klein, Chicago, IL; LA Louver, Los Angeles, CA; Leedy-Voulkos, Kansas City, MO; Frank Lloyd, Los Angeles, CA; Lu Xiao-Ping, China; Maeker, Pondicherry, S. India; Nancy Margolis, New York City, NY; John Natsoulas, Davis, CA; European Ceramic Center, Eindhoven, Netherlands; Netherlands Ceramic Institute, Den Bosch; Perimeter, Chicago, IL; Schopplein Studio; Shigaraki Ceramic Cultural Park, Japan.

Special thanks are also due to Cyril Frankel and Ben Williams in London; to Jim Skutt of Skutt Kilns, Portland, OR; Georgies Ceramic Supply, Portland, OR; John Paccini, Laguna Clay, Los Angeles, for supplying the variety of fire clays; Paul Soldner for the picture of the Soldner Clay Mixer; Deborah Smith and Ray Meeker.

INDEX